CONTENTS

Foreword
(Peter D. John)

Introduction   1
(Steve Wheeler)

1   ICT: Winning Hearts and Minds   7
(Steve Wheeler and Anne Winter)

PART 1: CURRICULUM DELIVERY

2   Promoting Literacy with ICT   26
(Dan Sutch and Peter D. John)

3   Promoting Numeracy with ICT   46
(Heidi Price and David Moore)

4   ICT and Music   60
(Robert Bennett and Will McBurnie)

PART 2: APPLICATIONS

5   Surviving the Internet   80
(Steve Wheeler)

6   Meeting individual differences: using ICT to support communication   94
skills for children with learning difficulties
(Mark Townsend)

7   Visual Literacy and ICT: 'I'm only looking…'   114
(Avril Loveless and Jess Thacker)

8   ICT and Creativity   132
(Steve Wheeler)

9   Personalising ICT   143
(Susan Waite)

PART 3: CASE STUDIES

10   Schools of the Future   161
(George Muirhead, Peter Hicks and Jonathan Bishop)

11   ICT in the Global Classroom   187
(Michelle Selinger)

References   201

Index   213

ACKNOWLEDGEMENTS

The editor, authors and publisher would like to thank the following individuals and organisations for permission to include their material in this volume. Every effort has been made to trace copyright holders and obtain their permission. However, the publisher and authors will gladly receive information enabling them to rectify any error or omission in subsequent editions.

National Council of Teachers in Mathematics (NCTM) Illuminations Software
Department for Education and Skills, National Numeracy Strategy
B-Squared
Priory Wood School
Northern Grid for Learning
Inclusive Technology Ltd
Broadclyst Primary School
do2learn
Crick Software
CFS-Technologies
Widgit Software
Pupils of Buckingham Middle School
Woodford Junior School
Woodfield Primary School
The Educator Online, Online Assessments

We are told daily that we are in the throes of a technological revolution where the computer and associated multi-media technologies will change – for good or ill –the nature of work, leisure, communication, politics, and even human interaction itself (Greenfield, 2003). This 'technological revolution' – and I use the word guardedly – is seen as marking the beginning of a knowledge or information society and thus ascribes to education a central role. It therefore poses challenges to educators of all types to re-think some of their accepted verities so as to deploy technology creatively and productively in ways that respond to the changing patterns for learning that will accrue.

The chapters in this impressive volume address these challenges head on. They do this in a number of ways: first, the authors focus on the role of ICT in contemporary education and the need for new pedagogies to grow alongside the new technologies. Second, they propose that new technologies and new forms of literacy and numeracy can serve as efficacious learning tools which might produce a more engaged, connected and educated society. Third, they help us to speculate on the role of ICTs in education generally, asking: what do we do with them? What useful purposes can they serve? What sort of skills do students and teachers need to effectively deploy them in their classrooms? And what sort of effect might they have on learning?

The chapters give much food for thought in other ways. I am currently trying to develop a theory of 'new pedagogy' that calls attention to the classroom uses of new technologies and the ways in which they blend with various teaching and learning styles (John and Sutherland, 2004; John and La Velle, 2004; Olivero, John and Sutherland, 2004; John, 2005). This theory sees the limitations of educational proposals based primarily on technology without adequate emphasis on pedagogy, and on teacher and student engagement. This volume goes a significant way to developing this theory and does so by cleverly avoiding both technophobia and technophilia. It also rejects technological determinism and sees the key as being based on the 'person-plus' model (Perkins, 1993) where teachers redesign technologies for education so that participation can be enhanced and education reconstructed in the interests of the learner. Many of the ideas embedded in the chapters also relate closely to the work of John Dewey and are guided by the pragmatic and experimental view of teacher professionalism. In fact, this book encourages all kinds of explorations by carefully navigating the reader through the possibilities and pitfalls of extended and exploratory uses of ICT.

The chapters in the book are predicated on the idea that ICT can help students enter new 'knowledge worlds' associated with the subject curriculum more powerfully than conventional classroom tools. It also champions the idea that computer literacy needs to be taught from an early age. The authors show that high levels of student engagement are associated with the continued use of ICT in classroom settings, and that students – even the very young – can work for extended periods of time individually and collaboratively investigating planned and unplanned tasks. Additionally, the authors demonstrate that students experiment with their own ideas more often when using ICT than when using more conventional approaches such as textbooks, worksheets, and teacher talk. Furthermore, students of all ages appear to use their ideas more creatively in lessons and become genuine 'subject learners' when ICT is integrated carefully into both the teachers' planning and classroom teaching. Finally, the chapters highlight the importance of classroom structure and the need to rethink conventional layouts and designs.

Throughout the book the authors emphasise the need for teachers to understand the affordances of ICT and the importance of building them into their own planning and pedagogy. This concept of affordance is popular but little understood. Originally, Gibson's (1979) neologism meant a focus on the action possibilities available in an environment to an individual – independent of the individual's ability to perceive this possibility. Donald Norman (1988) appropriated the concept by talking about the perceived and actual properties of an object thus adding to and fundamentally changing Gibson's (1979) original definition. The term has in recent years become bound up with ICT and its malleability has led to widely differing uses of the term. This discussion is taken further in the book and running throughout the chapters are a number of observable threads linked to the concept.

By weaving these affordances and a detailed discussion of them into each chapter, the book provides extensive guidance and evidence to support the work of teachers in school. It attempts above all to engage in a conversation with teachers about their work and culture, the technologies that sustain it, and the implications of new pedagogies for those technologies (Olson, 2000). It is premised on the idea of 'evidence based practice' where research generated knowledge is deployed to help practitioners think about, plan and execute effective learning in classrooms and beyond. Each chapter is based on a curriculum area or focus which is wholly recognisable to practitioners of all types (although the main focus is on primary teachers). The findings are also presented in new and exciting ways that engage teachers with the process of teaching with ICT.

To conclude, often it seems the pressure for change in education stems more from the demands of technology and the economy than from philosophy, values and evidence. In fact, much of the so-called 'technological revolution' comes from an economic imperative that demands new skills, competencies, literacies and practices that will enable the UK to compete in the new 'knowledge economy'. This 'technological revolution' provides educationists with a challenge: whether to rethink teaching and learning to promote participation and serve social needs or whether education should be structured in order to serve the needs of the economy and corporate institutions. This book addresses this challenge head on and comes down firmly in favour of the former (although not at the expense of the latter). As a result, it is accessible, creative and above all intelligent. I urge you to read the whole as well as dipping into its many fascinating parts.

INTRODUCTION
STEVE WHEELER

Introduction

Producing a book about information and communication technologies (ICTs) can be a risky undertaking. In a continuously changing industry where technologies are superseded or replaced so rapidly, it is difficult even for the manufacturers to keep pace. The result is that the computer you buy in the store today may already be several months out of date. Books on technology are notorious for going quickly out of date. If you are reading this book several years from its publication date, some of the technologies and applications contained within its pages may appear quaint, or even antediluvian. Nevertheless, there is an inherent constant within educational ICT. It is simply that computers in schools can be, and often have been, used in a multitude of creative and imaginative ways to enhance the learning experience and motivate children to learn. For good reason then, this book focuses more on the pedagogy of ICT than it does on the technology.

Transforming primary ICT

In 2002, the Department for Education and Skills (DfES) published a slim volume entitled: *Transforming the Way We Learn*. This publication was a celebration of the UK Government's National Grid for Learning (NGfL), and provided the reader with an optimistic review of what could be expected in schools concerning the deployment and implementation of ICT over the coming years. However, as one social commentator once remarked: 'The future has been a disappointment.' Although valiant efforts have been made to try to embed ICT within the curriculum, a visit to many primary schools will confirm that, generally, teachers do not use ICT at all, or if they do, it is often reluctantly, and in a fashion that falls short of its full potential. This hardly represents a transformation of the way we learn.

Any Year 3 child will tell you about the lifecycle of the butterfly and its four stages, from egg to caterpillar, through chrysalis and finally to butterfly. This process of transformation occurs naturally as the conditions change, and schools are analogous to this example. Just like the butterfly, they have the inherent potential to be transformed if the conditions are right.

There is little doubt that ICT has the power to 'transform' the way we teach, and it certainly affords endless possibilities for the enhancement of children's learning. But the transformation has yet to be realised. Teachers now need to ask whether or not the power of information and communication technologies is being harnessed effectively. They need to consider the multitude of ways in which ICT can be successfully deployed in the primary classroom, and also the ways in which it could be poorly used or underused. In other words, teachers need to take stock of current practice and available technologies and consider whether ICT is being used to its full potential.

This book represents a serious attempt to reflect on these issues. Drawing on the expertise and knowledge of some leading theorists, visionaries and practitioners within primary ICT in the United Kingdom, it presents case studies, reviews and theoretical perspectives, providing teachers and, in particular, those in their initial teacher training or entering into their newly qualified teaching year, with a means by which they can rationalise the use of ICT to transform their own professional practice.

The book contains eleven chapters and is divided into three parts. The first part deals with how ICT might be used to transform the delivery of the curriculum, the second presents some useful applications of ICT in specific contexts and the third contains case studies of successful transformation of primary teaching and learning using ICT within local and global contexts.

Part I: Curriculum delivery

The first chapter focuses on teachers' attitudes and beliefs and the potential of these to influence the success or failure of ICT in the classroom. **Steve Wheeler** and **Anne Winter** offer an overview of some of the key factors that influence technology acceptance or rejection. These include teacher attitudes, diffusion of innovation, transparency of technology, technophobia and the principles of applying ICT to the primary context of teaching and learning. They conclude with a case study of one small school's adoption of a new technology – interactive whiteboards – and offer some guidelines on how to encourage teachers to use them confidently.

Chapter 2 by **Dan Sutch** and **Peter John** provides an overview of some of the important developments of ICT as a support for the teaching of literacy. They offer some examples of best practice in this key area of the curriculum.

Chapter 3 is written by **Heidi Price** and **David Moore**, who are numeracy consultants working with Plymouth Local Education Authority. This chapter takes a similar perspective to Chapter 2, but focuses on the teaching of numeracy, another core part of the curriculum. Combined, these two chapters offer teachers an effective strategy for the use of ICT in the promotion of literacy and numeracy.

This book has a strong thread of creativity running throughout it and Chapter 4 provides the reader with a particularly relevant focus. Former primary teachers **Rob Bennett** and **Will McBurnie** place ICT within a musical context, and offer teachers some creative ideas on how to use computers and specialist software to develop skills and competencies.

Part 2: Applications

Part 2 features a number of applications of ICT in primary education, and provides readers with ideas about how they can transform current provision in very practical ways.

Chapter 5 by **Steve Wheeler** deals with the thorny subject of uses and abuses of the internet, including how to protect children when they 'go online'. He poses a number of scenarios and case studies for teachers to consider as they determine the best ways to use the internet without compromising the integrity of their practice while protecting children from undesirable and potentially dangerous materials. He also touches on several issues of network safety including how to protect against hackers, the nature of malware (computer viruses) and the importance of firewall software.

Chapter 6 places ICT within the context of Special Educational Needs provision. Written by **Mark Townsend**, formerly a deputy head teacher in the special education sector, this chapter encourages teachers to consider a range of ideas, strategies and challenging scenarios to encourage the creative use of computers in inclusive education.

In Chapter 7, **Avril Loveless** and **Jess Thacker** approach the notion of visual literacy, and delve into how important this range of skills can be in the successful use of ICT in primary education. They suggest that the primacy of images is important for all concept learning, and stress the central role of ICT in the learning process.

In Chapter 8, **Steve Wheeler** builds on the Loveless and Thacker chapter, investigating some of the key ideas behind our current thinking about creativity. He challenges teachers to think more creatively as they deploy ICTs across the entire primary curriculum.

'Personalising ICT in the Primary Classroom' is the title of Chapter 9. Written by **Sue Waite**, this chapter is based on recent research in primary classrooms, and asks teachers to think about how they might personalise learning for their pupils using the power of ICT. She takes the reader on a concise but comprehensive tour of the most recent theories of individual differences and challenges teachers to use ICT in new ways to tap into the vast and fertile potential of the child's mind.

Part 3: Case studies

The third and final section of this book focuses on future trends in the use of ICT in primary schools and contains two chapters. In Chapter 10, two case studies of the innovative use of ICT are presented. Firstly, **George Muirhead**, Head Teacher at Woodfield School in Plymouth, offers his personal perspective on the way in which ICT has transformed his own inner-city school. He was instrumental in establishing the city's first completely wireless primary school. In this chapter, he candidly relates his experiences, shares his research findings and documents the benefits and limitations of this technology. The second part of the chapter is written by the Head and

Deputy Head Teachers of Broadclyst Primary School near Exeter, which has transformed its delivery of the National Curriculum through ICT. **Peter Hicks** and **Jonathan Bishop** provide the reader with a case study of a 'School Without Walls' in which each Year 6 pupil has exclusive use of a networked desktop personal computer. This success study is related in an accessible and relevant manner, offering teachers a glimpse of what may be in the near future of ICT in primary schools.

Our final chapter expands the transformational vision to a world perspective. In it, **Michelle Selinger**, who in her capacity as the Manager of Education for Cisco, writes about the many new initiatives that are taking place in schools around the world. She offers a number of strategies for the multicultural education of children, including the e-twinning of schools to enable pupils to use ICT in a truly global approach to learning. This international perspective on the use of ICT in primary education derives from her work in educational systems across four continents and provides a truly inspirational conclusion to the volume.

I sincerely hope that this book will provide teachers who are about to embark on their careers with some of the knowledge and inspiration needed to transform primary teaching through the use of ICT.

Steve Wheeler
Plymouth
February 2005

Contributors

Robert Bennett is Senior Lecturer in Education and ICT at the University of Plymouth. He is Team Leader for the BEd (Hons) Primary Specialist Pathway degree and also responsible for coordinating undergraduate and postgraduate School Experience. His research interests include the use of ICT in music education, investigating teacher confidence and e-learning.

Peter Hicks and **Jonathan Bishop** are currently Head Teacher and Deputy Head Teacher respectively at Broadclyst Community Primary School, Exeter. Between them they have created the 'School without Walls' which integrates teachers, pupils, parents and the community into a truly connected learning community. Together they created the first true Home School Learning initiative and Broadclyst School became the first in Britain to link together learning in schools and learning in homes. Their school holds an influential position as it is setting out a new model for education – one that is exciting and dynamic, one that employs successfully the medium of the age and one that delivers excellence for all.

Peter D. John is Professor of Education and Dean of the Faculty of Education at the University of Plymouth. He is co-director of the ESRC Interactive Education Project, and director of the ESRC Video-Asset Project and the TTA funded Video-Inspired Dialogue project. He is author of numerous articles and chapters on professional knowledge and practice, ICT, pedagogy and professional development and the use of video in teacher education. He is co-author of the forthcoming *Learning Lessons with ICT* (London: David Fulton) and *Interactive Education* (London: Routledge).

Avril Loveless is Reader in ICT in Education at the University of Brighton. She is editor of the international journal *Technology, Pedagogy and Education*, has given many international keynote addresses and is currently involved in collaborative projects with colleagues in the UK, Europe and Japan. She is well known as the author of several books on the subject of educational ICT.

Will McBurnie is Principal Lecturer in Education and Music at the University of Plymouth having previously taught in schools. He teaches on undergraduate and post-graduate teacher education programmes and runs the Faculty of Education's MA degree in Music Education. His research interests embrace many aspects of teaching and learning in music.

David Moore has been a Primary consultant in Plymouth for the last three years. He has worked on developing the leadership of maths across the city and been involved in writing and delivering courses related to maths during that time. He has also been involved in developing web-based materials to provide examples of cross-curricular links with maths and other subjects. Currently he is involved in a maths project working on developing materials to support children with special needs.

George Muirhead is Head Teacher of Woodfield Primary School in Plymouth. He has a wide experience of running a variety of primary schools from a 30-pupil rural primary to a 430-pupil inner-city junior school. His interest and passion has always been to plan for the future not the present and he is currently head teacher of the only all-wireless laptop primary school in the City.

Heidi Price has been a Primary consultant in Plymouth for the last two years. She has worked on developing the leadership of maths across the city and been involved in writing and delivering courses related to maths during that time. She has also spent time researching into the use of formative assessment and children's mathematical development. Currently she is involved in a maths project working on developing materials to support children with special needs.

Michelle Selinger is Education Strategist in Corporate Citizenship for Cisco Systems. Prior to joining Cisco in 2001 she worked at the University of Warwick where she trained teachers in ICT and education and directed the Centre for New Technologies Research in Education (CeNTRE). Her research interests include the pedagogical and cultural implications of global e-learning programmes.

Dan Sutch is currently a Learning Researcher at Nesta Futurelab. His main research interests include investigating the roles within technology-rich learning contexts, the opportunities of mobile technologies in transforming learning experiences and the use of new technologies in developing learners' communication and language skills. Prior to joining Futurelab, he taught at St Michael's Primary School in Stoke Gifford, where he used a variety of ICT tools to develop pupils' interest in language, including using Virtual Learning Environments to enable access to a wider range of learning styles.

Jess Thacker is a primary school teacher in Burgess Hill. She has written and directed numerous short films and documentaries. Working with young people, she has collaborated and taught on several community film projects. Jess is interested in finding ways to enrich the primary curriculum through film and photography.

Mark Townsend is Senior Lecturer in Education at the University of Plymouth where he teaches on a number of initial teacher training programmes including the BEd (Hons) Primary ICT Specialist Pathway degree programme. He also teaches extensively on the Foundation degree for teaching assistants, and set up the first online module for this programme. His research interests include e-learning and how ICT can support children with special educational needs. Before this he spent 20 years working in special schools, including time as a deputy head teacher.

Sue Waite is a researcher in the Faculty of Education at the University of Plymouth. Her current research interests include the role of collaboration, critical thinking and reflection in undergraduate learning, ICT in primary teaching and learning and the inclusion of pupils with learning difficulties in mainstream schools.

Steve Wheeler is Senior Lecturer in Education and ICT at the University of Plymouth. He helped to set up the BEd (Hons) Primary ICT Specialist Pathway degree programme in the university's Faculty of Education and also teaches on several other undergraduate and postgraduate teacher programmes. His research interests include e-learning, creativity and individual differences in learning.

Anne Winter is a primary teacher specialising in ICT. She is currently researching creativity through ICT in Foundation Stage pupils. Her academic interests include teacher motivation, comparative education and the use of interactive whiteboards in the primary school.

PART 1: CURRICULUM DELIVERY

1 ICT – WINNING HEARTS AND MINDS
STEVE WHEELER AND ANNE WINTER

> *The real problem is in the hearts and minds of men …*
> Albert Einstein (1879–1955)

This chapter will enable you to:

- consider how ICT has the potential to transform primary education;
- explore the reasons some teachers resist the use of ICT;
- understand some of the issues of the 'digital divide';
- appreciate some of the causes and implications of technophobia;
- begin to formulate a strategy for more effective adoption and use of ICT in your school.

Introduction

The arrival of information and communication technology (ICT) in the primary class-room has produced some astounding outcomes. For many, teaching and learning have been transformed, with new methods and practices often emerging as a direct result of the use of computers. The internet has unleashed countless new resources and caused teachers to rethink what teaching and learning are all about. Electronic records and databases enable the classroom practitioner to access a wealth of useful information that was previously out of reach. Tedious and mundane jobs can be automated, liberating teachers to concentrate on the more creative aspects of their professional practice. ICT is quite simply transforming primary education, and it is doing so at many levels.

Teachers have met the rapid uptake of computers in schools with both positive and negative responses. From a positive perspective, ICT brings a number of clear advantages for the teacher and the learner, which encompass new resources, new ways of teaching and new ways of learning. The internet, for example, can provide children with access to a vast repository of information, learning resources and experiences. The use of interactive whiteboards can enhance lessons by providing teachers with a range of new delivery methods and teaching resources. Use of e-mail can cut down response time from days to minutes, with teachers connecting to each other, school governors, Local Education Authorities, suppliers, specialist teachers and advisers and, of course, pupils and their parents. In short, the introduction of ICT has the potential to radically alter the face of teaching and learning in schools.

Less positively, ICT has been instrumental in alienating many teaching staff, causing them to question their role as educators, and engendering a great deal of disquiet and anxiety for the future. In a revealing study, Preston and colleagues noted that despite the demands of the ICT curriculum, less than 10 per cent of teachers were using anything other than word processing more frequently than once a month (Preston *et al.*, 2000). Even now, five years on from Preston's study, teachers seem not to be using ICT in great numbers for creative teaching. With any change comes uncertainty and, in the case of the computer, this change has been all pervasive. It is no wonder that some teachers feel threatened by technology. It is clear that ICT is becoming a more important part of the delivery of the school curriculum, and is set to become a core subject in UK secondary schools by 2006. Knowledge of how to use computer technology is now assumed for teachers entering the profession and for those already in it. The UK government spent £230 million from the New Opportunities Fund (NOF) on the training of teachers in the effective use of ICT, with the objective that all teachers would be competent users by 2002 (Wheeler, 2001). This initiative was only partially successful.

It is our intention in this chapter to examine the benefits and limitations of ICT in primary education, and explore the ways in which you, as a future ICT co-ordinator and educational technology champion, can sensitively, but authoritatively, affirm the place and importance of ICT as a key teaching and learning resource. A useful starting point will be to examine the psychological aspects of teachers' responses to new technologies.

Technophobia

No matter how good a technology is, it will fail if people either find it too difficult to use or perceive no use for it. There is little point hoping for a 'transformation of ICT' in primary schools if teachers do not use technology. Extreme negative responses to ICT may be the result of fear or anxiety. Such adverse reactions to technology are often referred to as technophobia, a widespread phenomenon, affecting as much as half the population (Brosnan, 1998), a statistic which can be generalised to teachers. It has resulted in the rejection of technology by some and reluctant acceptance by others. It is well known that the majority of primary school teachers are female. According to Brosnan's research, females also tend to report a higher level of computer anxiety than males (Brosnan, 1998, p. 23). If these are sound findings, then technophobia should clearly be viewed as an important predictor in the success or failure of primary ICT.

Technophobia ranges from the outright fear of new technology through mistrust of technology, to various levels of irritation and frustration caused by 'misbehaving' computers. How often have you actually shouted at your computer, or felt a strong desire to hit it? Notwithstanding, technophobia may also be a rational response to the computer. Teachers rightly express their wariness of new technologies if they either see no relevance or utility for them, or if they feel they lack confidence in their use. Some teachers avoid using computers because they have had bad experiences with them in the past, or have heard horror stories of lost data files or virus attacks. Then there are those who would dearly love to try out new technologies to explore potential, but do not know where to start. The reasons are many and varied.

With a few notable exceptions, most primary schools in the UK now have computers with connection to the internet and a host of other electronic resources available. Teachers may wish to improve the use of this ICT provision in their school, or they may be aiming to introduce a new technology such as an interactive whiteboard or a wireless network into the classroom. They may be quite successful in this endeavour, but they may also need to prepare themselves for a mixed reaction from their collea-gues. Some may adopt the technology quite readily and quickly embed it into their teaching practice. Others may respond more reluctantly and only use ICT if they feel they have to. Still others may shy away from it entirely, arguing that they see no need for the new technology, or that it will take too much of their time to master it.

Time to reflect

What factors do you think would cause teachers to avoid using a particular technology or idea? Make a list.

Where and when have you observed any of these in schools?

Several factors have been identified as reasons for the underutilisation of ICT in schools. Lack of staff development, lack of availability and access to ICT resources, lack of support from ICT developers and school administrators, as well as classroom management issues and problems are all possible reasons according to Lim (2001). Venezky (2004) suggests that two clear reasons emerge as barriers to the adoption of ICT with teachers either doubting the value of ICT or being put off by technical problems.

One of the prevailing issues in primary schools is the percentage of a school's budget that is assigned to the purchase, maintenance and support of ICT. Some teachers may feel aggrieved that much needed resources are being directed toward computers and peripherals. These feelings are likely to be exacerbated if these teachers see little or no concrete return in improved learning outcomes. They may also be likely to oppose the upgrading of ICT at a later stage.

Diffusion of innovation

One of the most useful explanations of the adoption of new technologies and ideas in any given social grouping can be found in the work of Everett Rogers. In his seminal book *Diffusion of Innovations*, Rogers offered a sociological profile of the process whereby new ideas and technologies are adopted, along with a useful model for the management of change (Rogers, 1983). Rogers identified several groups of individuals whose behaviours led to the adoption of a new idea. Although not explicitly founded upon a psychological explanation, Rogers's model is none the less couched within a behavioural context – the willingness of each group to adopt new ideas, and the effect of social comparison and peer pressure that result.

In Figure I.I below, Rogers shows that there are five categories of response to the introduction of change (innovation). Those who are the first to adopt an innovation – approximately 2.5 per cent of the population – usually do so with little reservation about the utility of the innovation (Rogers, 1983, p. 248). They are the ones, for example, who might be seen queuing outside an electronics store early in the morning of the release of a new hi-fi system or mobile phone. Innovators are sometimes obsessive in their eagerness to try out new ideas and often possess a technical knowledge at least equal to that of the manufacturers and designers of the product. They also tend to have a little more disposable income to hand to purchase new technologies. Some have perhaps a little unkindly labelled these individuals as 'anoraks' or 'nerds', but it is the Innovator sector of the population that enables the manufacturer to recoup a little of the initial manufacturing costs so they can produce more units. These individuals may even see computers as the potential answer to every problem, and for this reason they could be referred to as 'techno romantics'. Innovators are also generally financially better off than those in the next category.

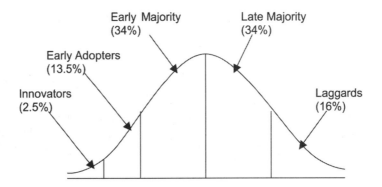

Figure 1.1: Adaptation of Roger's diffusion of innovations model

Rogers calls this category the 'Early Adopters', making up approximately 13.5 per cent of the market. Early Adopters are generally a little more respectable in the community and may be opinion leaders whom others follow (Rogers, 1983, p. 249). Early Adopters generally take the view that to maintain their high social standing they must continually make judicious decisions to adopt new ideas. They often serve as role models for the larger section of a community. This 'technophiles' group can be characterised as instigating a fairly quick uptake of the new technology perceiving as they will the long-term benefits, and regarding the comparatively high cost of the new technology as no barrier.

The third sector of society to adopt a new idea or technology is known as the Early Majority, and makes up around 34 per cent of the market. Early majority members are essentially deliberate in their decisions to adopt a new idea or technology, and tend to watch the early adopters for the lead (Rogers, 1983, p 249). By the time this section of society buys into a technology, prices have already begun to fall and have become more affordable due to economies of scale becoming more efficient and favourable on the part of the manufacturer. At this stage of adoption, the technology has probably penetrated sufficiently into the consciousness of a society that it is no longer in danger of ending up a 'fad' or a passing phase. In technological terms this group could be identified as 'techno realists' in that they seek evidence of real and pragmatic outcomes before committing themselves to adopting the new technology.

The next grouping of people buying into a new idea or technology is referred to by Rogers as the Late Majority, which constitutes another 34 per cent of the population. Late Majority adopters tend to be sceptical about new ideas, and remain at the periphery of new technology use until the vast majority of their peers have already committed to the new idea (Rogers, 1983, p. 250). At this stage, the technology is no longer 'new' and may have already gone through several reiterations, becoming smaller and more compact, efficient and easier to use, and with advanced technical support and user networks. At this stage the technology is being mass produced and the price is affordable to the average citizen with minimum risk. Members of the Late Majority are the 'techno sceptics' in the world of technology – those who require a great deal of convincing before they begin to view the technology as an essential or desirable item to buy into.

The final 16 per cent of society is called the 'Laggards' by Rogers. He sees this group as possessing no opinion leadership within its ranks, and a sector exhibiting cautiousness that overrides most of the decisions that are taken by the rest of society (Rogers, 1983, p. 250). Laggards may also fall into the lowest income group within the community, and are therefore easily able to justify their caution. It is interesting to note that marketing agencies that are tasked with advertising a new product or technology generally ignore the Innovators and Laggards for two different reasons. Innovators will buy into the new product regardless of any media hyperbole, while Laggards are unlikely to purchase the product no matter how hard it is sold to them. It is entirely possible that some Laggards may turn into 'techno Luddites' if they are provoked to take action against a new system or technology that they feel is in any way threatening their security.

Recent studies have shown that this pattern of diffusion of innovation has held true for the adoption of ICT in schools. Venezky (2004) offers a useful review of this effect across schools in several countries.

Change agency

All changes bring uncertainty and anxiety, and if negative repercussions are to be avoided, the management of this change should be conducted in a sensitive manner. Without the changes brought about by ICT, education may be in danger of stagnation, but with them teachers and pupils will be required to quickly acquire new knowledge, and adapt to new skills and methods of working. Understandably, these changes have brought with them a culture of uncertainty in which teachers constantly struggle to keep up with the seemingly breakneck speed of change. Change will bring casualties.

In his groundbreaking book *Future Shock*, Alvin Toffler warned that:

> As a person's sense of strangeness and incongruity … grows, a second phase, 'psychological arrival' takes place. Characteristic of this are anxiety and depression; increasing

self-preoccupation; ... general withdrawal from society in contrast to previous activity; and some degree of hostility and suspicion. (Toffler, 1970, p. 88).

This statement may be more relevant today than when it was first written.

Change agency then needs to be conducted with sensitivity and empathy. ICT has a more fundamental contribution to make than its simple functionality as a tool to enhance teaching and learning. There are many benefits it can bring to the classroom, including motivational advantages, the generation of deeper understanding through the promotion of cognitive engagement, and the encouragement of collaborative learning approaches are just some of the positive spin-offs (Dede, 1998; Wheeler, 2001; Forcheri and Molfino, 2000). Successful change agency will almost certainly require deep contemplation of the benefits and limitations a given technology brings to the classroom. Teachers who are successful ICT champions tend to think through the issues before presenting their colleagues with a clear case for the introduction of a new ICT. Change agency fails when a new technology is introduced simply because it 'seems like the thing to do', or 'we have the money so let's spend it'. Such strategies tend sadly to culminate with potentially useful equipment gathering dust in a cupboard somewhere.

Time to reflect

From your own personal experience using the computer, list as many advantages and disadvantages as you can...

Advantages   *Disadvantages*

Teacher beliefs

Teachers' beliefs about teaching and learning using ICT are central to integration (Mumtaz, 2000). The extent to which they value ICT skills and see them as relevant and useful directly relates to the extent to which these skills are practised and used in their work (Simpson et al., 1999). If teachers believe that ICT adds no value to their teaching, that is if they see it as neither relevant nor useful, then they will not use it. If the school's technology resources are high-quality, relevant and compatible, training has been given, technical support is readily available, access is open and yet the teachers still do not see the value of using new technologies then they will still not be used.

Furthermore, there is the deeper-seated issue of professional practice. If teachers see no need to question or change their practice, they may just as unwillingly adopt the use of ICT (Preston, Cox and Cox, 2002) or even reject it. Psychological research has suggested that an individual is more likely to perform a behaviour when there is a high probability of a positive outcome (Ajzen and Madden, 1986; Doll and Ajzen, 1992).

Two teachers talking …

The power and potential of Information and Communications Technologies are yet to be fully realised in schools. Many barriers to full exploitation of educational technologies exist, including technological constraints such as bandwidth limitations and lack of hardware, political issues such as funding and regulation of activities, and human issues, such as lack of knowledge and skill. As we have already indicated, perhaps one of the most difficult areas to address lies within the psychological domain. Specifically we mean the attitudes, philosophies and perceptions of teaching staff. Imagine this scene at a secondary school somewhere in England. What follows is a fictional conversation between two teachers in a staffroom during a coffee break. Although it is fictional, you are likely to hear most of these arguments at some time in schools. Although the conversation is set in a secondary school, many of the issues are equally relevant to primary education. Read through the following scenario, and while you are doing so, think about the issues that are being raised and arguments that are being made by both parties.

Microchips or Mr Chips?

John Singleton is the newly appointed deputy head teacher at Broadfield Community School. The school has 962 pupils on roll and a head teacher who will be retiring within the next six months. Mr Singleton will be acting up once the head teacher retires and may apply for the job. In the meantime, he has been given the task of deciding what the main priorities are for next year's resources budget. He only has enough funds to finance one department adequately. The choice falls between Physical Education and ICT, both of which have a recognised need for new equipment.

One morning, as he is making his coffee in the staff room, Mr Singleton overhears a conversation between two of his senior staff. Jane Armitage is 28, and is the ICT co-ordinator for the school. She is also Head of Mathematics. She is in conversation with Roger Bailey (aged 50), who is Head of PE. Mrs Armitage comes from a progressive educational background, which contrasts with Mr Bailey's more traditional approach, one he has successfully practised through almost 30 years of instructor experience, first in the Royal Marines and later in the secondary education sector. Listen in with Mr Singleton to their conversation …

Mrs A: … and I still say that we need more computer terminals in the ICT suite … we have two, sometimes three pupils sharing each machine.

Mr B: Look Jane, it's no good you banging on endlessly about computers – all the kids do is play games on them anyway …

Mrs A: Hang on. That's not strictly true. They do a lot of very constructive stuff, particularly online with the internet. You ought to come and have a look some time.

Mr B: ... and I bet they download porn and all sorts of horrible stuff when your back's turned too ...

Mrs A: No. Definitely not! We have special software to block out that kind of material ...

Mr B: Hmmm. You can't be certain that it works though, can you...?

Mrs A: ... besides which, when the pupils are engaged in meaningful work ...

Mr B: Meaningful? Such as...?

Mrs A: Well ... some of them are building their own personal web pages at the moment. It's really creative ... they learn an awful lot... there's a lot of skill involved in that kind of project. Others are running computer simulations where they are government ministers. They can see what would happen if they had to make decisions that affected millions of people, and then they discuss these results – good collaborative stuff. They can explore and discover for themselves without us breathing down their necks! Then there are the specialised software packages ... take Success Maker for instance – that's great with the SEN pupils. Helps them with their reading problems and...

Mr B: (*interrupts*) Look, in my experience ... which, OK, is very limited ... computers just keep breaking down. I can never get them to work for me. So I've given up. It's all very frustrating. Computers are ... they're ... electric idiots, that's what they are!

Mrs A: They only do what you tell them to do Roger. Listen ... I can get you some tuition if ....

Mr B: Not really interested. I've lived without computers for 40 years and I'm not really thinking about starting now. I've other things to do with my spare time ... what little I've got...!

Mrs A: But we all use computers everyday without really knowing it. Your clock radio, the digital watch you're wearing ... the microwave in the kitchen. They're all controlled by microchips...

Mr B: Ah.... that's different though isn't it. They're useful.

Mrs A: (*smiling triumphantly*) You know, I think you're a little scared about computers ... go on, admit it!

Mr B: (*frowns*) Not scared. Just can't be bothered. (*He thinks for a few seconds*) Some people are a little worried about the things though. I've heard colleagues saying that there are elements of teaching that will be 'taken over' by those machines. I've always said you can't beat good old 'drill and practice' methods to reinforce learning...

Mrs A: Well, I can only quote from Arthur C. Clarke ... you know, the science fiction writer... 2001 and all that? He said: 'Any teacher who can be replaced by a computer ... should be!'

Mr B: Well, he *would say that*, wouldn't he? What does he know about teaching anyway? All he writes about is little green men and space travel and the like ...

Mrs A: Actually, he is a very accomplished scientist too ... what he's saying is that teaching is not about giving information ...

Mr B: *Some* of it is!

Mrs A: ... it's about facilitating learning. Getting kids to think for themselves. To get them to construct their own meaning and knowledge. Providing them with the best possible learning environments...

Mr B: (*laughs*) Sounds like you've swallowed a DfES circular!

Mrs A: No, really, I think those principles are very important.

Mr B: Fair enough. No disrespect, but I happen to believe that far too much money has been spent on computers in this school already. The kids are becoming computer geeks, and ... have you seen them lately? ... some of them are seriously out of condition! What about some more cash for new gym equipment? We're really struggling with the old kit. We need new sports equipment – the old stuff's falling apart at the seams! We need new mats and we also have a pressing need for more outdoor sports gear. It's not fair. It's PE that need more resourcing I'm telling you.

Mrs A: But PE isn't even a part of the core curriculum!

Mr B: Ah, but it should be though. Research is showing that if kids are fit and in good physical condition, they think and work better in the classroom...

Mrs A: So invest in some ICT equipment for the gym then. Record-keeping, pacing, timing, computers can do them all.

Mr B: (*exasperated*) Oh, come on, give it a rest! You can't tell me that computers can teach PE better than me!

Mrs A: Roger, you've missed the point. You can use computers to make classroom management easier. More importantly, we're using computers to get the kids to think for themselves. To problem solve. To work collaboratively and so on ...

Mr B: I can do that without a computer!

Mrs A: Well...... Nic Negroponte, the *Wired* magazine man, reckons that in a few years people will be using the internet more than they watch TV. He wrote that in 'Being Digital'...

Mr B: Well Nic Nitro... or whatever his name is ... probably wrote that to sell a few more books, didn't he? I'll stick to what I know best – drill and practice. I can teach the kids how to develop their fitness and instil in them a sense of fair play. They follow the rules I give them and they learn how to play a sport and be competitive. It's simple. It's effective. And I don't need computers for that now, do I?

Mrs A: Roger, you are such an old dinosaur. There really is no way to get through to you is there?

Mr B: Gee, thanks, I'll take that as a compliment. Anyway, got to dash! Got a five-a-side to referee! (*Both teachers leave the staff room.*)

John Singleton has listened to this discussion with a great deal of interest. In fact his coffee has gone cold. He has seen the resources budget for the next year, and has to make up his mind soon what he will be spending it on. He knows that to make sense of the very partisan perspectives he has heard, he must begin teasing out the key issues that have been made by both teachers.

Time to reflect

- *Which do you feel is the strongest argument and why?*
- *Can you identify any of the underlying philosophies, beliefs or learning theories that may cause these teachers to adopt their positions?*
- *If you were in Mr Singleton's shoes, which department would you be more likely to fund, and why?*
- *Start by writing down what you think the key issues are.*
- *What other issues have emerged?*

Digital divides

At the time of writing, a high proportion of homes in the UK (along with homes in many other western industrialised societies) have one or more computers and a large percentage of these are connected to the internet. Increasingly, children are using home computers that are at least as sophisticated as the ones they encounter in school. This ideally leads to children continuing their access to information and digital resources beyond the confines of the traditional classroom, and much has been written about this extra-mural phenomenon. However, there are still many children whose parents do not have computers at home, either for economic, social or other reasons. This leads some teachers to question the equanimity of schools encouraging children to use home computers for learning as an extension of school experience, while their less well off peers are clearly disadvantaged. This is one aspect of what is becoming known as the 'digital divide'.

There has been much talk of the 'digital divide' in society – the 'haves' and 'have nots' of information. However, such a binary may be an oversimplification. Not only is this a socio-economic issue relating to those who do or do not have access to ICT, but other far more complex and multi-layered issues are present. The digital divide speaks of what the British Educational Communications and Technology Agency (BECTa) (2001) has termed 'multiple digital divides', including those who 'will' and 'will not', as well as those who 'can' and 'cannot' – those who have the ability to use computers and those who do not. Digital divides also exist in terms of the language used to understand, utilise and exploit the power of the technologies, otherwise referred to as 'digital literacy'. There are also the more subtle, but nevertheless important, skills such as visual literacy, a topic addressed by Avril Loveless and Jess Thacker in Chapter 7. In any given school a number of digital divides may exist for both staff and pupils, and these can vary in their extent and influence over how and when information and communication technology is used successfully for teaching and learning.

Digital literacy

Exploiting the huge potential of the Information Age is a task set before all of us. Being able to access information at the time and place where it is required is more possible than ever before, with the advent of wireless technologies, broadband connectivity and intelligent agents. Digital literacy is the means through which this can be accomplished. Gilster (1997) provides a host of strategies available to anyone with access to a connected computer, including setting up personal 'news feeds' on their desktop, mastering the art of internet searching, evaluating the usefulness and veracity of a website, and generally being able to place the worth of a web resource within the wider context of information sources, such as books, journals and multimedia.

In short, digital literacy is all about making the technology work for you, finding new and interesting ways in which information technology can enhance life and improve the quality of teaching and learning. The digitally literate teacher will be convinced of the efficacy and usefulness of the connected computer. Below are some of the general possibilities of ICT in a contemporary context.

ICT as a practical utility

The practical worth of ICT can be assessed by how much it impacts upon one's own experience. For primary teachers, ICT can be assessed in terms of how much it can impact upon learning outcomes, and how much it can enhance, or improve upon, previous teaching methods and learning activities. School cupboards up and down the land are full of old equipment that is either redundant, or simply 'didn't work properly' when it was first used. This is a perennial problem for schools. Shiny new equipment holds a lot of promise until it refuses to connect when plugged in. Brightly coloured software is an exciting prospect, until it freezes on the screen and you are required to unplug the computer simply to free it up and get it working again. At the bottom of this problem are the twin culprits: absence of support and lack of training. For ICT to become a successful proposition in any school, it needs to be not only simple to work, but easy to correct if and when it malfunctions.

ICT as embedded in the curriculum

In any given school, ICT is becoming embedded or integrated into the curriculum. No subject has been left untouched by its versatility and appeal. Innovative teachers are using networked computers to enable their pupils to communicate with each other and children from other schools as a means of accessing a myriad of learning resources and as a way to express creativity (Wheeler, Waite and Bromfield, 2002). Interactive white boards (IWBs) are increasingly being used to present teaching resources in new and exciting ways across all subjects, and digital cameras are used to capture images that can then be manipulated, stored, retrieved and presented electronically. Sensing equipment and software is used in science as an exploration of the natural world. In forward-looking schools, ICT can clearly be said to be an embedded discipline within the national curriculum subjects at Key Stages 1 and 2.

ICT as a discrete subject

When ICT becomes a subject in its own right, specialist teachers will claim this particular domain as their own. Inevitably, the digital divide will grow between those teachers who specialise in the use of ICT, and those who don't because they believe they don't have to. There will always be an amorphous mass of teachers holding the middle ground – those who view ICT as just another teaching resource or learning aid. Just like the marketeers of new technology, we feel that it is this middle ground that holds the future success of ICT in schools. An important principle holds true here: to take hold and flourish, ICT must be viewed as a transparent, almost invisible aspect of professional practice, just as other more familiar tools such as the pencil, eraser and notepad have become.

ICT as transparent or opaque technology

What do we mean by 'transparent'? In order for ICT to become an integral part of school life, teachers need to see 'through' the technology and what it can do for them and the children within their classroom. Transparent technologies require little learning but pay back a lot in terms of information or service (Wann and Mon-Williams, 1996). If you are an experienced motorist, then your vehicle has become a 'transparent technology' which requires little mental effort for you to use. If you travelled to work by car and your route is familiar, you probably have little memory of the journey. However, when you first learned how to drive, your car was an 'opaque technology' – a lot of mental effort (concentration) was required to prevent you from driving onto the pavement! A transparent technology is one in which a minimum amount of cognitive effort is required for a maximum payoff.

A key skill teachers will need to develop to aid the growth of ICT in primary schools is the ability to use the unique attributes and affordances of digital technologies transparently. This must be achieved in such a manner that ICT becomes seamlessly embedded into the delivery of the curriculum, which achieves the necessary criteria without a return to the old and probably outmoded practices of drill and practice of traditional education (Forsyth, 1999; Wheeler, 2001). It is the current opacity of ICT that is perhaps one of the most trenchant barriers to its uptake and successful use in the classroom. Teachers are justifiably reticent about using technologies that they are either unfamiliar with or in which they feel they have to invest a great deal of time in mastering.

ICT should be like using a wrist watch – you forget you are wearing it and can't remember how many times you consult it during the day, but if it is missing, you soon notice! This is what we mean by transparency. However, ICT should not create a dependency culture, but should be used transparently as a means to an end – that is excellence and innovation in the teaching and developing of young minds.

Teacher attitudes and the adoption of innovation: a case study

As we have seen, teacher attitudes towards the use of new technologies vary, but they can often be deep seated. Anne Winter, who was a Master's degree student and is a qualified primary teacher, conducted a case study on the introduction of interactive white boards (IWBs) into her small rural school in 2004. It is presented here to illustrate how attitudes influence the adoption of innovation and how perceptions of usefulness and transparency contribute to the success or failure of adoption.

At the time of writing IWBs are at the leading edge of technology roll-out for primary schools, so this is a pertinent focus. Recent research supports the belief that IWBs are an effective learning aid. IWBs have been used effectively in a number of subject areas, in particular in the teaching of literacy and numeracy (Smith, 2001). Interactive whiteboards were considered to have helped learning 'a little' or 'a lot' by 92 per cent of pupils, in a recent report, the joint highest percentage of all the technology types (South Texas Community College, 2002). IWBs have been shown to motivate children (Mosely and Higgins, 1999; Valdez et al, 1999; Beeland, 2002; Denning, 1997).

The school selected for this study was effective and improving, with all members of staff sharing a commitment to succeed. In 2002, according to the Ofsted Inspection Report, the school was in a strong position to raise standards by ensuring that computers became an integral resource that supported learning in all subjects of the curriculum (Ofsted Report, 2002).

In July 2003 an interactive whiteboard with projector was installed in the school hall. The head teacher and the ICT co-ordinator anticipated that the IWB would be a key learning resource. It was hoped that the IWB would help to integrate ICT skills throughout the Primary Curriculum. The hall computer was networked to the other workstations in the school so that pupils' work could be retrieved, viewed and worked on. The IWB was connected to a desktop computer, a DVD player and a video player. The computer had internet access and appropriate software to support and enhance numeracy and literacy lessons.

All members of staff participated in an in-service training day led by the school's ICT co-ordinator. Held at the school, the training was focused on the teachers' needs, and was facilitated through a variety of teaching approaches. As part of the training day, teachers had to plan to use the IWB in one of their lessons. This was planned on the day and the resources were prepared. All teachers delivered their planned lessons.

Six months after the training day it was apparent that the style of training given on a one-day training course had had very little impact on teachers' use of the IWB in school. Since the delivery of those initial planned sessions, the IWB had been underused. One teacher used it daily to show a fitness video for the children to exercise to. Another teacher occasionally used it to screen DVDs. The remaining teachers had not used the IWB since their training day.

In December 2003 another IWB and projector were installed, this time directly into a year 4/5 classroom. It was connected to a desktop computer at the back of the classroom. The class teacher did not use it in the six months following installation. It would be interesting at this point to examine some of the identified positive factors that influence successful deployment and use of new technologies in schools. Cox, Preston and Cox (2002) have offered the summary presented in Table 1.1.

Table 1.1: Summary of positive factors needed for successful implementation of ICT

Positive factors needed for successful implementation of ICT	Evidence
Coherent planning and deployment of ICT resources, ideally on a school-wide basis (PwC, 2001)	Resources located in a variety of areas throughout the school. Resources allocated according to the school management plan.
Hardware and software are of high quality and compatible, allowing efficient electronic transfer of data school-to-school and school-to-LEA (Whelan, 2000)	All areas of ICT scheme of work are resourced well with software and peripherals. E-learning credits have allowed software provision for other subject areas. All workstations are connected to the internet and all classes and teachers have their own e-mail accounts.
Technical support is available (PwC, 2002; Fabry and Higgs, 1997)	A technical support firm is ready to come and fix any problems quickly. The phone number is displayed in the school office.
Training is available, of high quality and taken up by teachers (PwC, 2001; Fabry and Higgs, 1997)	All teachers have had training to use the whiteboard in the context of their own needs and the school systems.
There is access to hardware, software and school networks for all teaching staff, when and where it is needed (PwC, 2001; Fabry and Higgs, 1997)	Teachers have access to all resources both in their classrooms and in the computer suite.
Successful implementation of ICT needs to address three interlocking frameworks for change: the teacher, the school and policy-makers (Mumtaz, 2000)	The government has given extra funding for technology via e-learning credits and NOF training. Ofsted and the School Management Plan have highlighted the need for further integration of ICT.
If teachers perceive ICT to be useful to them, their teaching and their pupils' learning, they are more likely to have a positive attitude to the use of ICT in the classroom (Cox, Preston and Cox, 1999)	

The last factor in Table 1.1 is possibly the most vital for us to consider. Do the teachers see using IWBs as a positive experience? Or do they view the IWBs in a negative light?

Preston, Cox and Cox (2000) identified a number of factors, which contribute to teachers' perceived usefulness of ICT (see Table 1.2).

Table 1.2: Factors in teachers' perceived usefulness of ICT.

Positive factors	Negative factors
Makes my lessons more interesting	Makes my lessons more difficult
Makes my lessons more diverse	Makes my lessons less fun
Has improved the presentation of materials for my lessons	Reduces pupils' motivation
Gives me more prestige	Impairs pupils' learning
Makes my administration more efficient	Restricts the content of the lessons
Gives me more confidence	Is not enjoyable
Makes the lessons more fun	Takes up too much time

In our case study, we wanted to know how closely the teachers felt aligned towards the positive or negative perceptions listed by Cox et al. We distributed a questionnaire and then followed up with individual interviews with each teacher, using the positive and negative factors identified by Preston, Cox and Cox (2000) as the basis for our questions.

The statement teachers showed most agreement with was 'Would using the IWB reduce pupils' motivation?' Most of the teachers believed it would not and most also believed it would not impair learning. They also expressed their beliefs that IWBs would add interest to lessons. Half the teachers believed that using the IWB would make their lessons more interesting, while the other half thought that it would possibly make their lessons more interesting. Two thirds of the teachers agreed that using the IWB would make their lessons more diverse.

There has been much evidence to suggest that IWBs do indeed motivate pupils (Mosely and Higgins, 1999; Valdez et al., 1999; BECTa , 2002). Beeland (2002) found a statistically significant preference for the use of IWBs in the classroom – particularly for engagement and motivation of learners. In an exploration of the use of ICT at the *Millennium Primary School* in Greenwich it was widely reported that ICT had improved pupils' motivation, concentration, confidence, self-esteem, communication skills and enthusiasm (BECTa, 2003a). Pupils are motivated by positive experiences of using the technology for a range of activities and 80 per cent of teachers who used ICT regularly found that pupils were well motivated (Denning, 1997).

cont.

The teachers agreed unanimously that using the IWB could inject more fun into their lessons and most thought that using an IWB could improve the presentation of materials for their lessons. One teacher replied that using the IWB would not improve the presentation of materials for her lessons. Most did not agree with the statement that using the IWB was counter-productive due to insufficient technical resources. One teacher did not know and one teacher thought that using the IWB was counter-productive due to insufficient technical resources.

At the end of the interview three teachers added that they would like further training. One teacher said she would enthusiastically welcome more training. Another teacher said she would like to have opportunities for both hands-on training with the trainer in the classroom and opportunities to observe peers where teaching using an IWB is embedded in the classroom practice. One teacher said she would like to have the time to go through the curriculum to plan for opportunities where teaching with the IWB would be beneficial.

When asked 'Would using the IWB give you more confidence?' these teachers qualified their case with deciding on either answering in the present 'No', because they do not feel confident in their present use, or they answered for the future 'Yes'. Although they did not feel confident 'now', they could envisage a time when they would feel confident in using the IWB successfully.

The quality of added interaction in teaching is one area where lessons may be made more diverse with the addition of an IWB. Two thirds of the teachers agreed that using the IWB would make their lessons more diverse, the other third were split between not knowing and stating that using the IWB would possibly make their lessons more diverse. Studies show that the most effective uses of ICT are those in which the teacher and the software can challenge pupils' understanding and thinking, either through whole-class discussions using an IWB or through individual or paired work on a computer (Preston, Cox and Cox, 2000). The IWB can provide a medium for a more dynamic and interactive lesson; teachers need to explore in which aspects of the lesson the greatest gains are to be found. The IWB is an effective medium in a teacher-led whole-class learning environment and for reviewing lessons; it is also useful for teacher-led group work and, when used in this way, children respond with enthusiasm (Smith, 2003).

More laptops are being made available to teachers each year through the government initiative 'Laptops for Teachers'. The combination of an IWB and a laptop computer is seen as particularly effective in reducing the time needed to prepare some lessons (Bush, Priest and Coe, 2004). Teachers gain maximum impact from their laptops when used in conjunction with IWBs (BECTa, 2002). Four of the teachers in this study thought that using the IWB would not make their administration more efficient. Although half the teachers in this study have laptops they do not use them for planning their lessons. Most teachers thought that using IWBs could improve the presentation of materials for their lessons. All the teachers we interviewed thought that using the whiteboard could make their lessons more fun. Jo Ryman, Lead Consultant of the IWB pilot initiative, asked children for their opinion. Year 5 children at an Oxfordshire primary school said: 'Learning is more fun because we have interactive games and screens that help us to learn.' The whiteboard software allows you to create resources which pupils will find motivating and fun (BECTa, 2004). Two thirds of the teachers interviewed thought there were sufficient technical resources available in the school to use the IWB effectively.

At the end of the interview at our school half the teachers added that they would like further training. One teacher said she would be very enthusiastic to receive more training. The length of time spent on training is important: it has been found that one-day courses are inadequate (McFarlane, 1997) and that ongoing support and advice is more valuable that one-off training (Williams, 1998). Teachers need the opportunity to use and reflect on what they have learnt during a course and they should be encouraged to reflect on, and make decisions about, their own ICT development needs on an ongoing basis (Williams *et al.*, 1998).

Teaching tip

Are you aware of any teachers in your placement school(s) who are making good use of an interactive whiteboard? If so, it might be helpful to ask them for permission to go and observe a lesson or at least meet them for a demonstration.

Making contact with an expert interactive whiteboard user and observing them using it may be the most effective way (and certainly the quickest) of gaining inspiration and top tips for using the technology yourself.

In the case study, another teacher said she would like to have the time to go through the curriculum to plan for opportunities where teaching with the IWB would be beneficial. In order to raise standards in ICT, and for ICT to contribute to the raising of standards in other subjects, it is important to make clear and coherent links between the delivery of the Programme of Study for ICT and the wider use of ICT within the curriculum. The long-term plan for ICT should link with subject plans, showing where ICT skills, knowledge and understanding will be developed, before they are used within a curricular context (BECTa, 2004).

All teachers interviewed disagreed with a very high number of the statements for the potential usefulness of ICT. We conclude from this that they are not yet convinced that IWBs are a tool useful enough to enhance their teaching. There may also be a trade-off between usefulness and time required to learn to use IWBs effectively, and that this leads to a failure to adopt the technology.

Hooper and Reiber (1995) identify five stages in the process of embedding ICT. These are:

- **familiarisation;**
- **utilisation;**
- **integration;**
- **reorientation;**
- **evolution.**

Familiarisation is characterised by a teacher becoming increasingly aware of ICT and having attended some in-service training, but rarely (and often reluctantly) trying to use it in their classroom teaching. During the stage of integration a teacher becomes increasingly aware of the benefits of technology, and begins to incorporate it into teaching, often 'replacing' former activities with ICT alternatives. This begins to have a beneficial effect on teaching and learning, although use remains fragile and the teacher is often set back, for example by technical hitches (Hooper and Reiber, 1995). The teachers in the case study are using ICT in these early stages. Their negative perceptions of how useful ICT can be to their teaching may limit their progress beyond these into reorientation and evolution – where ICT becomes an embedded and transparent aspect of teaching and learning.

Promoting the adoption of new technologies

Even though they could see the positive potential of ICT, the teachers in the case study generally doubted that using ICT would augment their teaching. The school in the study still makes less use of the IWBs than it could do. If this is indicative of the teaching profession as a whole, this view makes it unlikely that other initiatives will persuade teachers to use IWBs or other new technologies to their full potential. Adopting a collaborative working approach and the support of a head teacher for the success of school development are seen to be vital (Ager, 2000). To enable and encourage more optimistic attitudes towards any new technology we suggest a three-stage plan of action:

1. Positive practice

    – Teachers visit other schools within the local Academic Council where the technology use is embedded throughout the curriculum.
    – Time is given for teachers to meet 'peers in good practice' to discuss where the technology is best used.

2. Collaborative Planning with Peers

    – Teachers pair up and discuss opportunities for using the technology in different curriculum areas.
    – Teachers begin to use resources based on the technology for numeracy and literacy and other key teaching.
    – Time is given for the paired teachers to see each other teach and share ideas.

3. Repetition and Reflection

    – Stages one and two are cyclical.
    – Reinforcement of key ideas and opportunities for discussion with both fellow schoolteachers and model practitioners.

Conclusion

ICT will become a transforming power in education if teachers see practical applications, but there will be no transformation if the technology is difficult to use, is beset with technical problems or takes too much time to learn. Leadership is important to the success of early adoption. Training and peer support should be provided and practical opportunities offered to practise the use of a new technology.

We hope that some of the ideas we have presented in this chapter will inspire you to become a champion of ICT when you start teaching. We also hope that this chapter will equip you to better succeed in encouraging your future colleagues to adopt and explore new ways of using ICT to enhance the learning experience of the children they are teaching.

2 PROMOTING LITERACY WITH ICT

DAN SUTCH AND PETER D. JOHN

It's not computer literacy that we should be working on, but sort of human-literacy. Computers have to become human-literate.

Nicholas P. Negroponte

This chapter will enable you to:

- **make informed choices about the appropriate use of technologies to enhance your teaching of literacy;**
- **consider the principles of designing 'ICT-rich' literacy learning environments;**
- **blend the examples of 'best practice' offered with your own teaching and learning style.**

Introduction

Primary Literacy is an area that can be greatly enriched by well applied, appropriate technologies. A wide variety of opportunities exist that can deepen the learning experiences of students while at the same time encouraging investigation, playful discovery and reflective learning. Of central importance, however, are the shifts taking place in the definitions of literacy. Originally stemming from the Latin *litteratus* meaning 'one who knows letters', this formal definition has changed in recent years and is now bound up with what Lanham (1993) calls 'digital literacy'. This he defines as 'being skilled at deciphering complex images and sounds as well as the syntactic subtleties of words' (Lanham, 1993, p. 161). Viewing literacy in this way involves developing the capacity to communicate (composing and interpreting) through varied communicative forms (multimodality). This definition will be used throughout this chapter.

Models of literacy

Definitions of English and English teaching have been long contested (Eagleton, 1983; Cox, 1991; Davison, 2000). In recent decades, however, literacy has become fore-grounded and arguments have focused on the idea of literacy pedagogy (Matthewman *et al*, 2004) and what it entails. These debates have cohered around three particular models: the 'Literacy Strategy' approach; the critical literacy approach; and a set of ideas built around 'New Literacy Studies'. The first, and most easily recognisable, is the National Literacy Strategy (NLS) which was introduced into primary schools in 1997 and secondary schools in 2000. The ideas underpinning it are drawn from a blend of cognitive and functional discourses that focus on the acquisition of the basic skills of language competence (Lankshear, 1997). The critical literacy approach, on the other hand, emphasises literacy as a social and political construct embedded in a cultural or socio-cultural milieu. This model stresses the need for children to be able to critique the power relations that envelop language thereby empowering and transforming learners (Friere and Macedo, 1987).

The 'New Literacy' movement or 'post-critical literacy' studies, on the other hand, bring together a composite of traditions and frameworks. Although originating in cultural studies its emphasis is firmly on the 'new' where changing out-of-school practices and advances in technology are reshaping the whole concept of literacy. This conception stresses the increasing diversity of practices or 'literacies' which will lead, it is argued, to new forms of pedagogy (Matthewman *et al.*, 2004).

Literacy and ICT strategies

These models or approaches to literacy have given rise to a range of teaching strategies that merge usefully with new technologies. Furthermore, current research has identified several key ways that ICT can support teaching and learning while recognising the heuristic value of the National Literacy Strategy (Kress, 2000; Cope and Kalantzis, 2000; Davison, 2000; Lankshear and Knobel, 2003). They include shared reading and writing strategies; whole-class word- and sentence-level work; group and independent work; media studies; and reflective and plenary sessions. Each will be dealt with in turn.

Shared reading and writing strategies

The opportunity to enable learners to read at a stage above their own ability level links to Vygotsky's (1978) theory of the zone of proximal development, where, through discussion with a more advanced other, a learner can develop their ability within an activity. Sharing texts is an important part of this aspect of the literacy lesson both in terms of shared reading and as part of shared composition. A number of visual display technologies can enhance this process.

- **Data projectors and visualisers can make any text big enough for whole-class sharing. The data projector, for instance, provides class-wide access to any digital resources while the visualiser can make any object a shared resource, for example the writing on the back of a packet of cornflakes, the blurb on the back of a DVD box or a section of text from within a magazine or a book.**

- **An additional affordance of the data projector is its ability to connect to a number of other technologies that can interact with the projected image, for example, interactive whiteboards, laptops, desktops, tablets and slates.**

- **Annotating text to highlight teaching points using highlighter functions, changing font colour or size can also relate directly to the teaching aspects taken from the National Literacy Strategy (NLS) framework. Framing this around discussions about these objectives, the technology can then act as a visual guide for the learners and as a recordable map of the lesson progress for the teacher.**

- **Enabling students to annotate, embellish and dynamically change texts within a shared context can be achieved simply by providing students with the opportunity to share ideas with peers using word processing technologies.**

Whole-class word and sentence-level work

Assessing and teaching to individual learning styles (or individual approaches to learning) has been highlighted as a key way of personalising learning opportunities within the classroom. Ofsted suggests that 'Taking students' learning styles into account (in this way) when planning and executing ICT lessons can greatly impact the learning that takes place' (Ofsted, 2004). Interactive whiteboards, for instance, can provide a kinaesthetic approach to interacting with language. Consider the two screen shots below in Figures 2.1 and 2.2 (taken from a Key Stage 2 classroom). Figure 2.1 shows how students can build words by dragging word parts together, before verbalising the word and explaining its meaning based upon its component morphemes. Figure 2.2 provides students with an opportunity to sort words into separate sections of the board – again using fingers (or stylus depending upon whiteboard make). This process asks students to read the words and to sort them into appropriate sections based upon phonic principles, while simultaneously becoming aware of the morphological roots of the words – recognising the word family that links the word spelling. This process was designed to highlight how phonic spelling strategies can be enriched with alternative spelling strategies to spell words with (for example) silent letters.

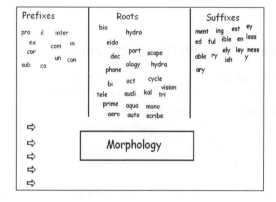

Figure 2.1: Word parts

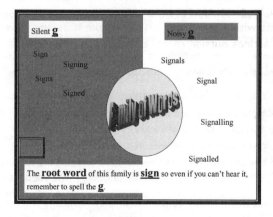

Figure 2.2: Family of words

These examples have been taken from word-level work, but a similar approach can be taken when manipulating words within sentence-level work. Using tablet technology or an interactive whiteboard allows this to become a collaborative task where students are able to share ideas while composing words and sentences kinaesthetically.

Time to reflect

What sorting and constructing activities can you think of that might encourage students to understand words and to make sense of spelling rules?

Traditional worksheet activities often ask students to add correct endings for tenses by selecting the appropriate plural ending or graphical representation of a phoneme. Computer-based worksheets can develop these activities more dynamically by supporting students with drop-down menus and the use of adaptable content frames and feedback based upon student input. Using options such as 'Forms' in Microsoft Word allows teachers to create worksheets that are designed specifically to meet teaching objectives within their specific classroom, worksheets that can be tailored to the specific needs and abilities of their pupils.

Group and independent work

An important aspect of the literacy hour is designed to facilitate small-group support so that pupils develop their own literacy practice. Below are short descriptions of digital tools that can be used by both the teacher and the learner to engage in group and independent work. When reading this section of the chapter, think about how you could develop these activities so that they are appropriate for the class you are working with and consider the classroom management strategies needed to ensure that the activities maintain their focus on learning.

Writing for real audiences has been highlighted by many theorists and researchers as being a key aspect of 'good practice' (Halliday, 1975; Kress, 1982; Graves, 1983). Much of this work has stemmed from the ideas of Vygotsky (1978) who stated that students should be given opportunities to write for a real audience because this provides students with a real reason to undertake authentic classroom tasks while validating their actions outside of the classroom. An example includes 'e-mailing a Viking' (www.InterActiveeducation.ac.uk) where a changed writing style of the students was observed with interest by the class. The children were asked to 'e-mail a Viking' after exploring the historical period in history. The 'Viking' was a support teacher who responded to questions put by the children. The immediacy of the strategy was accentuated by the excitement of the students as they awaited a personal response to their messages. A similar classroom-based project entitled 'e-mail an author' was equally successful. Here students e-mailed Sydney Northcote with their story ideas, opening paragraphs, plots and endings. The feedback to the students was quick, personal and sent from an external expert that linked the classroom activities with real-world authors. A 'real audience' to critique, embellish or question work, can be easily created by setting up links between other classes in the same school, between classes in different schools and even between schools in different countries.

Gamble and Easingwood (2001) claim that such examples illustrate how the act of writing has fundamentally changed. They argue, somewhat pessimistically, that *The content of the message and the medium now become important, often to the detriment of traditionally important elements such as grammar, punctuation and spelling.* However, as Triggs and John (2004) suggest, the personalised feedback from another author provides greater opportunities for creative copying that can actually enhance rather than derogate the more traditional elements of literacy.

Other examples of using new technologies to access new audiences can be seen through the use of Virtual Learning Environments (VLEs), school web pages and e-mailed school magazines.

Media literacy

A key part of literacy teaching is developing students' ability to communicate with a given audience. Providing an audience with a description, be it a narrative, a traditional tale or an instructional text, requires the ability to encode a message for an audience that is presented in a way that can be decoded in an accessible fashion. This highlights the merging that is taking place between the fields of literacy and media literacy. A key question remains: does a child who can tell a story through storyboards demonstrate an ability to communicate in the same way that a child who writes a story can? While no absolute answer can be given, it is becoming clear that new technologies can and do have the capacity to transform the very nature of storytelling in new and exciting ways.

Media Stage, for instance, is a virtual television studio where the user can manipulate characters, scenery, lighting and camera angles while inputting their own story through speech or a text-to-speech engine. Composing a story in this environment requires a different set of competencies from the author, yet the base requirement remains the same: the ability to construct and tell a story for a given audience. The use of video is an interesting area of development that can add to the use of role play within a literacy setting.

Planning is also an important element in the organising of effective writing. Determining purpose and audience at the outset is important; thus allowing the student to build on these foundations through a clear organisational process. Mind-mapping software allows learners to create a concept map of their ideas that can be easily organised into themes and a coherent pattern for writing. Many of these software packages provide students with the option of changing these concept maps into a linear planning tool. This tool can also be useful in whole-class brainstorming and sorting activities. This relates back to Moseley *et al.*'s (1999, p. 8) acknowledgement of *the capacity to present or represent ideas dynamically or in multiple forms [and] the capacity to present information in changed forms.*

Providing students with opportunities to use other methods of planning for writing can also be enriched through the use of digital technologies. Storyboarding software is well recognised as is the use of presentation software such as Microsoft's *PowerPoint* to illustrate a story with textual commentary. This allows the students to add illustrations to adorn a story as well as providing the opportunity for a range of images to be used as inspiration for a written narrative. *PowerPoint* can also provide different points of support for a young writer, encouraging a linear development from image as the dominant mode of communication to image as an aid to a more competent writer. This could be used as a support structure for writers at different stages of development or to enable more detailed reflection upon components of writing, for example asking more competent writers to focus on the detail of an image to aid their descriptive writing or providing weaker writers with an opportunity to tell a story through a different mode.

The spellchecker is another interesting generic tool. In the same way that the calculator is not designed to improve the understanding of division but is meant to give students the ability to calculate quickly, so the spellchecker's primary function is not to improve the understanding of spelling but to aid the performance of writing. However, there are benefits in using spellcheckers to aid the understanding of spelling as well as to support wider writing skills, for example, by giving immediate feedback to the user when the computer detects a spelling error and the options for corrections are given.

Consider the following sentence:

I sore the medals and I received to.

Real word errors are not noticed by the spellchecker (sore/saw and too/two). The words 'hte' and 'recieved' are mistyped, both of which were corrected automatically by my spellchecker. 'Hte' is a typographical error caused by poor typing skills and the auto-change function allowed the author to carry on writing without being disturbed by a process error (rather than an error of understanding). However, being unable to apply the well known rule 'i before e, except after c' may well be embedded as no mistake was seemingly noticed by the computer and nothing highlighted to the writer. Spellcheckers can provide support to writers of all abilities and also be used to develop understanding of spelling, but as with all of the technologies described in this chapter, the spellchecker must be used appropriately. One method of appropriate use is to combine spellcheckers with a thesaurus as a way of checking spelling corrections; students who favour more visual approaches to learning can use a visual thesaurus.

Chu (1995) and Wild (1995) have suggested that interactive storybooks and electronic storybooks can be motivational for younger readers. These technologies can support the reader to ask questions that are encouraged during guided reading sessions, such as thinking further about descriptions and meaning within the text. They can also encourage 'active reading', provide feedback relevant to the reader and assist the reader by verbalising the text as well as providing contextual explanations of meaning. The design of these resources can also be reversed to provide an interesting writing framework for students to develop interactive texts for peers.

Reflective and plenary sessions

Using technology as a method of recording discussions, problems and questions for later reflection relates directly to the role of the plenary session. Through the use of visual display technologies, all students' work can be shared with the class combined with a meta-commentary about the processes. In fact, students can easily lead this session by working on a machine attached to a data-projector throughout the lesson.

In addition to the examples above, further key principles of the use of ICT as an aid to teacher demonstration are given below.

- **Highly visual images, animated text and pictures**

  Including adding images to explain instructions and aid explanation.

- **Sound**

  An aid to independent work as the student can access instructions as necessary. The teacher can also pre-program feedback, instructions and guidance before the sessions. Sound is also used as part of many software packages to explain and exemplify written words.

- **Highlighting a teaching point**

  Using packages such as MS *PowerPoint*, practitioners can make their own ICT-based resources for classroom use. The teacher can then focus the resources to a specific teaching point for each lesson. This is very difficult to replicate with commercial materials as it is so specific to individual lessons and teaching styles. However, using hyperlinks and easy-to-use packages such as MS *PowerPoint* and MS *Word*, teachers can ensure resources are dynamic and ICT rich but also focused upon teaching tasks. There are various websites where teachers share resources and developing an understanding of how to alter shared resources and how to evaluate examples provided by other practitioners is an important part of the digitally literate teacher's toolkit.

ICT and the 'literacy learner'

There are a number of benefits accruing to 'literacy learners' in terms of both hardware and software. Below are a number of detailed examples.

- **Highly visual images, animated text and pictures**

  Students can move text boxes together to build phonemes, syllables, words, sentences or paragraphs such as instruction lists. Joining morphemes together to create 'hard words' is an abstract concept that is made tangible through the students grabbing text boxes and dragging them to join onto affixes. This malleability is enhanced with the use of an interactive whiteboard where a more kinaesthetic joining of components can be made.

- **Multi-sensory interface**

  The ability to take advantage of meaning presented in different modes is a key affordance of ICT in this area of learning. Textual communication is supported through oral, aural and visual depiction of meaning to enhance the learner's understanding or opportunity to understand. The animated interface created by hyperlinks and html is also useful in motivation and supporting students' work, as is the opportunity to use different screen colours, fonts, text size and colour.

  The screen interface also affords the students a different environment for their reading. The use of a multimedia interface can also aid reading.

- **Kinaesthetic learning**

  Hand/eye coordination required by manipulating the mouse offers another opportunity for students to engage with their work in a different way. The use of an interactive whiteboard requires students to stand while working and affords the opportunity of using both hands to create meaning. The use of ICT in this way enables students the chance to access different learning styles in literacy work.

- **Improved presentation**

  The screen typed text produced by students ensures clear division between letters, allowing students to clearly recognise letter strands. Students who have poor fine-motor skills and poor handwriting will be given the opportunity to present work in a clearer fashion. This can also be linked to creatively copying work from other sources, being able to build on knowledge of texts around you: books, magazines, posters and many classroom displays that are available as the basis of creative copying are print based and providing students with the opportunity to replicate this style is useful in early stages of writing.

- **Printed text**

  For a weak speller there is limited opportunity to see correctly spelt handwritten work; a few lines of the teacher's marking may be the only real opportunity to view correctly such work. However, posters, books, magazines, television subtitles, classroom displays and most other text which is generally correctly spelt are almost always computer-generated. Students have the opportunity, when working on a computer, to generate their own printed text that allows them to creatively copy correctly spelt work that they have already experienced.

- **Speed of feedback**

  The use of ICT offers immediate feedback that is difficult to replicate through traditional classroom methods. The computer spellchecker immediately highlights incorrectly spelt words. Text concordancing with quick internet-based searches brings in detailed results to student hypotheses within seconds. This allows students to focus upon analysing their results to reach conclusions rather than spending time collecting data. Certain software programs provide feedback in response to student actions. These can be personal and timely in providing students with an opportunity to develop their own understanding through interaction with such programs.

- **Continuity of product**

Taking into consideration the affordances mentioned above, students are offered a chance to work on a computer without having to be concerned about handwriting or presentation. This enables the students to continually focus upon an area of learning rather than an area of presentation. The state of 'flow', where learners are engaged, motivated and involved in their work, can be facilitated by technology that provides various tools for the learner.

- **'WOW' factor**

As with the affordance offered to the teacher/demonstrator, the motivational aspect of using ICT rich environments is still strong and acts as a tool to encourage student work.

- **QWERTY keyboard**

The use of the QWERTY keyboard can lead to a number of changes to the students' writing speed and the way in which they construct individual words. The kinaesthetic learning of separating each individual letter by physically having to move the hand to each letter requires students to concentrate on the make-up of each word. There is discussion about whether primary students should be taught to touch type using a QWERTY keyboard, a tool used for data entry by the majority of adults. Yet consideration needs to be given to a wide variety of input methods available to students of the future: stylus, finger (on whiteboards), voice, movement (Eye-cam).

Case studies

In this section four examples of the ways in which technology can be used to enrich learners' experiences of literacy are presented. The examples or vignettes have been selected because they demonstrate the different affordances of the technology being used and the 'pedagogical affordances' (John, 2005) that help the technology be integrated into teaching and learning.

Vignette I: investigating 'shun'

In this case study from a Year 5 class, ICT is used to:

- **enable a clearer presentation by the teacher;**

- **facilitate quicker searches by the students;**

- **provide greater opportunities for collaborative working;**

- **improve ways of collating research findings and the presentation of them.**

The outline lesson plane is shown in Figure 2.3.

Timing	Description	Role of digital technology
10 minutes	**Reading and recognising 'shun'** Whole-class reading of a poem containing lots of words with the 'shun' sound in.	Data projector/laptop providing clear view with appropriate font type, colour and size and appropriate background colour.
10 minutes	**Word play I**: students 'brainstorm' and exemplify words with 'shun' sound	
10 minutes	**Pseudo words** 'How would you spell prushun'? Students offer possible (phonically regular) methods.	
15 minutes	**Investigation I** Is there a rule that can help us know which spelling of 'shun' we should use? Students write as may words with the 'shun' in them while looking for any rules.	Web searching for letter strands, searching texts using 'find' option in Word. Excel tables used to record results.
5 minutes	**Mini-plenary** Whole-class discussions about spelling rules; sharing data; offering data that conflict and enforces spelling rules.	Cut and paste to record all words in appropriate columns in spreadsheet. Data projector displays for class to see.
5 minutes	**Investigation 2** Students asked to investigate 'shun' sound and to form spelling rules for their homework.	Use of school research methods as well as student's own use of technologies.
Varied: homework	**Language Investigation**	Weekly homework, students set a minimum amount of investigation (20 words) so that they can present their data, their spelling rule and their analysis of the data.
20 minutes (next session)	**Plenary** Discussion of language investigation, teacher highlights any spelling rules that have been proved and whole class present exceptions and qualifications of the rule.	Cut and paste to record all words in appropriate columns in spreadsheet. Data projector displays for class to see.

Figure 2.3: Lesson plan for session entitled: Investigating 'shun'

The broad aim of the lesson was to enable pupils to investigate the syllable pronounced 'shun'. The specific purpose was to let the children explore the possibility of being able to use words containing this syllable when the writer has no visual memory of the word. For example, if they were to write 'mission' without previous knowledge of the word, how might they decide whether it was mission, mittion, mition, micion, micean or mician?

Many students went about this task by working through any text they could find, searching for any word that had a 'shun' sound in it and then writing it in their language book. The majority of students wrote these words in categories depending on their spelling strands. The independent self-study which was at the core of the task resulted in a huge amount of data being collected by the class as a whole. Catherine, for example, far exceeded the rest of the class by collecting over 2,000 words that contained a 'shun' sound.

Other students used internet searches to find words, and then wrote families of words to extend their word count. This highlights the way in which the students' understanding of words was developing, in particular, being able to use words they already knew to help form related words that they did not know.

An example of the recording system used is set out below.

Sion	Tion	Cian	Cean
Profession	Ambition	Musician	Ocean
Fusion	Motion	Physician	Crustacean
Intrusion		Politician	

Figure 2.4: Example of data collection method

The next session began with students sharing the findings from their language investigations and providing examples of rules that the students believed would be helpful when trying a new word that had a 'shun' sound in it.

The analysis by the students presented the following guidelines for use:

Cian is used mainly for jobs where the root word ends with a 'c' (i.e. a job in music is for a musician).
Cean is only used for words that involve water.
Sion is used when the root word ends with 's' or 'd'.
Tion is the most common form of 'shun'.
'Shun' is only used in shun, shunt, shunts, and shunted – so don't use it anywhere else!

These guidelines were presented following a class discussion and were not influenced directly by the teacher. Although the topic of investigation was initiated by the teacher (with reference to the class results from the formative assessment process), the students decided to carry out the research themselves with some working in groups and others individually. Some chose 'ICT-rich' research tools while others relied solely on pen and paper. The excitement of the class at reaching a set of class agreed guidelines was notable. With a class list of words, created from individual research projects, the students were able to create their own hypotheses about the English language. Throughout, the students were collaboratively constructing new knowledge through a process of investigation which led directly to the writing of a large number of words that the students had no visual memories of.

Vignette 2: predicting phonic letter strands

As with the previous vignette, this example was part of an investigation into finding ways of selecting the appropriate letter strands to represent an irregular phoneme. A skeletal lesson plan is presented in Figure 2.5 to show a sense of the timings of the main events of the lessons.

Timing	Description	Commentary/examples
10 minutes	**Phonic play 1**: students 'brainstorm' words that are phonically regular. **Phonic play 2**: students 'brainstorm' and exemplify the phoneme /e/	Mind-mapping software to record answers.
Various – throughout session	**Reading and recognising phoneme /e/** Lower ability students use teacher made PowerPoint 'activity' of highlighting phoneme /e/.	Students select phoneme within a word, correct selection reiterates selection and moves to next word.
10 minutes	**Pseudo words** 'How would you spell Thr/e/t? Students offer possible (phonically regular) methods.	Threet, threat, thriet, threyt, etc.
15 minutes	**Investigation 1** Is there a rule that can help us know which spelling of the /e/ phoneme we should use? Students write as many words with the /e/ phoneme in them while looking for any rules.	Students use different resources to find words and various methods for recording including tables and groupings, and seemingly unstructured recording.
5 minutes	**Mini-plenary** Whole class discussions and discussions about spelling rules; sharing data; offering data that conflicts and enforces spelling rules.	Cut and paste to record all words in appropriate columns in spreadsheet. Data projector displays for class to see.
5 minutes	**Investigation 2** Students asked to investigate one spelling rule for their homework. Students write their spelling rule and begin to use time to collect more data.	Web searching for letter strands, searching texts using 'find' option in Word. Excel tables used to record results.
Varied: homework	**Language Investigation** Weekly homework, students set a minimum amount of investigation (20 words) so that they can present their data, their spelling rule and their analysis of the data.	Web searching for letter strands, searching texts using 'find' option in word. Excel tables used to record results.
20 minutes (next session)	**Plenary** Discussion of language investigation, teacher highlights any spelling rules that have been proved and whole class present exceptions and qualifications of the rule.	Cut and paste to record all words in appropriate columns in spreadsheet. Data projector displays for class to see.

Figure 2.5: Lesson plan for session entitled: Investigating the phoneme /e/

This lesson took place towards the end of the final year of the research project. Students were asked to consider whether there were any spelling rules to help them build the sound /e/. For example, if they attempted to write the word 'bossy', and they had no visual memory of the word, how would they choose to write it? Using 'synthetic phonics' the students presented the possibility that the word could be spelt: bossee, bossy, bossey, bossie, bossea, bossei, or even bossiegh. The students then began to collect words that included an /e/ sound and then categorised them into groups according to letter strands. With this bank of data, each student compared and contrasted with data collected by others within the class community. The students were asked again to suggest methods for attempting new words that included the /e/ sound.

Differentiation was achieved by the use of a 'teacher-constructed' hyperlinked presentation that allowed lower-ability students the chance to read and recognise the phoneme /e/ as an introduction to their investigation (see Figure 2.6). The slides were hyperlinked so that the student would only move to the next screen when they had selected the exact letter strand that represented the phoneme /e/.

Screen 1: Introduction to the task

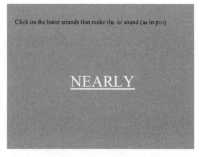

Screen 2: Presentation of word

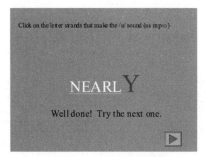

Screen 3: Reaction to correct selection

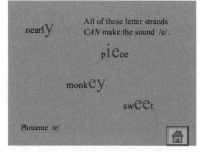

Screen 4: Reviewing letter strands

Figure 2.6: Teacher-made activity for reading and recognising the phoneme /e/

This style of the student task was designed to take advantage of the affordance of hyperlinks and to make the teaching point visually 'jump out' at the learner. The on-screen action was activated by the learner and the final screen (screen 4) presented words with particular letter strands (in this case the phoneme /e/) highlighted in an exaggerated manner.

Below is a description of an activity undertaken by Joe during his investigation.

Joe's hypothesis: The spelling strand 'ey' only makes the sound /e/ when at the end of a word.

Joe tested his hypothesis using skills he brought from outside the classroom. This skill showed a good understanding of ICT and high levels of data analysis. Joe opened the internet and accessed the 'Ask Jeeves' website. In the query field he entered 'diction-ary' and in the next query field he entered five tests, each time recording the results through cut and paste methods, printing and pen and paper marking.

Figure 2.7 shows a table detailing his test.

	Text entered into query field	Reason for test
Ist test	????ey	Search revealed list of words with ey letter strand at end of word.
2nd test	???ey?	Ey letter strand towards end of word.
3rd test	??ey??	Ey letter strand in middle of word.
4th test	?ey???	Ey letter strand towards beginning of word.
5th test	ey???	Ey letter strand at beginning of word.

Figure 2.7: Joe's method for data collection

The 'home-use' of ICT that Joe brought to the classroom was greeted with excitement by the class when he produced his results. Joe then spent nearly ten minutes explain-ing his research methods to the class community describing how he used a question mark (?) to represent an unknown quantity. Joe was only interested in searching for words with the letter strand /ey/ and was not interested in what the other letters were in the words he had discovered. Using this method of investigation, Joe found words from 'abomey' to 'winey' in a matter of seconds, creating a vast data bank for his analysis.

Joe then cross-referenced his investigation data with his own knowledge of phonics to see if he could prove his spelling rule. He presented it to the class and other students used their knowledge (developed through their investigations) to discuss his predic-tions.

Figure 2.8 gives a short extract of the conversation from the classroom combined with teacher commentary and discussion (in italics).

			Commentary and discussion
I	Joe	My spelling rule is that if you spell [the sound] /e/ at the end of a word it will be spelt ey.	*Joe presents a spelling rule that is incorrect although ey is a common ending for words.*
2	Ben	What about eye? That's not at the end of a word.	*Ben provides a word that doesn't follow Joe's rule (an incorrect word as eye is an /i/ sound, not an /e/ sound).*
3	Joe	Oh yeah.	*Joe accepts Ben's word even though it is incorrect.*
4	Ben	Oh no, that's not an /e/ sound.	*Ben realises his error and corrects his statement.*
5	Joe	Yeah, so I'm right. My rule's right.	*Joe then assumes his rule is correct.*
6	Claire	What about sea or bee?	*Claire finds two valid words that counter Joe's claim.*
7	Joe	Oh yeah.	*Words accepted by Joe.*
8	Claire	Or she.	*Claire offers another exception to Joe's rule.*
9	Joe	OK, so if you use ey at the end of a word it will say /e/.	*Using the new data, Joe alters his rule so that it includes Claire's new words.*
10	Claire	That's like a reading rule isn't it?	*Claire highlights a different stage at which such a rule would be useful — in decoding words for pronunciation, rather than for encoding words in spelling.*
11	Joe	Yeah.	*Joe accepts the new version of his rule.*

Figure 2.8: Interaction between students presenting spelling rules

The interaction presented in Figure 2.8 shows a common discussion that often takes place between students when a new rule is presented. During the lesson, students compare data to inform their spelling rules as they aim to create a new spelling rule. The teacher introduces a further incentive when he says that any new rules would be sent off to the editors of the *Oxford English Dictionary* to make them aware of the new finding.

It was not just the manner in which Joe was able to share his ideas within the class community that was impressive but his use of 'higher-order' thinking skills of prediction and analysis. Joe was able to enter into a discourse with the class community to reason about the structure of the English language in a detailed and knowledgeable way. During this one episode Joe had:

• **predicted a spelling rule;**

- encountered a vast number of words by using an intelligently positioned research tool;

- clarified his position through discussion with classmates.

This experience is far richer than the usual memory game of ten words per week and lent itself to Joe developing a complex understanding of the English spelling system. Joe's learning also impacted on his assessment results which showed a definite improvement beyond those predicted at the beginning of the year.

Vignette 3: Wordwalls

The analogy of *building language knowledge* and of *building words* develops the idea, mentioned earlier, of communicative tools. In a stage of the program *WordRoot* entitled *WordWalls*, a screen is presented with various words 'graffiti'd' on it. When the user selects a word it is either said aloud, contextualised or explained. This screen caused particular interest to the students and at the end of a language session, they asked if they could create their own *Wordwalls* during an ICT lesson. The *Wordwalls* created were entirely of the students' own choice and the community shared expertise in adding hyperlinks and in seeking specific content, for example various images or methods of recording sound.

Figures 2.9 to 2.13 provide a selection of the *Wordwalls* created, along with a short description.

Ceri and Gareth's investigations into how children of different ages pronounce the word 'dictionary'. By selecting the objects (for example 'Age 4') a sound recording is played of a child saying the word, saying the letters or the phonemes, according to their ability.

Figure 2.9: Ceri and Gareth's presentation

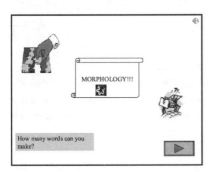

Fraser's opening page of his presentation of morphemes. He produced three other slides that showed prefixes, root words and suffixes that could be manipulated to form new words. Fraser used animated images from clipart to add to his work.

Figure 2.10: Fraser's presentation

Figure 2.11: Adam's presentation

Adam's presentation of analytical morphology: dissecting the word bicycle into its constituent parts of 'bi' (Greek meaning two) and 'cycle' (Greek meaning circle or wheel). Adam's hyperlinks explained these morphemes and then gave a literal and common definition of the word bicycle.

Figure 2.12: Tiffany's presentation

Tiffany's examination of the word decathlon (meaning ten contests). In a similar way to Adam's presentation, Tiffany invited the reader to investigate the meaning of each morpheme before giving a common and a literal definition.

Figure 2.13: Whole-class *Wordwall*

Whole-class constructed wordwall investigating how many ways of saying the word 'hello'. The investigation looked at audience and purpose (i.e. why you would use different words to say hello in different contexts and to different people). Each object (for example 'G'day') would trigger a sound recording of the student who suggested the word.

These *Wordwalls* offered the students a chance to represent their understanding of language in a multimodal presentational form that allowed them to follow their own personal interests and motivations. The presentations were shared between class members with the students explaining their work and helping each other to interact with their 'learning products'.

Vignette 4: Quorum Tools

In its evaluation of the first four years of the National Literacy Strategy, Ofsted claimed that *Good shared writing was much less common than good shared reading*

(Ofsted, 2002). New technologies can be used to support shared writing in a number of ways: from data projectors that allow sharing of the process and product of writing, and Quorum Tools that support multiple styluses working on one document, to using laptops and desktops that allow multiple authors to write within one presentation.

The example given below is taken from a year 6 class. The work was undertaken as part of a 'writing week' that saw collaborative narrative composition, enriched by science, numeracy and art activities that supported the theme of the writing.

Time to reflect

As you read through this example, consider how the technology enables:

- *collaborative process;*
- *editing and re-representation of ideas;*
- *negotiation and communication between authors;*
- *presentation of a real audience and a real reason for writing.*

The class worked together to create a collaborative adventure quest story. As a way of extending the current trend of writing 40-minute short stories, the teacher asked the students to work in pairs to construct two chapters that would be closely linked to chapters produced by the rest of the class. The genre of adventure quest is one which gives the reader the power to direct the main character's action at the end of each chapter by making a key choice that affects the story. Traditionally this will be offered with the response '... now turn to page *xx*', yet by presenting the story as on-screen text, the reader makes choices by selecting hyperlinks marked at the end of each chapter. During this series of lessons the students therefore created a shared construct of hyperfiction (Snyder, 2002).

The lesson had three main learning objectives:

1. To write following a set authorial style.

2. To construct a narrative fictional story following a given structure.

3. To hyperlink work to that produced by other students in the class.

The framework for the class book required each student to write their own chapter that had links to the overall story, was a self-contained adventure and started from the same scene as the preceding chapter ended, as shown in Figure 2.14, in which each chapter is represented by a single box.

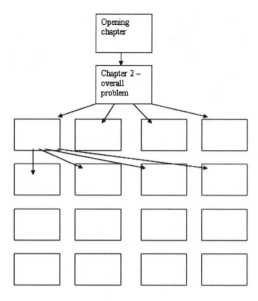

Figure 2.14: Schematic of the class book

Chapter	Activity	Role of technology
Opening	Teacher meta-cognitively models style and structure of writing using student suggestions and ideas. Discussion about make-up of class book, writing style, planning style, key characters (including description), allocation of chapters.	Visual display technology highlights shared work to whole class; word processor allows input, editing and reviewing. Font, colours, size used to highlight adjectives and adverbs (related to sentence-level work). Visual representations of make-up of book to aid understanding about class construct. Data projector/laptop ensured teacher could type work while maintaining eye contact with students.
2	Teacher as scribe, students offering sentences that fit with style, embellished by others in class. Discussion about orally constructed sentences and consistency of style. Students move from observers of writing process to inputting ideas.	As above, more use of editing functions as classmates added to/embellished sentences.
3–9 (including 4 ending chapters)	Students composing own chapters, working in pairs to share ideas and to develop content within class structure. Use of word processors using same font type, weaker writers copying teacher's introductory framework. The scaffolding process created by this learning situation was a powerful model that the students could copy creatively in order to construct their own narrative. Use of NetOp (management tool, to share ideas and discuss storylines, including how each chapter affects overall story.	Following dynamic worksheet created by teacher to mimic structure of writing. Developing student ownership of work. Creative copying – use of same text etc. Reviewing work by peers and teacher, editing of work. Use of NetOp for students to share ideas, share storylines and to question outcome of chapters.

Conclusion

As this chapter has shown, literacy is undergoing significant and rapid reconceptualisation and digital tools are accentuating this. These 'Silicon Literacies,' as Snyder (2002) terms them, mean that young children are growing up in a media-saturated age, and in consequence teaching will require an even greater emphasis on new modes of expression. One response would be to 'inoculate' children against the ineluctable tide of cyber-culture – this would involve a retreat into a world of bookish high culture where all forms of media and computer culture are derogated. An alternative, more progressive, response would be to bring the renewed emphasis on reading and writing abilities (resulting from computer-mediated technologies) to bear on the curriculum and practice of primary literacy. This is the approach taken in this chapter. It encourages teachers to help children to read, analyse, and decode a variety of texts while at the same time teaching them to be critical of the variety of media representations and discourses they encounter. The examples and practices outlined in the chapter also stress the importance of self-expression and creativity and show how ICT can blend with recognisable pedagogies to create what Rourke and Anderson (2002, p. 3) term *An act of encoding* where:

> *Ideas in textual format and communicating them to others forces cognitive processing and a resulting clarity that is strongly associated with scholarly practice and effective communication.*

3 PROMOTING NUMERACY WITH ICT
HEIDI PRICE AND DAVID MOORE

Computers are useless. They can only give you answers.

Pablo Picasso (1881–1973)

This chapter will enable you to:

- **explore how ICT can enhance children's numeracy learning;**
- **contextualise educational theory within ICT and numeracy;**
- **understand how ICT can fit into the National Numeracy Strategy;**
- **evaluate numeracy software and how it can be applied in a number of teaching contexts.**

Introduction

This chapter examines some of the key developments in the National Numeracy Strategy over the last two years within the context of promoting maths through ICT. It initially lays some of the theoretical background exploring the ways that ICT can be used in the classroom to enhance teaching and learning and then gives examples of ways to use the Interactive Teaching Programmes (ITPs) that are currently being developed to enable children to grasp difficult mathematical concepts. Finally this chapter suggests examples of ways of using ICT to develop mathematical understanding during different phases of the daily mathematics lesson.

How can we use ICT to enhance teaching and learning?

Pablo Picasso's quote at the start of this chapter tells us a lot more about human nature than it does about computers. However, one thing it does show us is that the computer operates on the basis of logic, and as such it is an entirely useful tool to promote mathematics learning. With careful planning and a rudimentary understanding of the capabilities of available software, ICTs such as the personal computer can be used with positive outcomes to promote good numeracy education at Key Stages 1 and 2.

When a teacher is embedding the use of ICT across the curriculum there are five stages that can be considered (Hooper and Reiber, 1995). This framework was introduced earlier in Chapter 1, but it will be useful to revisit it here within a numeracy context.

- *Familiarisation* – **a teacher is becoming increasingly aware of ICT, and may have attended some in-service training (INSET), but rarely (and often reluctantly)** tries to use it in his or her classroom teaching. At this stage the ICT may not enhance the teaching and learning as the teacher is not confident enough to rely on the technology.

- *Utilisation* – a teacher becomes increasingly aware of the benefits of technology, and begins to incorporate it into teaching, often 'replacing' former activities with ICT alternatives. This begins to have a beneficial effect on teaching and learning, although use remains fragile and the teacher is often set back, for example by technical hitches. Teaching and learning at this stage is enhanced.

- *Integration* – a teacher is becoming increasingly familiar with appropriate uses of ICT, and can integrate it into many aspects of his or her ongoing daily teaching. Teaching and learning begins to be very significantly enhanced.

- *Reorientation* – the potential of the ICT is now exploited to move into new areas and approaches that could not easily be replicated by more 'traditional' means. Teaching and learning begins to be significantly transformed.

- *Evolution* – the developmental and *creative* possibilities of the ICT are being fully explored. ICT use can grow and develop in response to the needs of the learner and the consequent teaching implications. Teaching and learning is very significantly transformed.

When considering the possibilities of enhancing the maths curriculum with ICT it is important to include calculators as well as computers, and extend to the whole range of audio-visual aids, including audio tape, video film and educational broadcasts.

The whole range of ICT can be used in various ways to meet two important goals in the teaching of mathematics:

- to support teaching;

- to motivate children's learning.

Before it can transform, ICT must be used to enhance good mathematics teaching. ICT should be used in lessons only if it supports good practice in teaching mathematics. Any decision about using ICT in a particular lesson or sequence of lessons must be directly related to the teaching and learning objectives for those lessons.

Teachers must ask themselves the question: does the use of ICT help to achieve teaching and learning more effectively?

ICT in the classroom to support teaching

In teaching, ICT can be used to enhance a number of teaching strategies:

Modelling

Using ICT, concepts and ideas can be presented in a variety of forms and very often in a dynamic way that can be used to model the concept or idea being presented. For example, using the Interactive Teaching Programme (ITP) for division it is possible to model the concept of division as grouping (see Figure 3.1). The dynamic quality of the ICT allows the link from the representation of the calculation with objects to the representation of the calculation with a number line to be clearly made.

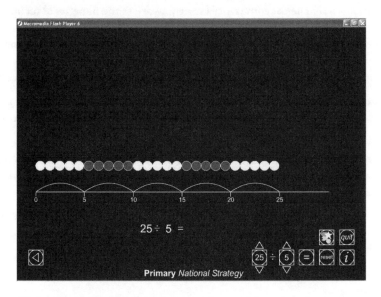

Figure 3.1: Interactive Teaching Programme used to model number division as grouping

Demonstrating

This is a teaching approach that can be exploited by the use of ICT in every subject. Using ICT the teacher can effectively demonstrate methods, illustrate procedures and set out instructions and processes for the whole group to observe. For example, the 'What's my angle?' program from the NNS ICT CD-ROM demonstrates how to place the protractor over an angle to measure it. This is a very powerful medium when presented using an interactive whiteboard, with children immediately able to observe the consequences of changes to angles.

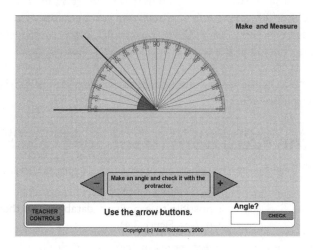

Figure 3.2: The NNS Protractor

Accessing and analysing

We know that children have preferred learning styles and that it is important to use a variety of approaches that incorporate these preferences. Sue Waite's chapter on individual differences in learning in this book is a useful elaboration on this theme. ICT can support visual, auditory and even kinaesthetic learning. It can allow access to data and information in a wide variety of forms and formats (sometimes involving the use of multimedia). Such data can often be manipulated to accommodate different learning styles and approaches. The use of ICT to quickly change and reconfigure data or information provides the teacher with opportunities to engage with children at a higher and/or deeper level and, in particular, facilitates analysis and interrogation.

The interactive website Illuminations (**illuminations.nctm.org/**) provides the teacher with a dynamic tool to explore the way changing the numerator and the denominator of a fraction affects its size (see Figure 3.3). Again the dynamic quality of this application allows the pictorial representation to change as the abstract numerical representation of the vulgar fraction is altered.

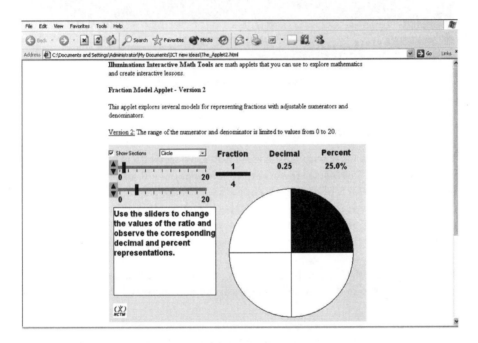

Figure 3.3: Illuminations software

Presenting, re-presenting and communicating

ICT opens up many new opportunities for presentation, re-presentation and communication. Information can now be presented in more exciting and engaging ways, creating motivating outcomes for a wide variety of learning objectives, e.g. by using the ITP for data handling. It is possible to examine a database and then re-present this as a bar chart or a pictogram (see Figure 3.4).

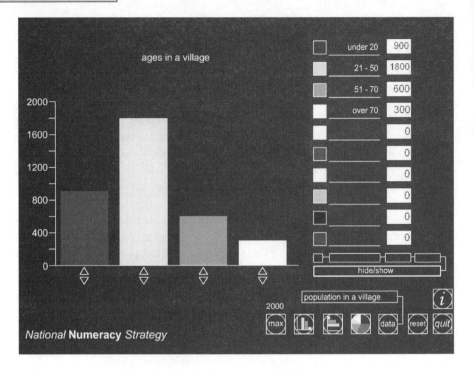

Figure 3.4: Bar chart and pictogram

Testing and confirming

This is perhaps the most potent aspect of interactive software in numeracy teaching. The power of ICT allows speedy access to information and instant modification of data. It is a powerful tool because it can enhance the development of children's skills of analysis and hypothesis. Children can be encouraged to deepen their level of enquiry and generate their own questions and hypotheses, which they can then easily test and confirm within a non-threatening environment.

Making an error should not be a problem, as children can quickly re-enter data, change parameters and try again, until they arrive at a successful solution.

The children can receive feedback on their attempts and act upon them without feeling judged. This affordance of the technology can promote greater risk taking and creativity. One example of this kind would be the setting up of an Excel spreadsheet containing a dynamic problem that allows the children to test out a variety of solutions to find the correct answer (see Figure 3.5). In this example the teacher may ask:

'Can you make both the answers the same in the green boxes?'

'What do you notice about the numbers in the blue boxes?'

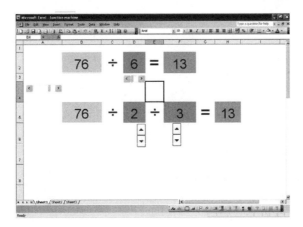

Figure 3.5: Dynamic problem displayed on an Excel spreadsheet

ICT as a tool for learning in mathematics

Historically, mathematics has always been a subject where the use of computers is widespread and in many schools computing was the purview of the maths teacher. Perhaps the view of mathematics as a set of rules to be learnt and as a subject where there is always only one correct answer has fuelled this link. However, many of the mathematical activities which children have engaged in using computers are highly directed tasks – this is sometimes referred to as 'drill and skill'. At their worst these programs use the power of a computer to do little more than animate what are essentially worksheets. Some of the more sophisticated programs respond to the child's incorrect responses with feedback and hints, but they still offer limited opportunities for children to pursue their own lines of enquiry or for teachers to plan for work to encourage problem-solving.

ICT has the potential to transform the way numeracy lessons are delivered and developed. The Primary National Strategy identified the eight key aspects of ICT shown in Figure 3.6 which allow work in all areas of the curriculum to be approached in alternative ways to those seen practised in traditional learning environments.

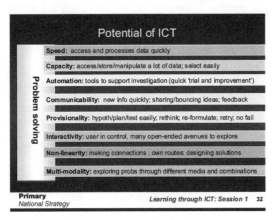

Figure 3.6: Potential of ICT in teaching and learning

Open 'content-free' software allows ICT to support children's mathematical thinking through these strengths of the technology. This includes several software applications such as spreadsheets. Take a few minutes to think through the problem in the Activity below.

Activity

Think about the following problem:

Farmer Jones has bought 100 pieces of fence.
Each piece is 1 metre long.

He wants to enclose the largest area of land that he can with this fencing.

What is the largest area he can enclose?

What shape would this field be?

In traditional pencil and paper approaches to the task children would have to perform a large number of calculations to solve the problem. If they performed all calculations accurately they would find the largest area.

The manner in which a spreadsheet such as Excel can conduct any number of calculations accurately and quickly at the touch of a key (speed and automation) allows children to explore a problem of this kind very quickly, reaching conclusions and moving towards a generalisable solution as, once the worksheet has been set up by the pupil to explore the initial problem, they can easily adapt it for finding solutions to related problems or those with a similar structure. For example: *What is the largest area that Farmer Giles can enclose with his 100 pieces of one-metre fencing?* Figure 3.7 shows how the spreadsheet could be used to perform this calculation, and generalise to other similar problem spaces.

	width of field	length of field	area of field	perimeter of field
1	1	49	49	100
2	2	48	96	100
3	3	47	141	100
4	4	46	184	100
5	5	45	225	100
6	6	44	264	100
7	7	43	301	100
8	8	42	336	100
9	9	41	369	100
10	10	40	400	100
11	11	39	429	100
12	12	38	456	100
13	13	37	481	100
14	14	36	504	100
15	15	35	525	100
16	16	34	544	100
17	17	33	561	100
18	18	32	576	100
19	19	31	589	100
20	20	30	600	100
21	21	29	609	100
22	22	28	616	100
23	23	27	621	100
24	24	26	624	100

Figure 3.7: Use of the Excel Spreadsheet

Using a program such as *Counter* children can explore a range of mathematical problems involving sequences of numbers fairly quickly, each time getting an accurate response, until they find a set of numbers which fulfil the desired criteria. Children's confidence can be boosted by early success in the solving of maths problems.

Activity

Examine the computer screen in Figure 3.8 and then consider the problem below:

Set one counter to 7, the other counter to 15.

Can you set the step size on each counter so that after the 4th step the two counters each read the same?

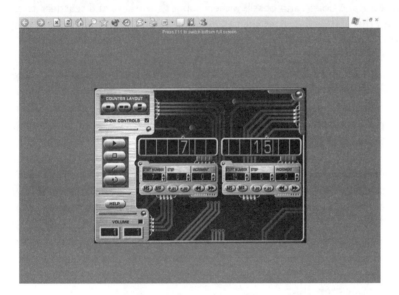

Figure 3.8: The Counter program

Children working on this problem can try a pair of numbers and if they do not work they can try another pair, only recording when they have a pair which fulfils the given criterion. This ability to try out an answer, find whether it is correct or not and then try another response if the first is not correct (known as 'provisionality') is again important in developing problem-solving skills such as reasoning and generalising, and also in providing motivation to persevere.

Learning contexts

We can identify three principal contexts of learning that can be observed in schools:

- **learning in a *community*;**
- **learning *collaboratively*;**
- **learning *independently*.**

Interplay between these three contexts has been well established in the literacy hour and in the daily mathematics lesson, but now needs to be further understood and exploited, both in these subjects and across the primary curriculum.

Time to reflect

How can ICT be used to support numeracy teaching when:

- *learning in a community?*
- *learning collaboratively?*
- *learning independently?*

Learning in a community implies that whole groups of children are engaged together in thinking and doing, and possibly their support workers and teachers too. Large-screen presentational devices such as interactive whiteboards and digital projectors could be utilised to involve the 'community' of learners in a common action.

Learning collaboratively could involve two or more children engaged in a common problem-based task. This could be supported by simple shared desk top computer resources and open, content-free software such as a spreadsheet. Alternatively, networked computers could be used to connect children's ideas for comparison or for the posting of solutions to maths problems.

Learning independently might be supported through the use of personal computers, or calculators. The use of the internet to access specialised maths websites and for exploration of number could also be encouraged as a supervised activity.

The Primary Strategy has identified some key aspects of learning across the curriculum which can be mapped across the three contexts we have explored above:

- **information processing;**
- **reasoning;**
- **enquiry;**
- **creativity;**
- **evaluation;**
- **problem-solving.**

Time to reflect

Think back to your own days in school (if you can) and try to remember how you acquired the above skills.

- *Was a technology or computer involved in the process?*
- *How difficult is it to teach these skills?*
- *How could the use of ICT transform the teaching of these skills?*

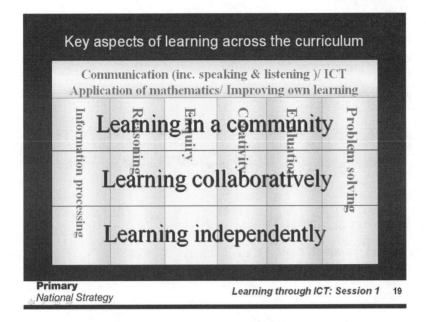

Figure 3.9: Key aspects of cross-curricular learning

Figure 3.9 demonstrates the way that we can enhance learning in all three contexts across each aspect. Overarching the curriculum is the methodology each teacher chooses to use to develop these aspects in the lesson. In this diagram they include the way teachers select the prominent means of communication, the way they use ICT to promote teaching and learning and the way they teach children to apply their understanding and encourage them to reflect on their learning.

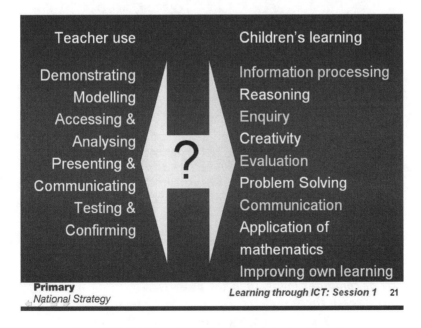

Figure 3.10: Bridging the gap between method and learning

An examination of Figure 3.10 should prompt you to consider how your own use of ICT can promote children's learning in the key aspects of the curriculum related to numeracy.

Teaching tip

When planning a lesson where ICT will be used, you may find that a good starting point will be to make a clear decision about which skills you would like the children to develop and through which style or styles this would be most appropriately achieved.

A lesson example

Let's take an example lesson where ICT is going to be used as the central teaching resource. The focus of the lesson is to teach the children to understand how to order numbers up to 20. The teacher chooses to use the Interactive Teaching Program software to show ordering of numbers, *demonstrating* the way to place numbers on the number line between two known values. The teacher knows that the children will be information processing the new skills and by choosing some specific questions he or she can encourage the children to develop skills in *reasoning* and *enquiry*.

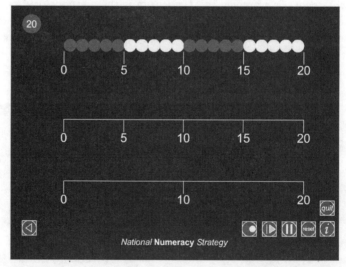

Figure 3.11: Software modelling the ordering of numbers

Using the learning task defined in Figure 3.11, the teacher can pose a series of questions to the children following a defined progression from simple to complex.

According to Bloom *et al.* (1956) there is a defined taxonomy (hierarchical list) of cognitive complexity that can be applied in teaching to develop thinking skills. Bloom and his colleagues proposed six levels of cognitive (or thinking) skills, progressing from the simple to the complex as follows:

- knowledge;
- comprehension;
- application;
- analysis;
- synthesis;
- evaluation.

Activity

The teacher asks the children several questions, progressing from simple to complex. Place these questions in ascending order of complexity according to Bloom's taxonomy:

'How could we find numbers between 0 and 100?'

'How do you know where to put 17?'

'What are the important guides that help you to place numbers in the right place?'

'Where would you put 17 on the first number line?'

'Can you put it in the correct place on the second and third number lines?'

'Do you think you could find any number position now?'

This is not an easy exercise, and you may disagree but here is our solution and rationale for the activity:

- The question: 'Where would you put 17 on the first number line?' is the simplest of the questions, and relates to the acquisition of *knowledge,* because it assesses whether the pupil knows where to place the number. The teacher would ask this kind of question first and often.

- The question: 'Can you put it in the correct place on the second and third number lines?' is a *comprehension* question as it tests that the child understands the mathematical principles involved in the task. This is a little more complex than the first question and would be posed once the teacher had established that the pupil could demonstrate an elementary knowledge.

- The question: 'How do you know where to put 17?' is an *application* question because it is testing the child's ability to make use of the principle articulated in the previous question. It is deeper and more probing than the first two questions, asking the child to justify his placing of the number on the computer screen.

- The question: 'What are the important guides that help you to place numbers in the right place?' relates to the skill of *analysis,* as it asks the child to decide what the reasons are for making the decision to place figures in the correct position on the screen. The pupil would be required to break down the operations and see how they fitted together to produce the correct answer.

- The question: 'How could we find numbers between 0 and 100?' is a question of *synthesis* in that it tests the child's ability to combine two or more mathematical principles together to enable him or her to arrive at the answer. This kind of question would be asked when the child is sufficiently advanced in his or her understanding to combine ideas to form a sophisticated appreciation of the task.

- Finally, the question: 'Do you think you could find any number position now?' requires the child to make a judgement based on generalisable rules, and is therefore *evaluative* in nature. This is by far the most complex of the cognitive skills that would be required to solve any problem based on the maths principle being taught. Questions of this type would be the last questions asked and would signal that the child had developed a fair expertise in undertaking mathematical tasks of this nature.

In the above lesson example, the software provides a dynamic setting for the children to explore number relationships, and frees the teacher to focus on 'higher order questions' to promote deeper learning. The children are engaged with the task in front of them on screen, and are prompted to progress in their mathematical reasoning by well placed and correctly sequenced questions that provide a tacit form of learning assessment. The first three questions are lower order and those most frequently used, and the later three questions build on acquired knowledge and understanding once the child becomes more expert. They are higher order questions which children find more difficult to answer spontaneously, and therefore require careful planning on the part of the teacher and a deeper level of cognitive engagement by the children.

Conclusion

ICT can offer many opportunities for developing children's mathematical understanding and improving their reasoning skills. As a teaching tool the dynamic properties of software such as the Interactive Teaching Programs produced by the Primary National Strategy allow the teacher to model mathematical ideas, adapting the images to the needs of the children during the lesson.

The eight key strengths of ICT outlined in this chapter can allow children, when working independently on mathematical activities, to focus on the higher order reasoning aspects of the problem-solving rather than simply on the calculations required. Where combined with good communication skills and well planned questioning techniques, ICT can act as a powerful influence on the reasoning and problem-solving skills of children as they learn. On its own, ICTs are useful tools. With good teaching support, ICT can be instrumental in transforming the numeracy provision in a school.

Useful websites

BECTa: **www.becta.org.uk** (accessed 4 December 2004)
King's College London Assessment for Learning Group: **www.kcl.ac.uk/depsta/ education/research/kal.html]** (accessed 4 January 2005)
National Curriculum in Action Creativity **www.naction.org.uk/creativity/index. htm** (accessed 10 January 2005)

Primary National Strategy: **www.standards.dfes.gov.uk/primary/** (accessed 8 January 2005)

Qualifications and Curriculum Authority: **www.qca.org.uk/ages3-14/66.html** (accessed 10 January 2005)

Reflective Teaching: **www.rtweb.info** (accessed 5 December 2004)

Resource materials on the Teachernet website – over 2000 lesson plans, materials on various topics and themes and information on delivering each key stage of the curriculum: **www.teachernet.gov.uk/teachingandlearning/** (accessed 16 December 2004)

4 ICT AND MUSIC – EMBEDDING ICT WHEN TEACHING MUSIC AND PROMOTING CREATIVITY

ROBERT BENNETT AND WILL McBURNIE

It's easy to play any musical instrument: all you have to do is touch the right key at the right time and the instrument will play itself.

J. S. Bach

This chapter will enable you to:

- appreciate some of the causes and implications of 'musicphobia';
- better understand how national initiatives, including the promotion of teaching with ICT, can be applied to music teaching;
- consider a rationale for teaching music and promoting creativity;
- explore the possibilities for using ICT to scaffold children's learning in music;
- begin to formulate a strategy for effective adoption and use of ICT in music teaching.

Bach to basics ...

Anyone who plays an instrument would tell you that Bach's statement is not true for most of us! Before we get to a stage of fluency, we have to learn instrumental technique and develop an understanding of music to create and interpret it. Bach is recognised as a musical genius: he could sit at the organ and improvise complex pieces as a matter of course. In Bach's career, throughout the first half of the eighteenth century, great strides were made in music technology with many of the instruments that we know and use today being developed. Nowadays when we use the term music technology we predominantly mean the use of ICT in music-making. Perhaps people today have a view that it is easy to make music using electronic keyboards and music software – all you have to do is press a button or click the mouse! To think of ICT in music in this way is to miss the point. Many musicians who incorporate music technology into their work still employ advanced instrumental skills. If music technology is incorporated effectively into music education it can provide a valuable and transformative tool for learning. This chapter is designed to help you develop a strategy to effectively adopt and use ICT in music teaching. A table listing key areas of music technology is included at the end of the chapter for your reference.

Causes and implications of 'musicphobia'

There are many reasons why Initial Teacher Training (ITT) students are likely to see fewer examples of primary music teaching in schools than other subjects. The emphasis on core subjects of the National Curriculum in recent years has frequently distorted the primary curriculum to the disadvantage of children's learning in the foundation subjects. The National Advisory Committee on Creative and Cultural Education (NACCCE) reported:

> Many of those who have contributed to our inquiry believe that current priorities and pressures in education inhibit the creative abilities of young people and of those who teach them. There is a particular concern about the place and status of the arts and humanities. (NACCCE, 1999, p. 8)

Many schools are now beginning to address this, refocusing on the requirement for a 'broad and balanced' curriculum. In the same way that some teachers have lacked confidence in the use of ICT, many primary teachers have not felt confident to teach music. Issues around 'technophobia' are addressed by Steve Wheeler and Anne Winter in Chapter 1. Primary teachers of music sometimes have concerns about ICT in music teaching because they believe that ICT can stifle children's learning in music: they see ICT as undermining the instrumental and aural skills that children should develop as 'the technology does it for you'. Good teachers see ICT as a tool for learning and know when and how to use it to promote learning in music.

To understand something of teachers' musicphobia can help us to promote positive learning experiences for children in music. A common cry from teachers is,

'I don't play an instrument,' or

'... I can't read music.'

If we considered an analogy with other subjects, would primary teachers not teach physical education because they considered themselves 'not in peak physical condition?' Would they refuse to teach art because they did not think of themselves as artists? To be able to do a handstand or turn cartwheels is not a prerequisite for teaching PE. To be able to draw with a sense of proportion, perspective and light is not a prerequisite for teaching art. Teaching music effectively, like art and physical education, requires particular skills in classroom management and raises different organisational issues to other curriculum areas. The recent developments in ICT provision have given primary teachers cause to review their organisation and management of all curriculum areas.

Like art and physical education, music requires the teacher to have an appropriate vocabulary to help children engage with the subject. Knowing how children learn in music is essential subject knowledge for primary teachers. If teachers develop skills themselves as musicians then this is a bonus for their teaching.

Key points

- Many schools are re-evaluating their planning to ensure a 'broad and balanced curriculum'.
- Good teachers see ICT as a tool for learning and know when and how to use it to promote learning in music.
- Teaching music effectively requires particular skills in classroom management.
- Knowing how children learn in music is essential to make effective use of ICT.

Time to reflect

*The real skill of using and applying ICT well is knowing **when** and **when not to use it**. Think carefully about how ICT could be used as a tool for teaching music. Make a list of ideas. Have you observed any good practice in this area when in school?*

How national initiatives can be applied to music teaching

ICT is an incredible motivator and is often viewed as being exciting and fun to use. It is common for children to want to use ICT. Computers empower children and give them control, they have kudos and are 'cool'. Findings from research carried out by Passey *et al.* (2004) into ICT use in primary and secondary schools is relevant to these points. Their key findings include:

- **ICT use by pupils and teachers in the case study schools led to positive motivational outcomes, supporting a focus upon learning and the tackling of learning tasks.**
- **Positive motivational outcomes were most frequently found when ICT was used to support engagement, research, writing and editing, and presentation of work. Where ICT uses supported internal cognitive aspects of learning, for example in the case of secondary design and technology, there were indicators that the motivation arising from the use of ICT was linked to enhancements in some subject-specific attainment.**
- **More positive motivation resulted when ICT use was focused on both teaching and learning, rather than when ICT was used to support teaching alone.**
- **Boys and girls were both motivated by uses of ICT. There was evidence that motivation from ICT use positively affected the work patterns of boys so that they worked in similar ways to the persistent pattern of girls.**
- **Motivation appeared to be independent of ethnic background, but socio-economic background impacted on occasions in terms of limited access or out-of-school support.**
- **There were indications that ICT impacted positively upon pupil behaviour inside school, and some impact on their behaviour outside school.**

These findings suggest good reasons to adopt ICT across the curriculum for supporting learners (children). There is, however, one major hurdle that stands in the way of a truly integrated ICT teaching pedagogy. That is the educator's (teacher's) confidence in, and personal perceptions of, ICT and music.

Guidance from National Curriculum Online suggests the following benefits of using ICT to teach primary music.

Using ICT can help pupils to:

- access, select and interpret information;
- recognise patterns, relationships and behaviours;
- model, predict and hypothesise;
- test reliability and accuracy;
- review and modify their work to improve the quality;
- communicate with others and present information;
- evaluate their work;
- improve efficiency;
- be creative and take risks;
- gain confidence and independence.

(**www.ncaction.org.uk/subjects/music/ict-lrn.htm**)

Legal requirements through the National Curriculum (DfEE/Qualifications and Curriculum Authority (QCA), 1999a) and the Standards required for Qualifying to Teach (Teacher Training Agency (TTA), 2002) are not sufficient to provide us with a rationale for embedding ICT in music teaching. Quite apart from the national imperatives for us to be embedding ICT in our teaching, good teachers will use ICT to help pupils achieve *musical* learning.

The text on page 64 illustrates key aspects of music learning and makes explicit reference to using ICT in the Programmes of Study for Key Stages 1 and 2 in the Music National Curriculum (England).

Embedding ICT across the curriculum has given us the opportunity to re-evaluate our approach to teaching and learning in the primary classroom. Through the implementation of the Literacy and Numeracy strategies a model of teaching and learning has been promoted which has included whole-class teaching, group, paired and individual work, and the use of plenaries. The strategies have also promoted the use of 'modelling' learning through demonstration and guided tasks. The parallel national developments in ICT provision have enabled us to engage with this model of teaching in a new way. Good teachers adopt ICT and combine these teaching strategies within their lessons to empower children to engage effectively as learners. Therefore, the main focus of this chapter is to help you become an effective teacher of music.

On its website offering advice to teachers of primary music, BECTa (2004b) provides guidance on *How to Support Children Using ICT in Music*. In addition to highlighting the benefits of having ICT activities before other musical activities, alongside other musical activities and after other musical activities, BECTa identifies the characteristics of good planning for ICT in music.

Well-planned ICT activities are:

- **appropriate to the musical task;**
- **suitably matched to pupils' expertise and ability;**

What the National Curriculum music programmes of study for Key Stage I and 2 say:

At Key Stage I children should be taught to

(2a) *create musical patterns* and

(2b) *explore, choose and organise sounds and musical ideas* .

The complementary ICT opportunity here states that:

(2b) *pupils could use software designed to enable exploration of sounds.*

As part of responding and reviewing appraising skills children are expected to:

(3a) *explore and express their ideas and feelings about music using movement, dance and expressive and musical language* and

(3b) *make improvements to their own work.*

ICT opportunity here states that:

(3b) *pupils could use recording equipment to recall sounds and identify and make improvements.*

At Key Stage 2 children should be taught to

(2a) *improvise, developing rhythmic and melodic material when performing* and

(2b) *explore, choose, combine and organise musical ideas within musical structures.*

In the breadth of study section it states that:

(5d) *use ICT to capture, change and combine sounds.*

(DfEE/QCA, 1999a)

A cross reference to the ICT curriculum suggests that children should be taught:

(1b) *how to prepare information for development using ICT, including selecting suitable sources, finding information, classifying it and checking it for accuracy (for example, finding information from books or newspapers, creating a class database, classifying by characteristics and purposes, checking the spelling of names is consistent).*

(DfEE/QCA, 1999b)

- supported by helpful guidance notes so that pupils can work independently;
- appropriate to the level of support available from the teacher or other helper;
- enlightening, because they offer a unique way of learning;
- realistic for the time available;
- musically rewarding.

(BECTa, 2004b)

It is important to recognise that ICT is a rich resource for teaching and learning to be accessed, controlled and manipulated by teachers and pupils. As a trainee teacher you need first and foremost to develop the generic skills to become a good teacher. ICT is no substitute for poor teaching, but it can be embraced to enhance the quality of teaching. In making decisions about when and when not to use ICT, you should be clear about how ICT will help you:

- achieve the musical learning objective for your lesson;
- achieve musical learning that cannot be learned without it;
- support creativity, rather than stifle it.

Key points

- ICT is an incredible motivator.
- Computers empower children.
- Teacher confidence is a major factor that stands in the way of the use of ICT.
- Good teachers will use ICT and adopt ICT to help pupils achieve *musical* learning.
- National developments in ICT implementation have enabled us to engage with this model of teaching in a new way.
- ICT is no substitute for poor teaching.

Time to reflect

Are you musicphobic? Many children feel very motivated and empowered when using ICT. How can you develop confidence to teach music creatively with the aid of ICT? Design a simple personal action plan. For example:

Problem	Action	Success criteria
Have never used ICT in music teaching before.	Identify one piece of hardware and software available to you (in school placement or training base). Learn the basic functions of your chosen resources and develop familiarity and confidence in their use.	Can use an ICT resource in music teaching context.

Developing a rationale for teaching music and promoting creativity

Music and the National Curriculum

Our rationale for teaching music must be based around the National Curriculum for music as this sets out the legal requirements of the music curriculum. In keeping with the National Curriculum, music is seen as a subject that children learn through **performing, composing, listening and appraising**. Learning the subject is very much an **active process** with children learning to **recognise, control, organise, name and explore sounds and their relationships**. Implicit in the National Curriculum (NC) levels of attainment is a psychological basis for pupils' learning in music:

'Pupils recognise' (the beginning statement of NC levels I, 2 and 3)	equates to **perception** of music.
'Pupils identify' (the beginning statement of NC levels 4, 5 and 6)	equates to **cognition** of music, i.e. not only able to recognise the musical feature, but can name it on the basis of knowledge of its characteristics.
'Pupils discriminate' (the beginning statement of NC levels 7 and 8)	requires **metacognition** , i.e. an ability to think about thinking.

Flavell described metacognition:

> *Metacognition refers to one's knowledge concerning one's own cognitive processes and products or anything related to them, e.g., the learning-relevant properties of information or data. For example, I am engaging in metacognition if I notice that I am having more trouble learning A than B; if it strikes me that I should double-check C before accepting it as fact.* (Flavell, 1976, p. 232)

It is important that the processes of perception, cognition and metacognition are not viewed in a purely hierarchical way simply because they can be mapped onto the NC level statements. Pupils will develop these processes by engaging with them all long before they achieve the expected music NC levels for their end of key stage. Children's development in music is a gradual process that requires continual opportunity to engage practically with the subject. Swanwick and Tillman (1986) illustrated a view of a sequence of children's musical development through a spiral model (see Figure 4.1). Central to their model is the notion of children developing their musicality through revisiting the processes of controlling sounds and expressing themselves musically as they move towards an understanding of musical forms and a deeper valuing of music.

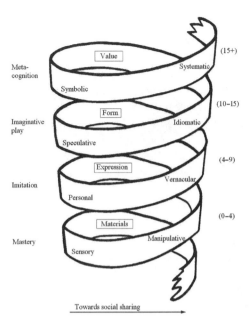

Figure 4.1: Sequence of musical development (Swanwick and Tillman, 1986, p. 331)

For years music has been taught with very limited use of ICT, record players and cassette recorders being the most obvious forms of technology to precede keyboards, computers and other forms of music technology available today. An important consideration for us is how ICT can be used in interactive mode rather than passive mode. In doing this, we need to consider when and how to adopt whole-class, individual, paired and group work and how to make effective use of plenaries in our music teaching. Traditionally children have learned music through singing, playing instruments, listening to established forms of music and using musical ideas and devices to create their own music. Commonly, music has been taught and learned in the primary school as a group or whole class activity. This was in keeping with the view that music making is fundamentally a social activity. Swanwick (1999) offers us three principles for teaching music musically:

- **we must treat 'music as discourse';**
- **have 'respect for the musical discourse of our pupils';**
- **put 'fluency first and last'.**

It is not difficult for us to understand 'music as discourse' as music saying something to someone, seeing music as a unique form of communication. In having 'respect for the musical discourse of our pupils' we should not lose sight of the importance of personal, individual meaning from music. The Swanwick and Tillman spiral illustrates this with the nodes on the left-hand side of the spiral at each layer (sensory, personal, speculative, symbolic) representing personal meaning and the nodes on the right-hand side (manipulative, vernacular, idiomatic, systematic) representing a shared social understanding.

Every level descriptor in the music National Curriculum relevant to primary children refers to children 'exploring' music. Expectations for level 1–3 say that 'pupils recognise and explore …' and levels 4–6 say that 'pupils identify and explore …' The notion of exploring is fundamental to learning music and reminds us that music is a creative subject. Just as Swanwick (1999) argues that we 'respect the musical discourse of our students', we need to encourage pupils to work creatively with music to achieve this. If music teaching is good, children should acquire knowledge and understanding of musical ideas, forms and devices through first-hand experience and have opportunities to make their own decisions about:

- **how to make sounds;**
- **how and when to change sounds;**
- **how their sounds can be organised;**
- **how their sounds can be combined;**
- **how their sounds can be used expressively and reflect different intentions.**

Ensuring that composing is a significant part of the music curriculum will help to address all of the above. Moreover, taking a problem solving approach to composing will help to develop the classroom culture required to enable children to talk, experiment, think, act and reflect musically.

In raising awareness of different learning styles, national initiatives such as the Key Stage 3 Strategy and the TeacherNet website have promoted the visual, audio, kinaesthetic (VAK) model of preferred learning styles for use in primary and secondary schools (see below). The model acknowledges that individuals have preferences for visual, auditory and kinaesthetic modes of learning. Trainee teachers need to acknowledge that the learner may well employ a combination of these learning styles. As music exists in time and is essentially perceived in the auditory mode, kinaesthetic and visual factors *linked directly to sound* become important in supporting children's learning in music. ICT lends itself to facilitate this. Musical structures can be created and manipulated through the use of ICT giving children the opportunity to see visual patterns that relate directly to the sounds they hear.

The TeacherNet website, on its 'Teaching in England' pages, describes the VAK model as the key preferred learning styles:

The VAK model
- The VAK model emphasises the preferences individuals have for visual, auditory or kinaesthetic learning.

VAK characteristics
- **Visual** – learners prefer to see information: they like reading text or looking at diagrams.
- **Auditory** – learners prefer to hear information: they like listening, talking.
- **Kinaesthetic** – learners prefer to learn by doing: they like moving, manipulating, touching.

(www.teachernet.gov.uk/teachinginengland/detail.cfm?id=523)

ICT as an aid to creativity

Elements of ICT can bring enormous benefits to all aspects of the creative curriculum. For most children at primary school, ICT is an exciting and ever-developing dynamic tool which they can use to realise things that would not be possible without it. Leask and Meadows (2000) stress the importance of viewing children as *creative* users of ICT. If we adopt a 'problem-solving' approach to composing, we can create a learning environment where children are encouraged to be imaginative and try out ideas. For example, an individual can compose a simple four part composition and use a computer to replay, edit and adapt the work by him or herself. ICT empowers children to work independently, giving them the opportunity to combine different musical elements, to try out musical ideas and to 'make mistakes' and correct them.

The National Advisory Committee on Creative and Cultural Education's (NACCCE) report gives this definition of creativity, which contains four important factors;

> First, they [the characteristics of creativity] always involve thinking or behaving **imaginatively**. Second, overall this imaginative activity is **purposeful**: that is, it is directed to achieving an objective. Third, these processes must generate something **original**. Fourth, the outcome must be of **value** in relation to the objective. (NACCCE, 1999, p 30)

The combination of the above factors can help to realise a piece of work that has the 'wow-factor '. With appropriate teacher guidance and integration of ICT this sense of high-quality creative work can be realised more and more often. In terms of National Curriculum Online *Spotting Creativity*, the complementary website to the NACCCE document, suggests that the teacher should look for children who are:

- **questioning and challenging;**
- **making connections and seeing relationships;**
- **envisaging what might be;**
- **exploring ideas, keeping options open;**
- **reflecting critically on ideas, actions and outcomes.**

(*www.ncaction.org.uk/creativity/spot.htm*)

It is interesting to notice how some of these statements bear more than a passing resemblance to the ICT National Curriculum programmes of study framework:

- **finding things out;**
- **developing ideas and making things happen;**
- **exchanging and sharing information;**
- **reviewing, modifying and evaluating work as it progresses.**

(DfEE/QCA, 1999b)

One of the most important aspects of using ICT is the facility to be able to edit work in progress through *undo, cut, copy, paste, drag-and-drop,* etc. features.

This is fundamental to achieving the *developing, reviewing, modifying and evaluating* segments of the ICT programmes of study. The obvious example to illustrate this is that of story writing where the young learner is able to make changes such as spelling or sentence structure and to edit and adapt aspects of his or her work quickly and efficiently with the minimum of fuss. This principle provides the learner with a *safe working environment* where it is okay to 'make mistakes' as these can easily be rectified without having to start again. Using ICT in this way enables the individual to solve problems, using trial and error and experimentation as methods to achieve a final outcome. This way of working is particularly advantageous for aspects of the music curriculum where children are encouraged to try ideas out and edit and adapt their work before a final performance.

Key points

- **There is a legal requirement to teach music.**
- **Children's development in music is a gradual process achieved through revisiting and refining musical ideas.**
- **The use of ICT should support 'interactive' approaches to learning music and acknowledge VAK learning styles.**
- **Music is a unique form of communication allowing children to develop both personal and shared meaning.**
- **ICT should be incorporated to encourage children to explore and work creatively with music, taking a problem solving approach to composing.**
- **ICT can help high-quality creative work, adding a 'wow-factor ' to a lesson.**
- **ICT provides a 'safe environment' where the learner can explore, try out ideas and 'make mistakes' that can be easily modified.**

Teaching tip

When planning for music make a conscious effort to use ICT creatively and also ask yourself these questions:

- *Is my use of ICT truly 'interactive'?*
- *How do the features of my chosen ICT application lend themselves to using visual and/or kinaesthetic modes to support internalising music?*
- *How best can ICT help in the creation of the 'wow-factor' in music-making within my lesson?*
- *How can I best provide the children with a safe learning environment in which they can explore possibilities and be creative?*

Using ICT to scaffold children's learning in music

The term 'scaffolding learning' is a metaphor that comes from Vygotsky's idea of 'zone of proximal development' (ZPD). Ager (2000) discusses this and its implications for teaching with ICT. Vygotsky's definition of the ZPD is:

the distance between the actual development level as determined by independent pro-
blem solving, and the level of potential development as determined through problem sol-
ving under adult guidance or in collaboration with more capable peers...

The zone of proximal development defines those functions that have not yet matured
but are in the process of maturing, functions that will mature tomorrow but are in an
embryonic state. (Vygotsky, 1978, p. 86)

The art of scaffolding learning is to provide structures and frameworks to help pupils achieve the next step in their development. The scaffolding of learning can be described very simply by using the metaphor of a building site. Scaffolding is used to support a new structure as it is being built. The ultimate aim of the building project is to build a strong and reliable final structure. Along the way and during every stage of this meticulously planned process differing forms of scaffolding are used to shore up, support and in due course contribute to the new product. Clear parallels can be drawn in education. The learner has a goal to aim for and the teacher uses a variety of methods to scaffold the learning process until this final goal is achieved. Adopting the national strategies in primary teaching, teachers plan lessons to support the learning of all the pupils in their class. An important issue when scaffolding learning in music is to still allow the children's creativity to flourish. While we may provide appropriate scaffolding, we will always want the children to make their own decisions about the 'detailed finish'.

In developing your models for scaffolding, not only is it important for you to consider different learning styles as articulated in the VAK model above, but you should also be aware of Gardner's theory of multiple intelligences. Gardner viewed intelligence as:

the ability to solve problems, or create products that are valued within one or more
cultural settings. (Gardner, 1993, p. 14).

Gardner identifies musical intelligence as one of seven types of intelligence, which are summarised here by Smith (2002):

- **Linguistic intelligence involves sensitivity to spoken and written language, the ability to learn languages and the capacity to use language to accomplish certain goals. This intelligence includes the ability to effectively use language to express oneself rhetorically or poetically; and language as a means to remember information. Writers, poets, lawyers and speakers are among those that Howard Gardner sees as having high linguistic intelligence.**

- **Logical-mathematical intelligence consists of the capacity to analyse problems logically, carry out mathematical operations and investigate issues scientifically. In Howard Gardner's words, it entails the ability to detect patterns, reason deductively and think logically. This intelligence is most often associated with scientific and mathematical thinking.**

- **Musical intelligence involves skill in the performance, composition, and appreciation of musical patterns. It encompasses the capacity to recognise and compose musical pitches, tones, and rhythms. According to Howard Gardner** musical intelligence runs in an almost structural parallel to linguistic intelligence.

- **Bodily-kinaesthetic intelligence** entails the potential of using one's whole body or parts of the body to solve problems. It is the ability to use mental abilities to coordinate bodily movements. Gardner sees mental and physical activity as related.
- **Spatial intelligence** involves the potential to recognise and use the patterns of wide space and more confined areas.
- **Interpersonal intelligence** is concerned with the capacity to understand the intentions, motivations and desires of other people. It allows people to work effectively with others. Educators, salespeople, religious and political leaders and counsellors all need a well-developed interpersonal intelligence.
- **Intrapersonal intelligence** entails the capacity to understand oneself, to appreciate one's own feelings, fears and motivations.

In promoting his concept of multiple intelligences, Gardner makes the distinction between *intelligences* and *domains*, domains being:

> '... disciplines, crafts, and other pursuits in which one can be enculturated and then be assessed in terms of the level of competence one has attained.' (Gardner, 1993, p. 20)

Gardner emphasises his view that we use multiple intelligences within any domain.

> A person with musical intelligence is likely to be attracted to, and to be successful in the domain of music. But the domain of musical performance requires intelligences beyond the musical (for example, bodily kinaesthetic intelligence, personal intelligences), just as musical intelligence can be mobilized for domains beyond music in the strict sense (as in dance or in advertising). (Gardner, 1993, p. 21)

This is something that is important for us to consider: we can appreciate the value of learning in one subject, supporting learning in another subject.

> While from my present vantage point the best way to start to understand the human mind is to examine its different frames, its separate intelligences, in the end we just also learn to yoke those intelligences together and mobilize them for constructive ends'. (Gardner, 1993, p. 24)

One of the major challenges of primary teaching is the spread of ability within the class and also the individual learning styles that different children prefer. It is often hard to meet the full needs of all *individuals* in your class. Ager (2000) discusses how the use of ICT can help to support differing learning styles and so support the needs of the individual.

The use of colourful and vivid multimedia presentations using animations and audio and movie clips can help to greatly engage, inspire and enthral the learner in keeping with the VAK model. The advent of increasingly affordable interactive whiteboard (IWB) technology and user-friendly software is making this type of exciting learning environment a reality in many schools today. One of the main aims of the Primary National Strategy is to tailor education to ensure that every pupil achieves and reaches the highest standards possible. It also promotes personalising the school experience to enable pupils to focus on their learning.

Both Vygotsky and Gardner refer to problem-solving as a significant characteristic in their respective definitions of *ZPD* and *intelligence*. If composing tasks are set as problem-solving activities, music teaching can function with a sound basis for **how** children will learn music.

Whole-class teaching

So what does good whole-class teaching in music look like and what part can ICT play in making it a more *dynamic, exciting* and *personal* experience for the learner? The National Numeracy Strategy describes positive features of direct teaching. Good direct teaching is achieved by balancing different elements:

- directing;
- instructing;
- demonstrating;
- explaining and illustrating;
- questioning and discussing;
- consolidating;
- evaluating pupils' responses;
- summarising.   (DfEE, 1999, pp 11-12)

Although the above quote comes from the National Numeracy Strategy, the list of elements is true for all good direct teaching, no matter what the subject. In addition to the introduction to the lesson, these elements are highly pertinent to the plenary sessions. The National Literacy Strategy defines the plenary as:

a separate session when the whole-class is brought together. (DfEE, 1998, p. 13)

In music, we can benefit from having plenaries within the lesson as well as at the end of lessons. Plenaries within the lesson are a useful strategy to scaffold learning in music: you can ensure pupils remain on task, have opportunity to continually review and reflect upon their musical ideas and are encouraged to consider alternatives.

The National Literacy Strategy describes the plenary:

It should be used to:

- *enable the teacher to spread ideas, re-emphasise teaching points, clarify misconceptions and develop new teaching points;*
- *enable pupils to reflect upon and explain what they have learned and to clarify their thinking;*

- enable pupils to revise and practise new skills acquired in an earlier part of the lesson;
- develop an atmosphere of constructive criticism and provide feedback and encouragement to pupils;
- provide opportunities for the teacher to monitor and assess the work of some of the pupils;
- provide opportunities for pupils to present and discuss key issues in their work.'

(DfEE, 1998, p 13)

The well-chosen use of interactive whiteboards to provide the focal point for the management of learning in music can lead to interesting, relevant, clear and lively whole-class sessions that not only help to fire the children's imagination but also cater for differing learning styles and the individual needs of the learner. Using ICT effectively promotes children's motivation and encourages a high level of interest. The teacher is able to model learning situations clearly and effectively. The use of interactive whiteboards can also make whole class teaching interactive: it can be visually, aurally and kinaesthetically stimulating and engage children in learning. It would be true to say that the use of ICT in this way turns the notion of whole-class teaching from a *passive* exercise to an *active* experience. In teaching music you should always look to use the interactive whiteboards to make instant links between visual representation and sound.

Individual, paired or small-group learning

Traditionally there has been limited opportunity for individual learning in music within the classroom situation other than through collective group or class activity. This has been partly due to the fact that for children to combine musical ideas, they have needed to be part of a group: to learn how their musical part might fit within a piece, they have needed others around them playing the other parts! ICT lends itself to offering a realisation of 'the other parts' for children to explore how their part might fit.

Having considered Vygotsky's ZPD, Ager argues that there are significant implications regarding scaffolding and the use of ICT:

> ... collaborative work between two or three children in front of a computer working on any type of problem-solving activity can create an environment in which the children within the group can provide the scaffolding that they each need in order to progress.
> (Ager, 2000, p. 12)

When using music ICT, it is important that you frame the learning situation: you need to be clear about how the capabilities of the resource will help children to achieve the intended learning outcomes. Some software, for example Blackcat's *Compose*, can be set to four different levels: each level builds on the tools introduced in the previous level. You can design problem-solving questions tailored to the ZPD of the learner.

If composing tasks are set as problem-solving activities, children can effectively engage in using ICT for music learning through paired and small-group work. Sutherland *et al.* (2002) conducted research into the use of ICT in primary English, mathematics and music through three case studies. In the music case study, which involved children in a composing project using *Dance eJay* music software, there tended to be a pattern to the lessons with teacher input at the beginning, paired work at the computer and a sharing and discussion of work and ideas at the end. They found that:

- *pupils commented on how sharing ideas and listening to each other's work aided them with their own compositions;*
- *the "new technologies" being used [in all three case studies] are all relatively open-ended environments in which pupils can construct and express their own ideas;*
- *visual feedback from the respective computer environments seems to have been crucial in helping pupils to see structure and form;*
- *'environments were structured by the teacher for pedagogic purposes, to enable pupils to focus and play with particular ideas and not others.*

(Sutherland *et al.*, 2002)

So ICT *can* greatly enhance collaborative work in a face-to-face local setting. What about collaboration in a wider perspective? The use of the internet can open up the opportunities for truly global communication and collaboration. At present 99 per cent of UK primary schools are connected to the internet, and over half of these at broadband speeds. The possibilities for collaborative work are limited only by your imagination. Projects are achievable which would have been impossible to attempt even ten years ago. A good analogy here can be found in the present-day car-making industry. Different parts of the final vehicle can be made all over Europe (or even the world). Workers never meet face to face, yet the final results fit together very efficiently.

Through the use of complex IT management and communication systems the progress and quality of the end product can be tracked and monitored. It could prove to be very exciting to work on a collaborative music performance project with children from different countries and diverse cultures. What better way of bring a multicultural music lesson to life than with the aid of a video link with a performer in another continent?

Employing adult support

Vygotsky was very clear about the importance of 'adult guidance' in helping children achieve their potential (See Vygotsky, 1978, p. 86 with reference to the above). You should not forget that teaching assistants and parent helpers can play an important part in scaffolding learning in music. You need to ensure that they are clear about intended learning outcomes and the ways in which they can support children to engage in musical problem-solving.

The knowledge, skills and confidence that teaching assistants and other adult helpers bring to the classroom is likely to vary greatly. Having children teach and train the adult helper in the use of music hardware or software can be a useful exercise for both parties. Not only will the adult gain familiarity and understanding of the technology, but the child may consolidate her understanding and grow in confidence by 'knowing more' than the adult. Equally, an adult helper with expertise in music can help scaffold children's learning by modelling and offering musical insights to help children make their own decisions.

Useful expertise for teaching assistants and adult helpers to develop include:

- **knowledge of specific software and hardware to ensure children make best use of these;**
- **employing questioning and listening skills to encourage children to express their musical ideas and to experiment;**
- **understanding of the elements of music and the associated vocabulary to develop with children. (see Table 4.1 for examples).**

Table 4.1: Examples of the elements of music and associated vocabulary

Element of music	Description and associated vocabulary
Pitch	Melody, high – low
Duration	Beat/pulse, rhythm pattern, use of silence (rests); long, sustained (sostenuto); short (staccato)
Dynamics	Loud (forte); quiet (piano); gradually louder (crescendo); gradually quieter (diminuendo)
Tempo	Fast (allegro); slow (andante, adagio, lento, largo); getting faster (accelerando, stringendo); getting slower gradually (rallentando), getting slower immediately (ritenuto)
Timbre	Sound colour (e.g. recognising sound of specific instrument)
Texture	Layers of sound; combinations of instruments; harmony
Structure	Form (e.g. binary, ternary, rondo); relationships of one section to another

Key points

- **Exploit ICT to scaffold children's musical learning.**
- **Consider Vygotsky's ZPD, Gardner's multiple intelligences and VAK learning styles as theoretical perspectives to underpin your music teaching.**
- **Make problem-solving approaches to composing a significant feature of your music teaching.**
- **Use whole-class introductions and plenaries in your music teaching.**
- **Make effective use of adult support to scaffold children's musical learning.**

When whole-class teaching ...	For paired or small-group work ...
... what types of statements will you need to encourage a problem-solving approach?	... what types of questions will you need to encourage a problem-solving approach?
For example: We need to think about the types of sounds that we could use to create the right mood for ...	For example: Can you find a musical pattern that will describe ...? Are there other sounds that will fit with.....?
... how could ICT support?	... how could ICT support paired or small-group work?
For example, when composing music for a story: Use the IWB to demonstrate chosen software and highlight important elements of the story. Select different children to come to the front and sequence elements, etc ...	For example, when composing music for a story: Use chosen software in pairs or small groups to explore and try out musical ideas in keeping with the story.

Figure 4.2: Composing as a problem-solving activity

Conclusion

We recognise that some of our readers will be musically literate and confident whereas others may be less sure of their ability to teach music. We hope that this chapter will have given you insights into approaches that can be effective for you. As trainee teachers you are developing and applying generic teaching skills that are appropriate to children's musical education. You are continually finding out more about specific ICT resources and are developing a framework to embed this in your teaching. By considering musical elements and their associated vocabulary within a problem-solving context for composing (see figure 4.2), you will be able to develop your skills of music teaching.

You are entering the profession at a time when schools and teachers are addressing the place of the arts in a broad and balanced curriculum. It is appropriate that you consider what you have learned about the teaching and learning process from recent national initiatives and consider how these can be applied to music teaching. Keeping the theoretical perspectives in mind when planning and evaluating your music teaching will help you to continually develop and refine your own rationale for teaching music and embedding ICT. We hope that this chapter has provided a basis for you to do this.

Summary

In developing your rationale for fostering children's creativity in their music learning you need to consider how you use ICT:

- in a problem-solving approach to composing music;
- to encourage children to explore, apply musical imagination and work creatively;
- to support children's musical development through perception/cognition/meta-cognition;
- to help create a safe environment to solve musical problems;
- as a powerful tool for musical communication;
- to supplement the tools we have for teaching music rather than replace existing resources;
- with an effective theoretical underpinning to scaffold musical learning (Gardner, Swanwick, Vygotsky, VAK model);
- to promote enthusiasm, excitement and enjoyment for learning.

Useful websites

- www.blackcatsoftware.com/
- www.2simple.com/music/
- www.bbc.co.uk/radio3/makingtracks/games.shtml
- www.creatingmusic.com/
- www.findsounds.com/
- www.ncaction.org.uk/creativity/spot.htm
- www.ictadvice.org.uk/
- www.ncaction.org.uk/subjects/music/
- www.m4t.org/
- www.musicteachers.co.uk/
- www.teachingideas.co.uk/music/contents.htm

Key areas of music technology

	Examples
Audio recording	Cassette/mini-disc/CD recorders, mp3 recorders, etc.
CD-ROM and interactive audio CDs	The Orchestra, BBC Music Magazine CDs, (children and teachers can make their own with PowerPoint!)
DVD player/recorder, video player/recorder, camcorder, digital still camera, short movie clips	Create or play stimulus for composing
Hi-fi and portable systems	Enable connection of peripheral devices, e.g. computer, mini-disc, mp3 devices, DAB radio, etc.
Internet	Online interactive software, teaching resources
Microphones, effects units (including reverb, delay, pitch-shift), mixing desk	Explore pitch relationships vocally with pitch-shift effect
MIDI (Musical Instrument Digital Interface) files	Backing tracks
MIDI input devices	Keyboards, drum machines, guitar pick-ups
MIDI	An agreed industry standard enabling MIDI devices, such as keyboards, computers and drum machines, to exchange digital information to make music
Multi-track recording	Porta-studio, hard-disk
Music games software	Music Ace
Music keyboards	Single-finger chords, fingered chords, memory (chord banks, melody banks), use of auto-rhythms/styles, exploiting range of 'voices', samples, rhythm pads
Notation software	Sibelius, Finale
Sequencing software	Steinberg Cubasis VST, 2Simple Music Toolkit, Blackcat Compose
Video editing software incorporating sound	MovieMaker, iMovie

5 SURVIVING THE INTERNET: ISSUES OF USE AND ABUSE

STEVE WHEELER

Some say Google is God. Others say Google is Satan.
Sergey Brin (Stanford University)

This chapter will enable you to:

• appreciate the issues of internet safety and child protection;

• identify problems and solutions related to the above;

• explore and develop strategies to improve school internet use;

• better understand problems such as viruses, spam and hacking.

Introduction

In an age of increasing vulnerability and anxiety, primary school children's use of the internet is of enormous concern to parents and teachers alike. Stories about how the internet has been used for sinister and unsavoury activities regularly appear in the popular press and on television, and sadly it is often children and young people who are the victims. In this chapter we explore the key issues, dangers and questions of internet use, and evaluate it in the context of a variety of teaching and learning activities. You are asked to think creatively about the potential of the internet for learning, countered with possible solutions to protect young minds while liberating them to explore freely. What kind of messages should teachers send to parents about how children are using the internet in school? What assurances can teachers provide? What are the questions parents are asking? What are the things teachers need to know before using the internet in teaching? Included in the text are several scenarios related to this topic for you to think about.

The internet: a global phenomenon

There is no doubt about it: the internet is the most influential communication technology in the history of humankind. All that has gone before has been swallowed in its embrace. Paul Levinson calls it the 'medium of media', because it encompasses radio, television, textbooks, images, telephone and e-mail communication, serving a worldwide, real-time audience (Levinson, 2003). The internet is a network of networks connecting millions of users, computers and information databases, and constitutes an almost infinite number of learning resources distributed around the globe. It is rapidly expanding at such a rate that the number of users at any point in time can only be loosely estimated, but latest figures suggest around 600 million users – or one in ten people on the planet (TES, 2004b). Its educational potential is immense and its transformational power is yet to be fully realised.

But a start has been made, and it's not just about accessing information. Schools throughout the industrialised world and elsewhere are using the internet to publish web pages that present news of events and photographs of school trips and are a means of providing information (for example, homework tasks).

Teachers are also realising that they can exploit the power of the internet to provide their pupils with a potentially huge 'real' worldwide audience to show off the work they do – a sort of 'shop window'. As a virtual meeting place, the internet is second to none in its potential for connecting people across the globe.

There is also much discussion about the notion of 'cyberspace' – an idea first introduced by the science fiction writer William Gibson in his novel *Neuromancer* (1995) which describes the imaginary or 'virtual' space within which all computer-based materials, communication and the world wide web itself reside. Teachers are exploring the idea of cyberspace as an environment in which pupils' experiences can be transformed and enlivened. Using the internet's resources, for example, children can visit museums in Europe, America and Australia, tour the battlefields of the Second World War and climb to the summit of Mount Everest, all in one day, and all without leaving the computer suite.

It is easy to eulogise over the internet, but what is its true nature? There are of course bad aspects as well as good. Many internet sites we stumble on can cause us to question its usefulness. From explicitly pornographic sites to sites promoting racism and hate, to sites showing how to construct explosive devices – it is all out there if someone has thought about creating it. So is the internet inherently evil? The answer is probably the same for any medium, including television or film. One theory suggests that all media are neutral until content is placed in them (Clark, 1994) and, despite its unique attributes, the internet appears to be no exception. The internet has the potential to harm or nurture, to misinform or educate. Knowing how to achieve the latter is a skill many teachers are trying to acquire, and it is this set of issues that forms the basis of this chapter. Let's start by examining a problem that may be familiar to some teachers …

What a web we weave …

The scenario below has been written to help you to explore the issues surrounding web-based 'publishing' of children's work, personal information and achievements, and communicating with 'e-pals' using the internet. Step into the shoes of a teacher in the following reflective exercise:

Imagine that you are teaching a group of 30 Year 6 pupils, and you have a networked suite of 12 computers, each linked via broadband to the internet. One of your teaching activities with your group over the last few weeks has been to introduce them to Microsoft *FrontPage* and to show them how to use the software to create web pages. As an exercise, you have asked each child to create his or her own personal web page. Each child must therefore:

- learn how to use **MS** *FrontPage* to create the pages;
- decide what he or she wants to put on the web page;
- gather together a number of links to favourite websites;
- consider the design, colour, layout and general appearance of their website;
- write about how they went about the task and what were the worst and best bits;
- search out, contact and enter into e-mail conversation with children of a similar age from other parts of the world.

You have told the class that each page can contain whatever each child wishes to put into it, as long as they let you see it first. Several have already forged ahead with great enthusiasm, creating pages that show their photographs, personal details such as their interests and hobbies, favourite pop stars and/or footballers, links to their favourite websites and details of their family life.

The children are excited. A few have asked you for permission to publish some of the school work that they are particularly proud of onto their web spaces. They have scanned in images of their drawings and paintings, and some have included imaginative story writing work and poems they have written. Each child has also been given a personal e-mail address and has been encouraged to contact school children in other parts of the world to develop electronic pen-pal or 'e-pal' conversations. Are any alarm bells ringing for you yet? Read on …

The problem

Parents of some of the children in your class have recently come to hear about this project and have expressed their concerns to your head teacher. The parents have complained that using the internet leaves their children open to possible danger from undesirable individuals who may take advantage of the information displayed on the websites. They are extremely worried, and the head teacher wants some answers.

Time to reflect

You now have to deal with this problem before it gets out of hand. Your task is to defend your project so that your head teacher is satisfied that you have done all that is necessary to protect the children you are teaching. You also need to be in a position to address the concerns of the worried parent. You can do this by:

- *presenting a detailed account of the potential and actual benefits of the activities in terms of positive learning outcomes;*
- *detailing some of the possible pitfalls or dangers and how you intend to manage or overcome them;*
- *taking steps to minimise or eradicate any potentially difficult or damaging aspects of the project by revising the tasks. (Hint: What kind of things should children not be encouraged to put on their websites?)*

How to address the problem

What areas will you start to address? What will you need to take into consideration? As a start, you may like to take the following steps:

Step 1: Plan – Think about how you may want to tackle this problem. What strategy will you need to develop? Who might you need to talk to? What resources might you need? How long will it take?

Step 2: Do – Write down your actions for the above tasks, and think how your ideas might be applied if you really *were* the teacher in the scenario.

Step 3: Review – To help you to solve the problem, think about how you would feel if you were the parent of one of the Year 6 children. What would you wish to know from the teacher? Why might you be concerned about the project? What assurances might you require from the school?

Step 4: Reflect – What could be the possible limitations of the strategy you have formulated? Also, what are the apparent benefits, for you, your pupils and their parents, and the school? How would these be measured?

My Solution

If you have completed the above exercise, you will have formulated some kind of strategy to address the problem, and you will have reasoned through all your ideas to come up with a solution. In my opinion, your strategy should have one important item at its centre: Consultation.

However, you probably want me to elaborate a little on this. So I would like you to consider the following: it would be advisable for you to ensure that all those who are involved in such a project are well informed. Your head teacher should be informed about your intention to do the project, and your rationale should be prepared with the head teacher in mind in the first instance. He or she is responsible for all the teaching and learning activities that take place within the school and is accountable to the governing body. The parents of the children should also be informed, and you should make yourself available to talk through the issues with them if required.

Furthermore, ways of directly involving parents, either by inviting them to an online demonstration of their child's web page work or by engaging them as volunteer helpers during the project, may also prove to be useful. It is obviously more desirable to work with parents than against them.

Next, you will need to identify some of the more practical things you may wish to think about to address the problem. One important area is to understand how schools protect their pupils when they use the internet during teaching sessions. You can start by doing the following exercise:

Time to reflect

Have a word with your placement school's ICT coordinator.

Ask them what security and safety issues they have encountered or dealt with when teaching using the internet.

What protocols and measures have they put in place to protect pupils from danger?

Who was/is involved in the process?

Naturally, one of your major concerns must be to protect each child from any potential physical and emotional harm. There are two potential areas of threat:

- **contact with others going beyond e-mail;**
- **personal information and details being made available to others.**

Conversely, you will also need to consider the danger of the pupils losing out on a valuable learning experience if the project has to be drawn to a halt. It is a fine balancing act. Within the strategy you will be presenting to your head teacher you could think about the following ideas:

Plan:

- **In advance of the project, search for and organise contacts with bona fide schools where there are students of a similar age wishing to find overseas pen pals via e-mail (e-pals). They may be in another country (see chapter II for some ideas on this).**
- **Ensure that relevant software is in place to track activities and to filter out undesirable material from the internet.**
- **Consider using a closed (password-protected) intranet system for pupils to post their websites within.**
- **Encourage the group to practise e-mailing each other within the class, so that they begin to acquire the technical and compositional skills they will need.**
- **Try to ensure that every aspect of the project runs smoothly – that technical help is quickly available if something goes wrong.**
- **Consider involving interested parents as volunteers.**
- **Consider allowing any children of concerned parents to do other equivalent work without involving them in activities deemed to be unacceptable to the parents. (What kinds of activities could replace publishing a website or communicating electronically with other children in other schools?).**

Do:

- Act as a moderator of the information that goes into each child's website. (Negotiate with them the content and talk over the possible issues with each if you deem it necessary.)

- Help your pupils to develop the pages, showing them the best ways to present information that is safe, acceptable and informative. (Don't forget that any available teaching assistants, or volunteer parent helpers may also be able to support this.)

- Encourage the children to collaborate in groups so that the weaker or slower members of the group can benefit from those who are more able.

- Manage each child's 'e-pal' and search activities by screening the websites and discussion groups the pupils visit – inform them of some of the possible dangers if you feel it is necessary.

- Meet with any concerned parents to reassure them of the safety of the project – sit down with them at a networked computer and demonstrate to them some of the group's work and how it will benefit the children.

- Write down a list of all the possible skills the children may acquire and try to relate these to the curriculum and to their life skills needs in general.

Some possible solutions

From the above, you will see that there are many ways schools can get around the problems and potential dangers of using the internet. If photographs of pupils are needed, then permission should be asked of parents, and pupils should only be shown if they cannot be identified. Side profile or back views are often used by schools, and usually photographs can be anonymised in some way. However, you should also consider *why* pupil's pictures are needed for a website in the first place. If you can't use images of pupils, what are the alternatives? Can children present pictures they have taken or drawings they have made instead?

On no account should pupils' personal details be posted on a website and children should be warned not to disclose any personal information to those they may encounter in chat rooms and in discussion groups. Such e-contact activities are best conducted under supervision from the teacher or other responsible school staff, but teachers can't be everywhere at once. It is therefore a useful strategy to lay down ground rules for all children to remember and follow.

One of the best ways to protect children from internet abuse is to use a filtered or preferably self-contained internet system such as a school *intranet*. These versions enable children to work and communicate within a secure digital environment, and only authorised users (with the correct passwords) are able to see images and use resources contained in the system. Filtering software can also be purchased to screen undesirable materials and stop them from being downloaded onto children's screens. School ICT coordinators will know of these packages. There is much a school can do to decrease the risks to children as they use the internet.

Review:

- Regularly inform your head teacher and other relevant staff (e.g. ICT coordinator) of good progress as well as any potential or actual problems you have encountered during the project.
- Provide a rationale for the project. Work out what you are going to tell the head teacher about *why* you are doing the project.

In tackling this part of the problem, I first considered the reasons for getting the class to do this project. I decided to use a three-point plan, examining the pedagogical (teaching and learning), psychosocial and practical/technical issues.

Pedagogical issues

The key question is: was the project technology driven, or did it have inherent merits that the technology could be used to support? I looked at what the potential and actual benefits would be for the class. Could the skills they learned be used in several contexts? Would doing the project improve their communication skills? Would it encourage them to be creative? In short – what would they learn from it? Could other, less risky, non-technological methods be used instead?

Psychosocial issues

I then looked at all the things that the children might wish to post on their websites. How personal might they be? Would they be presenting acceptable selves to the potential WWW audience? What would be the merits of encouraging the children to do this anyway? I examined possible gender differences – would the boys be more 'up front' than the girls when choosing content?

Practical/technical issues

Once these issues had been considered, I then moved on to think about what possible dangers lurked in cyberspace for the children. Would there be a potential for emotional harm? Could there be the potential for physical harm through deception (e.g. paedophiles posing as young children, or males posing as females)? Might the children come across undesirable material (e.g. pornography or sites encouraging racial hatred)? What filters would the school need to put in place to counteract this threat? Finally I had a question about how robust the system was – would there be breakdowns and if so how long would problems take to resolve? Was there a technician or knowledgeable member of staff or parent available at short notice?

Some of the key questions

Let's examine some of the key questions related to the problem and answer each one in turn:

1. *Can the power of the internet be harnessed effectively to provide children with quality learning opportunities?*

The short answer is yes. An infinite set of possibilities is only now beginning to materialise for children. The internet is still growing, and so are they! Actually harnessing this power and using it to help develop young minds is often dependent upon the teaching strategies each teacher uses. Children generally enjoy using computers because they are ideal tools for experimentation – the 'what if ...' questions they often ask. Provided it is used safely and responsibly, the internet can act as a transforming technology, connecting children around the globe, and providing access to previously difficult or impossible to obtain information and resources.

2. *Do the undesirable elements found on the internet outweigh the advantages and benefits?*

There is general agreement that for young children some elements of internet content are potentially dangerous, and there is also a large amount of unhelpful or inaccurate information to be found out there in cyberspace. One of the new roles of the teacher must be to act as a human filter, vetting and pre-exploring websites and online resources, and then pointing students towards the most relevant and helpful areas. There are a number of electronic filters available for schools and parents to use to protect children from undesirable internet sites, and these devices are becoming more sophisticated all the time. Alternatively, if there is great anxiety, store useful websites in the computer's cache memory and then disable the internet connection while the children are using the computers.

However, a far greater danger is the threat from dangerous individuals who pose as children in chat rooms. This, I feel, is a question that will only be addressed by consultation between teachers and parents. What are your opinions on this?

3. *Can children engaging in e-pal communication with children in other countries really gain an insight into another culture without visiting?*

The richness of text can be quite astounding. There is so much that can be conveyed through written language, and people who meet on the internet very quickly get to know each other. Fiction writers have been fleshing out characters using only the written language for centuries. So I think it is entirely possible that children will be able to convey many aspects of their own cultures and traditions to each other using e-mail. The extent to which this is possible will be contingent on the imagination of the children involved. Remember that a large number of text based symbols (called 'emoticons') can be used to convey emotions including smiles :-), frowns :-(and winks ;-) . More ideas about using ICT to connect children of different cultures can be found in Chapter II.

4. *What kind of checks and balances is it possible to implement in order to ensure that children's web pages are appropriate and acceptable?*

The teacher is responsible for monitoring these kinds of activities. He or she should ensure that pupils do not post materials that have the potential to cause offence, and that they work in keeping with the ethos of the school to achieve the stated learning outcomes. There also needs to be a consideration about copyrighted materials being used – check with your library if you are in any doubt. The teacher's role here will be to act as a guide to the rules that apply.

5. *What may be the key reasons parents object to activities such as the one outlined in this tutorial?*

As I have already outlined, many parents are concerned that their children do not become involved in activities where they can be made vulnerable to contact with undesirable individuals. They are also concerned that their children do not enter websites that contain materials liable to offend, corrupt or mislead. Some parents may be concerned that their child should learn a wide range of skills, and that using a computer may be limiting. (For example, how will children develop their writing skills if they spend too much time using a keyboard? How will they practise their maths skills if they only use calculators to work out sums?) Some parents may hold religious or moral beliefs that using computers or the internet is wrong and may object on these grounds.

Teaching tip

Don't assume that all parents are completely familiar with the potential of the internet. For some, ICT, the internet and 'cyberspace' may be totally alien concepts, and all they may be aware of will be the media hype and occasional news items on television or in the newspapers.

Be prepared to patiently explain, demonstrate and generally inform parents of the potential of ICT and how their children (and perhaps they too!) can benefit from it.

Conversely, it is also worth remembering that some parents are expert at using computers, and may have knowledge and skills that surpass your own. If you don't know the answer, admit it, and then go and find out!

Let's now turn our attention to an examination of the benefits and limitations that such a project would yield for your Year 6 children.

Benefits

There are many benefits but some of the important ones for pupils may be realised in:

- **raised interest in computers and information technology;**
- **new and improved skills in organisation, presentation and communication;**
- **better appreciation of other cultures, languages and traditions;**
- **a sense of achievement and raised motivation;**
- **acquisition of better skills in information retrieval;**
- **more confidence in the use of electronic communications media (i.e. e-mail);**
- **development of better problem-solving skills.**

You may be able to think of other benefits the Year 6 project would deliver.

The obvious benefit of consultation is that all who should have a say have a chance to voice their opinions and concerns. Parents in particular have a vested interest and deserve to be kept informed. They will naturally be very concerned about the safety of their children and any potential dangers and they have a right to voice these concerns. However, most of them will usually also see the benefits of this approach to learning, developing as it does a range of transferable life skills and long-term benefits including information technology skills, organisational ability, cultural awareness and knowledge of other countries, language and communication skills, and design considerations (see comments above).

Limitations

For pupils, the limiting aspects of the Year 6 project will probably include: disappointment at not being able to finish the project on time; not having the skills to complete the project; potential exposure to undesirable materials; and technical failure leading to frustration and/or demotivation.

The process of consultation may result in everyone wishing to exert more than their fair share of influence, with the result that the project could then be in danger of grinding to a halt or simply not happening. Some parents may decide to withdraw their children from the project, which will mean that they will miss out on the experience. For you as the teacher of course it will mean extra work – you will have to find something else for your pupils to do which will engage them in equivalent experiences and at a similar level.

Evaluating web resources

I have already argued that the internet is not all doom and gloom. There is a huge potential for schools to exploit the internet's potential as a vast treasure house of information for pupils to explore. We have already explored the idea that, like any medium, the internet also houses a large amount of harmful, dangerous and undesirable materials. But what about information that appears to be useful or factual? Unfortunately, many people (student teachers included!) simply accept what they find on websites without question. There is a problem with this outlook as many sites are not always as accurate or useful as they first appear. It is important that teachers evaluate the quality of websites before they use them for teaching purposes. But how can they achieve this?

The Silver Standard

One method for evaluating the quality of a web site is by using the 'SILVER' standard. This is a tool I have created to test the usefulness and veracity of any resource found online. The acronym represents a systematic test of all the features you would expect to see on a good website:

- *S* = Structure of the website, and its organisation of content. Is the website logically presented and well written? Does the content have relevance and currency?

- *I* = Interactivity level. How much can you interrogate the site? Does the website have discussion areas or other interactive features?

- *L* = Links to other useful and reputable sites. Are there also links to this site from other reputable sites?

- *V* = Visual impact of the website. Is the site easy to read, or are the colours distracting? What about the size and format of the text? Do the graphics have a useful purpose?

- *E* = Ease of navigation – how easy was it to find your way round the website? Were there good signposts, buttons and hyperlinking within the site?

- *R* = Reputation of the site owner(s) and/or contributors. Are they known in their field(s) of activity? Who else uses this web resource? What are the user comments? How was the website recommended to you?

Activity

Search the internet for websites that have educational content. Select two websites that are similar in content or level, one of which scores highly on the SILVER standard and one which scores low. Document these in the boxes provided:

Website 1: *Title and/or URL:*

Your scores: S ...... I ...... L ...... V ...... E ...... R ......

(10 = Excellent, 0 = Poor)   *Total Score ....*

Comments:

Website 2: *Title and/or URL:*

Your scores: S ...... I ...... L ...... V ...... E ...... R ......

(10 = Excellent, 0 = Poor)   *Total Score ....*

Comments:

Which website came out on top as your 'best' site? What reasons do you have for choosing it as the best? Deciding which site is the best for your needs or for the needs of the pupils within your classroom is obviously a little subjective, but the use of a structured checklist should provide some objectivity to the process of selection. It is important that teachers visit and evaluate all web resources before they let the children loose on them. In essence, vetting the worth of a web resource is a professional accountability for all education professionals.

Teaching tip

Ensure that any website you are using, developing or recommending is accessible to children with special needs or disability:

- *Will children with various forms of dyslexia be able to read the text?*
- *What will a website need if it is to be used by children who are partially sighted or blind?*

Have a look at the 'Bobby' web-testing site **http://bobby.watchfire.com/bobby/html/en/index.jsp**, and then use it to test the two sites you identified above. How useful is the 'Bobby' site as a quality assurance tool? If you were to design your own website, what features would you place there? What features would you definitely avoid using?

Notes:

Features I would use:

Features I would not use:

Edward Miller has devised a comprehensive evaluation process to assess the quality of websites in terms of technical quality, reliability, navigation, interaction levels, and context.

Activity

Read the paper by Edward Miller (URL below) and reflect on the process he outlines for evaluating websites. How useful is his method in determining the worth and quality of websites?

(www.soft.com/eValid/Technology/White.Papers/website.quality.html)

Zombies, digital pathogens and hackers

There are several other potential dangers to consider when using the internet. Downloading material from some sites may expose users to computer viruses – programs specifically created to cause damage to computers and the files they hold. Digital pathogens (viruses) can also be introduced into your computer if you carelessly open attachments in e-mails when you are unsure of their origin. Increasingly, computer hackers are breaking into people's computers and causing serious disruption and damage. Have you ever wondered why there is so much unwanted e-mail (spam) out there and why it is on the increase? Some viruses are able to infect unprotected computers and take control without the owner's knowledge. The virus (or 'malware') writer will then be able to use your computer's processing power and internet connection to send spam to others. With more and more homes and businesses connecting via broadband, faster data transmission speeds are escalating the problem. If you are unfortunate enough to be a victim of a virus attack, and the spammer then uses your computer to send junk e-mail without your knowledge, then your computer is said to have become a 'zombie' computer. If you suspect that this has happened, or would like to ensure that it doesn't, you need to ensure that your virus protection software is up to date. Also make sure that you download any available 'patches' or software upgrades from your virus protection software supplier. Finally, install a firewall protection in your computer to guard against attacks.

Spam with everything

Spam is becoming an increasingly frustrating and annoying phenomenon in electronic communities and in some areas is reaching epidemic proportions. The equivalent of junk mail, but much more easily sent, spam has been known to arrive in such large volumes that it can close down a school's server (known as denial of service), overloading memory and preventing the school from using important functions such as reliable e-mail communication. It is thought that the use of the word 'spam' to describe junk e-mails derives from the Monty Python comedy sketch in which a café served 'spam with everything'. It is best not to be a target of spammers, because once you are targeted, your active e-mail address can be sold on or passed across to other spammers. Before you realise it, you are receiving dozens or even hundreds of spam messages each week offering you everything from huge prize winnings on a lottery to cut-price Viagra or breast enlargement. Wallace (1999) has suggested that the need to regularly delete spam is the psychological equivalent to 'weeding the garden'. As more junk e-mail pours in, you are required to invest regular time deleting messages to prevent your computer's mailbox from being overrun.

Schools can purchase spam detection software, and it is a good strategy to delete spam e-mail rather than opening it or attempting to reply to it. Open it and it could be infected with a virus. Reply to it and you may find it is 'bounced back' to you because there is no return address, or even worse, you alert the spammer to the fact that your e-mail address is active. Some e-mail software packages provide a useful feature within the tools menu to recognise junk e-mail and file it away for deletion in a 'spam' file.

When children play games online, the computer they are using may be particularly vulnerable to hackers. Many types of anti-virus software and firewall software are available for reasonable prices which can help to reduce the risks of viruses and hackers (For useful information on this theme visit the web resource at: **www.thinkuknow.co.uk/parents/3.htm**). For those who purchase protection software, regular updates are included in the cost, usually for a year or more, ensuring the computer is constantly immunised against most of the dangers posed by rogue internet users. Your placement school's ICT coordinator should be aware of these issues, and can offer guidelines to users within the school. A more comprehensive review on the dangers of using the internet and how to protect your computer from them can be found in the work of Steven Furnell (2003).

Conclusion

In this chapter we have examined many of the issues and problems associated with educational use of the internet. We started by exploring the potential dangers that children may encounter if left unprotected. You were asked to reflect upon a problem involving a project where a group of Year 6 pupils used the internet to create their own personal web pages. Consultation between teachers and parents was proposed as an effective means of promoting the excellent potential of the internet as a learning tool without compromising the safety of the children. The use of filtering and intranet facilities were offered as safe alternatives to 'open use' of the internet. Strict teacher monitoring of any internet activities was strongly advised. We also explored the potential of the internet through an exercise involving evaluation of website materials and you were offered a systematic tool to tackle this problem. Finally, we discussed the potential dangers and issues arising from computers connected to the internet, including hackers, viruses and unwanted e-mail. The internet is potentially one of the most fertile learning resources available to teachers, but it must be used with caution and a great deal of planning if it is to be exploited safely, and to its fullest extent.

Useful websites

Watchfire Bobby (assessing accessibility for people with disabilities to websites) (**http://bobby.watchfire.com/bobby/html/en/index.jsp**) (visited 21 February 2005).

Automatic website test software (**www.usablenet.com/accessibility_ usability /webtesting.html**) (visited 21 February 2005).

Miller, E. (2002) Website Quality Challenge. (**www.soft.com/eValid/Technology/ White.Papers/website.quality.html**) (visited 17 December 2004).

Advice for parents and teachers about how to protect young children when they are using the internet can be found at: **www.wiseupthenet.co.uk** (visited 10 December 2004).

For most people, technology makes things easier. For people with disabilities, however, technology makes things POSSIBLE.

Mary Radabaugh (1988)

This chapter will enable you to:

- **explore issues of Special Educational Needs in primary education;**
- **understand how ICT can be used to support the communication needs of pupils who have been identified as having learning difficulties;**
- **gain an awareness of the wide-ranging special needs that are now likely to arise at some time in the primary school classroom.**

Introduction

The importance of facilitating the development of communication skills must lie at the heart of all good teaching. Without these skills, pupils with difficulties will not only fail at the curriculum but, more importantly, they will fail at being able to communicate needs and choices. They will also fail to engage in the social discussion and interaction with their peers that we are able to take for granted.

However, the area of special needs is both extensive and complex. I have not intended to be overly prescriptive here in terms of which software applications should be used and how. Rather, the ethos is of examining the pedagogical processes involved in ways in which ICT can be applied to learning as effectively – and creatively – as possible to support communication development. The application of these principles is illustrated with reference to three, wide-ranging real case-study scenarios, which also serve to demonstrate some aspects of particular conditions, and point the reader to some useful additional sources of supporting information.

Finally, working alongside many teachers and teaching assistants, I have frequently come across many imaginative and transforming examples of ICT-based work created to meet specific needs of pupils – often adapting readily available software – and just a small selection of these have been incorporated to illustrate the text.

New technology, new independence

In the early 1970s, **Ma**rgaret Walker, **Ka**thy Johnson and **Ton**y Carnforth developed their communication language system based on signing and symbols, and named it after themselves – **Makaton** (Makaton Vocabulary Development Project). This development has probably done more than anything to enable children with severe and complex learning difficulties not only to communicate their basic needs but to express themselves in both functional and creative ways. However, running a close second to this must be the development of ICT, and the proliferation of software and other resources which are enabling these pupils to attain something like their true potential, despite the disadvantages they experience. This is not the place to try and document the very wide range of learning opportunities now available. Instead, it for us to consider the *principles* which underpin the use of technology and to engage with some of the dynamic and transformative outcomes that can be achieved. As Blamires (1999) identifies, we are aiming to provide for pupils, who would ordinarily be placed in disadvantageous situations in terms of being able to communicate their needs and ideas, the chance to improve the quality of life of individuals, and their range of life opportunities.

What are these principles? First and foremost is the acquisition of a definition and understanding of what is meant by Special Educational Needs (SEN), and indeed communication. In late 2002, the Department for Education and Skills (DfES) published a consultation document which provided for a slightly revised system of labelling of the various categories of SEN. The categories included updating the classification of children with behavioural, emotional and social difficulties (BESD), identifying the specific needs of children with dyslexia, dyscalculia and dyspraxia (Specific Learning Difficulties, or SpLD), and introducing a separate category for children on the Autistic Spectrum (Autistic Spectrum Disorder, or ASD).

What the categories do not tell us in great detail is the huge range of difficulties and indeed capabilities that pupils within each grouping may experience, nor the exact nature of their complexity. That is for us as educators to work out. It also fails to inform us about the increasing likelihood that pupils from all categories, including those with the profoundest disabilities, are increasingly likely to be found in the mainstream setting. The Code of Practice (DfES, 2001a) is the driving force behind the inclusion of many such children, and the Special Educational Needs Disability Act (SENDA 2001) ensures that we have a legal duty to educate children identified with learning difficulties in ways which have an equivalence to their mainstream peers in terms of access, outcomes and especially resources.

When this user talks, the computer listens (Kelly, 2003)

> The fundamental problem of communication is that of reproducing at one point either exactly or approximately a message selected at another point'
> (Shannon, 1949)

McKeown (2000) observes: *Language is highly prized in our society. Success and power are associated with good communication skills: the ability to speak, use language effectively and write in a clear and persuasive manner.* Where does this leave the pupil who is disadvantaged, through delays in developing cognitive or physical skills, or both? We need to consider very carefully a range of factors if effective communication systems are to take place, whether it be for the child who has profound and multiple learning difficulties (PMLD), or for the pupil who is performing at levels marginally below those of his peers. We then need to remind ourselves of the fact that some half a million children have speech and language difficulties (ibid).

- **Firstly, we need to be able to** *transmit and receive* **information (sensory, two-way, synchronous/asynchronous) which will therefore enable communication to be conducted in an effective and efficient manner. In children who have complex learning difficulties, these systems may be damaged or operating in ways which are different to their mainstream peers. We therefore need to be able to identify where the difficulties are implicit, whether it be in literacy, verbal or other areas of communication, and establish points of intervention.**

- **We also require an ability to** *store knowledge***: many children with special educational needs may experience difficulties with recall, especially within their short-term and working memories. It may be that what is important for some pupils, in order to develop learning, is not the establishment of a progressive curriculum in which knowledge and skills are taught step by step. Instead, it is teaching them how to access the tools which can be used to support their means of communication.**

- **Knowledge in itself may be of little value. We need to be able to process information so that it may be applied to different contexts. The development of communication systems that pupils can understand, interpret and adapt in ways which match their learning advantages are paramount at whatever level of learning they are performing.**

- **Lastly, the learner and educator need to be able to manage the development of communication. We should ensure that there are opportunities for carefully planning schemes for encouraging the acquisition of communication skills, and that these are used across all contexts. Observation and recording need to thoroughly document where strategies are succeeding and failing.**

Why use ICT for pupils with communication difficulties?

There are many reasons why ICT is an excellent tool for including all learners in the classroom, regardless of the levels of their ability to communicate, with technology frequently allowing pupils to transcend their disabilities, both cognitive and physical. BECTa (2000) identified some key reasons which help to explain the success of ICT:

- *ICT enables the pupil to be an active participant in the classroom, not just a passive observer.* **In mainstream classes, it will be necessary to differentiate lessons in order to ensure that all pupils are included in effective learning. ICT is a highly flexible tool which can be readily adapted to meet very individualised needs.**

- *ICT offers opportunities for differing learning styles to be met.* There is an emphasis on visual presentation in the new technologies, particularly those based on the internet, but increasingly sound is being used creatively to support computer-based activities in a meaningful way. By observing a pupil's learning style preferences, it is possible to differentiate tasks which match these preferences. (See Chapter 9 for more on individual differences and ICT.)

- *ICT is a motivating medium which has a certain 'street cred' about it.* There is dynamism in the presentation of the media used by ICT which has become widely embedded in youth culture. Research shows that over 70 per cent of children are regularly using gaming technology, while the market for mobile phones has extended into the lower primary school age-group.

- *ICT enables pupils to stay on task by focusing their attention and alleviating some of the physical pressures.* An inherent quality of ICT is what has been referred to by the Department for Education and Employment as *automaticity.* The computer will carry out many of the mechanical skills inherent in communication.

- *ICT enables pupils to develop independence.* Through use of the appropriate software and access peripherals, we can provide the pupil with an environment in which the minimum (or indeed no) adult support is required for interaction and learning to take place.

- *ICT affords privacy to work and develop at the learner's own pace.* The user is in control. Yes, some activities on the computer may be time-bound, but because of the asymmetrical nature of most technology-based learning (excluding live chat and video-conferencing here), the activities are always there to come back to. This reduces the pressure that many learners with difficulties feel when they are given a specific timetable to work within.

- *ICT can facilitate social communication and interaction, including pupils in a wider community.* ICT is a great promoter of collaborative learning (Tyrer et al., 2004). It is a tool which enables pupils to engage in the ethos of problem-based learning at any level. It also encourages them to work in teams which, given a stimulating learning scenario, will almost certainly result in considerable interaction and even discussion.

- *ICT can support the production of well-presented, high-quality outcomes.* For all children, and not just those with learning difficulties, the chance to edit and refine their work with relative ease is a key reason for justifying the use of ICT. Computers also allow all learners to create work, which when displayed on the screen or printed out is of high quality, and comparable to their peers' outcomes.

Developing an ICT-based intervention: the processes

In order for pupils with Special Educational Needs to learn effectively using ICT, we should ask:

- **What do we know about the exact nature of the pupil's difficulties?**

- What do we want the pupil to learn?
- How can ICT be used to impact on these difficulties – especially in ways which more traditional teaching methods and resources may not have been able to?

It is then possible to move forward in a planned and systematic manner through a series of process stages.

Being informed: where to obtain information about the nature of the pupil's difficulties

The first point of contact must be the school's Special Educational Needs Coordinator (SENCo), who will have detailed information about particular children's needs. An overview of pupil needs will be contained in a statement – if the pupil has one – and the majority of children with SEN will also have an individual education plan (IEP), with additional information from annual review meetings being especially important to identify key areas of individual learning. The school may also have strong support from a speech and language therapist who will certainly be able to offer advice on the various support methods and interventions.

Almost all the known medical conditions which affect children are represented by agencies and interest groups, with many being present on the internet: 'Contact a Family' is an excellent organisation which provides a directory of such web-based information, as well as outlines of medical conditions and disabilities, and can be accessed online at: **www.cafamily.org.uk**.

The importance of observation

In Figure 6.1, BECTa identifies what Ofsted might well be looking for when monitoring pupil responses while using ICT in the classroom.

As evidence of the effectiveness of teaching, look for the following responses from pupils:	
Responding positively to challenges	
Having good attitudes to work, exhibiting enthusiasm, commitment and enjoyment	
Persevering, concentrating	
Posing questions and solving problems effectively with ICT	
Making effective, relevant and creative use of ICT	
Using ICT to experiment, learning from mistakes and becoming independent	
Using ICT to improve their work, taking pride in the finished product	
Using ICT effectively to communicate ideas and find things out	
Showing respect for ICT hardware, software and data	
Collaborating, working effectively in teams and independently	

Figure 6.1: Ofsted checklist

This format may have its uses. However, within the context of recording how the precise needs of the pupils with complex learning difficulties are being met by their use of ICT it is irrelevant and indeed contributes little in the way of the detailed knowledge required to understanding exactly how such pupils may be using ICT. The professional judgement of teachers needs to be applied more rigorously to the observation and recording process if pupils' learning is to be optimised.

Identifying the pupils' strengths in their use of ICT

We need to consider what is important in terms of recording skill development and planning for the next steps.

- *Where is the pupil coming from, in terms of prior learning and acquired level of competent skills?* **Transfer of knowledge about pupils between stages of transition, such as from class to class, year to year and school to school, can be difficult to record and communicate effectively. Developmental checklists can certainly help in this, and increasingly there are standardised systems more readily available. It is possible to construct a checklist of skills, which are both developmental and implicit in terms of offering a basis for recording and subsequent planning – although it should be pointed out here that many pupils with learning difficulties do not always follow consistent paths of development and progression. Figure 6.2 provides an extract from a proprietary recording document, created by B-Squared.**

Computer Activities

Touch keys or a switch, mouse or rollerball etc

Track movement across a screen showing reaction at appropriate point

Tracks object horizontally across the screen operating the switch at the correct time

Tracks object vertically across the screen operating the switch at the correct time

Moves objects on screen

Match objects on screen

Can tolerate interruptions due to rearrangement of switch, positioning or changing software/ activity

Can recognise a computer image and a print of the same image not on the screen

Shows signs of attempting to make one-to-one correspondence between activity (by changing nature of switch use or by facial expression)

Understands one to one correspondence between switch press and action

Select from 2 box grid on concept keyboard with verbal prompt

Select from 2 switches with verbal prompt

Presses switch with fingers

Press a switch to make the screen change

Match letters and numbers to letters and numbers on screen

Match objects to pictures on screen

Match shapes to shapes on screen

Looks for object on screen

Figure 6.2: Computer activities checklist
(Reproduced by kind permission of B-Squared: **www.bsquaredsen.co.uk/**)

Plymouth Education Authority has also developed the BARE project (Below Age-Related Expectation), which is designed to help educators record the levels of achievement of pupils who are performing at levels below those identified by the core National Curriculum strands of learning.

- *What computer skills is the pupil capable of using effectively for the tasks involved?* **It is important to consider the range of ICT activities that a pupil may be able to use in order to access appropriate learning resources. Remember that ICT is not just about computers: the range of equipment that can be classified as ICT** includes tape and video recorders, photocopiers, mobile phones, video-games and anything that is programmable. There may be just as much worth in teaching a Foundation Stage pupil to use an infant cassette player as a means of developing independence as there would in using a computer. An example of this can be demonstrated by a teacher who wanted to develop independence skills in a pupil by encouraging their use of a children's cassette player to play tapes which contained instructions for playing games. The pupil had to not only listen to the tape, but learn how to follow instructions and organise the subsequent activities.

- *Does the pupil have an active role to play in both the recording of their skills, and planning?* **Both the Code of Practice (DfES, 2001a) and SENDA 2001 stress the importance of all pupils being able to take at least some responsibility for the decisions made about recording and planning judgements. For those with complex difficulties, this may be especially problematic but not impossible. The Record of Achievement format introduced in the late 1980s and modified following the Dearing Report of 1996 was designed to engage pupils in the recording and to some extent planning of their curriculum and personal learning goals. The use of '*I can* ...' statements, along with the integration of examples of pupils' work and perhaps digital photographs of them engaging in creative processes, especially if formatted in an ICT-based presentation, can provide a valuable system in which learner and educator can establish a dialogue about achievements, strengths and areas that need working on.**

What do we actually want the pupil to learn?

In the wide range of classroom contexts in which we are likely to find an equally wide range of learning needs and difficulties, the first answer could be, 'It's in the QCA Scheme of Work'. While the planning offered by the Qualifications and Curriculum Authority (QCA) does cover all the content that could be covered in the primary school, and drives the great majority of teachers' planning, these should, however, be considered in context of the overall needs of the pupil. It is of value to use such schemes as a starting point for thinking about learning activities. However, we need to also think about other important objectives, such as independence: *What can I do by myself*, and *How can I get my needs, feelings and thoughts across to you?*

We should also consider the depth of learning we wish the pupil to achieve. It is important that children, particularly those with complex learning difficulties, are not subjected to learning opportunities which are developmentally beyond where they are achieving. Byers and Rose (1996), McKeown (2005) and others have identified the significance of this, and have broken down the levels of learning into key stages:

- **Experiential: the pupil is placed in environments where they are able to experience different sensory stimuli.**
- **Acquisition: the learner is starting to acquire the skills and knowledge, although the retention of these may not be consistent or complete.**
- **Fluency: the skills and knowledge are becoming inherent for the learner.**

- Maintenance: the learner can retain what has been taught over increasing periods of time.

- Generalisation: the learner is able to consider acquired knowledge and skills in different contexts.

- Application and adaptation: the learner can draw upon their knowledge and understanding in more complex scenarios, being able to 'unpack' learning and reformat in ways appropriate to meeting problems and tasks beyond linear development processes.

Case study 6.1: Using ICT to support communication development for a pupil who has PMLD

Activity

Jack is a Year 6 pupil who suffers from severe brain damage caused by cerebral palsy. He has a range of sensory impairments; he is partially sighted, as well as being unable to talk. He has poor body control, and when sitting, has to use a specially constructed chair. Arm and hand movements are often uncontrolled, and much physiotherapy work has been directed at developing a more targeted use of his hands. However, he can express emotions, and has started asserting quite strong preferences for certain activities, e.g. music and playing with noise-making toys. His individual education plan (IEP) focuses on trying to develop his communication and independence at an appropriate level.

- *How can ICT help support the development of these objectives?*

- *Visit the Inclusive Technology website at www.inclusive.co.uk and examine the range of access devices available.*

Let's revisit our earlier question: What do we want the pupil to learn? I suggest that for this pupil it is essential that we offer him opportunities to learn how to:

- communicate his essential needs and feelings as independently as possible;

- develop his physical skills, in order that he can access the technology which will enable him to communicate his needs and feelings;

- consider *where next* in terms of skill development – within the areas of communication and access to technology.

Figure 6.3: NGfL Jungle Slide Show
(Image reproduced by kind permission of Priory Woods School, source: the Northern Grid for Learning.
(**www.northerngrid.org/sen/powerpoint.htm**)

In the activity illustrated in Figure 6.3, a slideshow created by the Northern Grid for Learning, which is a freely downloadable resource, enables various animated creatures and their associated sounds to appear every time a switch is pressed. The multi-sensory nature of the activity and the vivid use of graphics and movement have provided a highly stimulating learning resource which will engage and indeed motivate many pupils in the PMLD group, developing not just early communication skills such as visual concentration, tracking, anticipation and expression, but also associated skills in targeting switches access.

Interfacing the computer

For the pupil who has complex physical difficulties such as Jack's, it is imperative that we consider the most effective way that he can access technology. As Kelly (2003) notes, one of the biggest barriers for physically disabled children using the computer is the keyboard. Using a specially designed interface, however, it is possible to select a switch device which will meet a particular strength that a physically disabled pupil can then effectively use, whether it be activated by touch, movement, sound or even the blinking of an eye. They can also be used to operate toys, cassette players etc. with mains-adapted models also being available.

- **Touch-screens: the computer responds when the screen is touched. Touch-screens may come as devices which can be fixed to standard monitors, or be integral to a specially designed monitor (see Figure 6.4).**

Figure 6.4: A touch-screen in use   Figure 6.5: A variety of switching devices

(Images reproduced by kind permission of Inclusive Technology. **www.inclusive.co.uk**)

- **Switches: these are devices, which when activated, will make something happen (see Figure 6.5). A picture could be built up or objects made to move. With increased cognitive development, the pupil can use the switch to make choices and may use a combination of two or more switches to control the computer.**
- **Adapted keyboards, such as the *IntelliKeys* overlay keyboard (Figure 6.6), enables the computer to be accessed through the use of a flat tablet, based on a grid system of 'switches' which can then be programmed to operate software, using appropriate overlay graphics.**

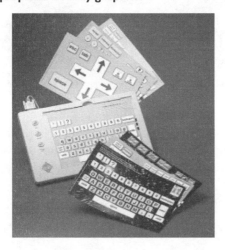

Figure 6.6: The Intellikeys overlay keyboard.

(Image reproduced by kind permission of Inclusive Technology. **www.inclusive.co.uk**)

Moving on ...

Jack has the potential to develop his cognitive, communication and physical skills through the use of ICT. Future activities could be designed to enable him to make a choice when a pair (or more) of objects are displayed on the screen. These could be further developed to integrate a system of needs identification— perhaps choosing an activity, food or other desire using a picture selection process.

Figure 6.7: Catch the cheese!

In Figure 6.7 a teaching assistant has used an open-content, and readily available, software program to facilitate the development of mouse control skills. When the pointer (enlarged) is placed over the cheese which moves randomly around the screen, the computer rewards the user by exploding the cheese.

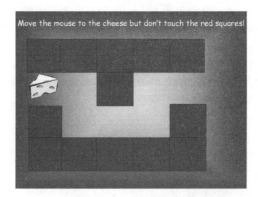

Figure 6.8: Cheese maze

In a more advanced development of mouse-control skills (Figure 6.8) the pupil has to guide the pointer through a variety of maze configurations in order to reach the cheese, with similarly dynamic rewards built in.

Case study 6.2: Meeting the needs of a pupil who is on the Autistic Disorder Spectrum

Activity

Jo is a Year 3 student who is high on the Autistic Spectrum Disorder. She requires a very structured learning environment, responding in difficult and indeed challenging ways when faced with something unexpected or inadequately prepared for. Her verbal language is predominantly echolalic, although she can name correctly the activities, events, objects, people etc. who are important to her. She suffers from no sensory impairments; indeed, she has a heightened perception of sounds, which can cause her distress at times. She will also react emotionally in ways which are quite different to her mainstream peers, by, for example,

Her teaching team are focusing on improving her levels of behaviour through developing her understanding of what is going on around her.

How can ICT help to facilitate her understanding of her learning environment?

Visit the National Autistic Society website at www.nas.org.uk and read the 'what is autism?' section

According to the National Autistic Society (online: 2005), it is estimated that there are some 500,000 families in the UK currently touched by autism in some way. Their difficulties, as a spectrum would suggest, are wide ranging, with Jo being more towards the higher end. The diagnosis of Autistic Spectrum Disorder (ASD) identifies these three key elements as being integral to the diagnostic process and forming the *triad of impairments*:

- *social interaction* (difficulty with social relationships, for example appearing aloof and indifferent to other people);
- *social communication* (difficulty with verbal and non-verbal communication, for example not fully understanding the meaning of common gestures, facial expressions or tone of voice);
- *imagination* (difficulty in the development of interpersonal play and imagination, for example having a limited range of imaginative activities, possibly copied and pursued rigidly and repetitively).

One of Jo's major problems arising from the condition is that of managing change – a difficulty facing the majority of pupils with ASD – and clearly change is an inherent part of the school routine. Such pupils find the transition between activities and associated staff almost impossible to manage, and educational objectives may well focus on creating resources which help the pupil to anticipate changes (in any form) to routine. The use of visual timetables which incorporate graphics, are a frequently successful way of managing this particular area of difficulty. Rebus, Makaton, the Picture Exchange Communication System (PECS) and the Picture Communication system (PCS) are popular sources of standardised symbol 'languages', although it is important to establish consistency in the use of symbols.

Further information on symbol languages

Widgit Software, at **www.widgit.com** offer communication software which can be supplied with the various symbol language libraries. Mayer-Johnson Inc. at **www. mayer-johnson.com** offers guidance on developing literacy skills using the PCS symbol system.

The PECS, developed by Pyramid Approach to Education, is designed to establish effective learning environments for children and adults with autism or related developmental disabilities and severe learning impairments.

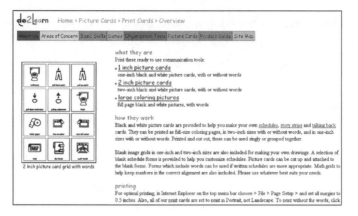

Figure 6.9: The do2learn website
(Reproduced by kind permission of do2learn: **www.do2learn.com**)

The do2learn website (see Figure 6.9) aims to support parents and educators of children with severe and complex learning difficulties, and provides access to a large number of varied resources. They offer freely downloadable symbol cards which cover a variety of school-based and social contexts.

Developing understanding …

As Jo develops her understanding of a graphic or symbol-based language, she will have at her command a form of expressive communication which will enable her to engage proactively in her environment. She will be able to attach meaning to symbols and use them to assert choices and preferences, express feelings and read instructions with understanding. It will also offer her a way of recording experiences. She will learn to use symbols and understand that images can have meaning. We will then have a teaching tool which is in a mutually comprehensible language, and one that both learner and educator can develop. It may then be possible to examine other areas of intervention, such as encouraging the development of her understanding of feelings and emotions.

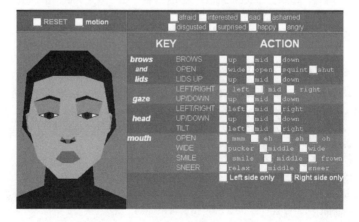

Figure 6.10: do2learn's animated face
(Reproduced by kind permission of **www.do2learn.com**)

In the activity shown in Figure 6.10, an animated face responds to commands which an adult types in. The face responds appropriately, and provides a good opportunity for the learner to acquire social language and a demonstration of appropriate expressions and behaviours.

Case study 6.3: Using ICT to support a pupil with dyslexia

Activity

Shaun is in Year 6, and has been diagnosed as having dyslexia. He demonstrates considerable difficulty with his writing skills, which usually results in his work being poorly organised, untidy, containing misspellings of many words, and the mirror-imaging of letters such as p and q, b and d. He displays equal difficulty with reading, 'tripping over' words especially which are outside the obvious spelling patterns, such as 'was'. He finds following large portions of text extremely difficult, and will often gain little understanding from what he has read. His lack of organisational skills transcends into other areas, and he will regularly be ill-equipped for tasks, which often involves losing equipment or forgetting to bring items to class.

However, as with many children who have dyslexia, he has many strengths which may be hidden or over-shadowed by the diagnosis and label he carries with him. He is, for example, an articulate boy who will regularly contribute to classroom discussions in an informed and thoughtful manner, and has a range of constructive interests.

Increasingly, Shaun is finding it difficult to keep up with the demands of the curriculum, and is beginning to lose interest in many aspects of his school work.

- *Consider how ICT can be used to help Shaun manage effectively the difficulties that dyslexia is causing him in his written work.*

- *Visit the Dyslexia Institute's website at: http://www.dyslexia-inst.org.uk and explore the sections on dyslexia facts, recognising dyslexia and helpful hints.*

What is dyslexia?

> *On a visit to China I felt outside society. I couldn't understand the written codes around me. Then I understood what it felt like to be severely dyslexic.*
>
> (Liz Brooks, formerly Executive Director, Dyslexia Institute)

According to the Dyslexia Institute:

> *Dyslexia is a specific learning difficulty that hinders the learning of literacy skills. This problem with managing verbal codes in memory is neurologically based and tends to run in families. Other symbolic systems, such as mathematics and musical notation, can also be affected.*

The Orton Dyslexia Society (now the International Dyslexia Association) (1995) adds:

> *Varying in degrees of severity, it is manifested by difficulties in receptive and expressive*

language, including phonological processing, in reading, writing, spelling, handwriting and sometimes in arithmetic.

About 10 per cent of the population have some form of dyslexia. Around 4 per cent are severely dyslexic, including some 375,000 schoolchildren, causing difficulties in learning to read, write and spell. Short-term and working memory, organisational skills, emotional difficulties along with the associated difficulties with literacy such as untidy writing, poor spelling and phonological awareness may also present themselves.

Dyslexia is biological in origin and tends to run in families, but environmental factors may also contribute to it, affecting all kinds of people regardless of intelligence, race or socio-economic class. Those who experience the condition will also possibly display unexpected performance in some areas of learning: for example, being low achievers in terms of reading ability but good at expressing themselves verbally in discussion.

The effects of dyslexia may largely be overcome by skilled specialist teaching and the use of compensatory strategies, and the earlier the intervention, the better the outcome.

How can ICT support dyslexic learners?

The innate nature of ICT enables many of the above areas of difficulty to be addressed at fundamental levels. There are many software packages available which will develop auditory discrimination skills and phonological awareness. These range from those which are based on 'drill and practice' routines through to adapting existing open-content software packages which target an individual's needs precisely. The latter offers the educator the opportunity to engage in creativity, but may also be countered by the time needed to develop such activities. Somewhere in between these two options there is a range of software packages which offer content frames, which can be set up to allow pupils to engage in learning scenarios which are personalised and structured to meet their individual needs and indeed interests.

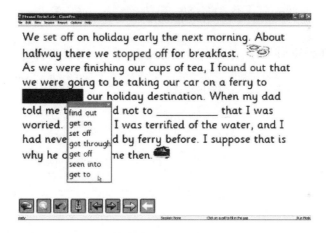

Figure 6.11: Crick Software's ClozePro program.

(Reproduced by kind permission of Crick Software : **www.cricksoft.com**)

The image in Figure 6.11 illustrates an example of how the use of software such as ClozPro can allow educators to carefully target specific learning objectives through the provision of open-content and cloze procedure formats. Within a selected framework, the teacher can determine the spellings and phonemes that a pupil needs to learn, and set them within an environment which can be based on the pupil's interests.

Certainly, good use of ICT to support dyslexia should embrace the following characteristics, although not all at once:

- **full speech support, so that all text on screen can be seen and heard;**
- **spoken instructions;**
- **opportunities to listen again or repeat an activity;**
- **a structured progression or word lists that can be selected to meet the needs of the user (on phonics and spelling programs);**
- **easy navigation around the screen;**
- **help menus;**
- **spellings, phonics and wordlists that are written in lower case, not CAPITAL letters;**
- **an uncluttered screen with a clear focus on the task;**
- **options to record the user's progress can be helpful;**
- **choices of screen backgrounds and colours can also be helpful.**

Developing skills

There are a number of technologies that are of particular use when working with students with dyslexia or dyslexic-type difficulties, and we should consider developing skills at using these particular tools:

- **assessment software, which allows the diagnosis of particular areas of literacy need;**
- **access to various formats of print styles and sizes;**
- **touch typing;**
- **specific skills work such as spelling patterns;**
- **planning tools, enabling the child to help organise how they are going to carry out an activity or series of activities;**
- **word processors, including predictive word processors, which offer a range of facilities, such as 'track changes' and 'drop-down menus'.**

Figure 6.12 shows an on-screen worksheet created by a teaching assistant working with a dyslexic pupil, using a readily available text-processing package, based on the package's 'drop-down menu' facility:

Colours

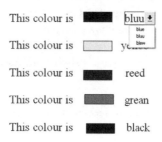

This colour is		bluu ▾
This colour is		ye...
This colour is		reed
This colour is		grean
This colour is		black

Figure 6.12: A colour worksheet for a dyslexic child

- **the use of software which offers predictive text facilities;**
- **speech reproduction and synthesis. It is possible to train speech recognition software, but many children with reading difficulties, for example, will be unable to digest the texts which they are asked to use when setting up such an option. However, an area that is of great benefit is the use of 'screen reading' software. CFS-Technologies offer a freely downloadable text reading facility which will reads aloud any given text with just one mouse click (see Figure 6.13).**

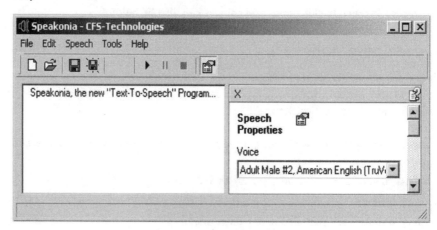

Figure 6.13: CFS-Technologies' text-to-speech program
(Reproduced by kind permission of CFS-Technologies)

Where next?

As in all areas of contemporary education, ICT is moving forward both rapidly and unpredictably, and perhaps, as Professor Stephen Molyneux (2003) stated, *the best way to predict the future is to invent it yourself.* However, there are certain trends emerging which will undoubtedly provide some dynamic opportunities for developing learning opportunities and environments which will enable pupils with the range of difficulties discussed in this chapter.

Accessing the internet, and active participation in online communities

Widgit Software, a specialist provider of software for pupils with such difficulties, particularly within the context of using symbol communication systems, has also been responsible for establishing the idea that those with low levels of literacy can become part of online communities.

Symbol World is a concept developed by Widgit Software, establishing an online community of learners who communicate primarily through the use of symbols (Figure 6.14).

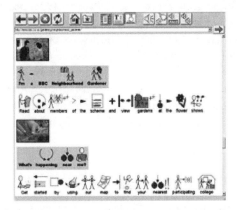

Figure 6.14: Widgit Software's Symbol World website
(Reproduced by kind permission of Widgit Software: **www.widgit.com/symbolworld**)

Widgit Software have now developed the first symbol-based web browser, *Communicate: Webwide*, with speech support, which enables the user to view many websites in a simplified layout, in a text view which can be configured to suit individual preferences, or have the contents of a web page automatically supported with symbols as well as speech (see Figure 6.15). The company also offers symbol-based e-mail systems.

Figure 6.15: Widgit's symbol-based web browser
(Reproduced by kind permission of Widgit Software: **www.widgit.com**)

The digital divide: barriers to promoting ICT

Lastly, we should consider barriers to using ICT for pupils who have special educational needs. Access equipment and appropriate software comes at a price. However, the tools described in this chapter are seen as being essential to enabling communication for the pupil with learning difficulties, and without them, such pupils must be severely disadvantaged.

Then there are the inhibitions that the educator may experience in developing the use of ICT. Many teachers feel they lack skills and confidence in the use of rapidly evolving technology, and are subsequently reluctant to develop its use, fearing that they may be beset by mistakes and even failure. But as Papert (1993) observed, errors benefit us: by reflecting on what went wrong and why, we can learn to fix them. Experimentation and play are certainly the best ways of developing an understanding of what ICT can do for us – as most of our pupils have discovered for themselves.

However, as we become caught up on the wave of enthusiasm generated by the educational society's obsession with the development of the new technologies, we should note George Brackett's observation (2003): *Technologies don't change schools – caring, capable people do.*

Some useful resources

British Education Communication and Technology Agency: **www.becta.org.uk**
CFS Technologies: **www.cfs-technologies.com/home/?id=1.4**
Cricksoft: **www.cricksoft.com**
Do2learn: **www.do2learn.com**
Widgit Software: **www.widgit.com**

The following websites provide good information on specific learning difficulties:

Action for the Blind: **www.afbp.org**
Association for all speech impaired children – AFASIC: **www.afasic.org.uk**
Autism Connect: **www.autismconnect.org**
Autism Spectrum Disorder Good Practice Guidance (DfES/597/2002):
    www.dfes.gov.uk/sen
British Deaf Association: **www.bda.org.uk**
British Dyslexia Association: **www.bda-dyslexia.org.uk**
Contact a family: **www.cafamily.org.uk**
Deafblind: **www.deafblind.co.uk**
Disability Code of Practice for Schools: **www.drc.org.uk**
Down's Syndrome Association: **www.dsa-uk.com**
Dyscalculia: **www.dyscalculia.org.uk**
Dyslexia Institute: **www.dyslexia-inst.org.uk**
Dyspraxia: **www.dyspraxiafoundation.org.uk**
ICAN: **www.ican.org.uk**
MENCAP: **www.mencap.org.uk**
National Autistic Society: **www.nas.org.uk**

NCDS: **www.ndcs.org.uk**

Promoting Children's Mental Health within Early Years and Schools Settings –
Guidance (DfES/0112/2001): **www.dfes.gov.uk/sen**

RNIB: **www.rnib.org.uk**

RNID: **www.rnid.org.uk**

SCOPE: **www.scope.org.uk**

SENSE: **www.sense.org.uk**

Supporting the Target Setting Process: Guidance for effective target setting for pupils
with special educational needs (DfEE/0065/2001): **www.standards.dfes.
gov.uk/otherresources/publications/targetsetting**

World Health Organisation: **www.who.int/en**

7 VISUAL LITERACY AND ICT: 'I'M ONLY LOOKING...'

AVRIL LOVELESS AND JESS THACKER

> *Looking is not indifferent. There can never be any question of 'just looking'.*
>
> Victor Burgin (1982)

This chapter will enable you to:

- **think about why it is important for trainees and teachers to be aware of visual literacy and the implications for primary education and professional development;**

- **consider some of the current definitions and discussions of visual literacy and ICT;**

- **appreciate the range of approaches to promoting visual literacy and the types of information and communication technologies which can be used with young children;**

- **evaluate a case study of the use of ICT to support visual literacy in the practice of a PGCE Primary student.**

Introduction

'Visual literacy' is a term that is used by many people within many disciplines, including art, education and media and communication studies. It is one of those terms that seems to engage a common understanding, but actually generates a range of definitions. There is a sense that we are participating in a global 'knowledge society' in which ICT plays an essential role as a medium and a tool, and that there is an association between the visual representation of information and the use of these tools for navigation, communication and expression of meaning. Teachers play an important, if changing, role in our society as it develops and deals with globalisation, and they need to address the character of ICT in their work as it reflects the purposes of the education system within their society. They have to consider how these technologies influence their professional and personal lives, as well as their practice in more formal classroom and school settings. This chapter will therefore address some of these issues by considering debates about the implications of visual literacy and digital technologies, and relate these discussions to approaches that primary trainees and teachers may wish to develop in their own work. These discussions are not abstract, theoretical or confined to the ivory tower of higher education, but can influence how we understand and express our ideas in our visual environment, in our communications and in our engagement in teaching − from the classroom to our professional and personal communities.

Time to reflect

Think about a 'typical' day in your life, from waking up to going back to sleep.

- *Can you identify the different types of visual representation of information or ideas that you encounter during the day, from the design on your breakfast cereal packet to the advert on TV you might watch at the end of the day?*
- *How many icons and signs do you interpret and act on during a day?*
- *How did you deal with visual information on any ICT screens you may have used, from a web-browser to a mobile phone?*
- *Have you captured visual images using ICT?*
- *Have you manipulated visual images using ICT?*
- *Have you communicated ideas with visual images using ICT?*
- *What do you need to know in order to be at ease with these visual representations?*

Thinking about visual literacy

As an undergraduate university student I was challenged and changed by a BBC television series called *Ways of Seeing*. This series and the following book, made by John Berger and his colleagues, altered the way in which I looked at the world of images – from fine art to adverts. It also altered the way I 'looked' at myself as a person doing the looking, as a woman in a particular culture, time, place, social class and political arena (Berger, 1972). I realised that not only did I bring my own experience and identity to the act of looking, but I was able to gain insights into the way in which visual images were used in the wider world. Although I did not know the term 'visual literacy' at that time, I realised that the ideas in this book went far beyond 'art appreciation', and had implications for the ways in which I would engage with the visual world, both looking at and creating images and visual environments. Later, as a primary school teacher I expressed this approach to visual literacy in the ways that I designed and decorated my classrooms; and encouraged the children to look at and create images that engaged attention, raised questions, expressed meanings and gave them a sense of control and choice in the understanding and use of visual language.

Thirty years later, as I sat chatting in a café, I was delighted to discover that this same book had had a similar impact on some of my friends, each with very different backgrounds and personal histories. All of us, in our own ways, had taken those ideas and incorporated them into our work as teachers, broadcasters, researchers, writers and designers. We hope that, just as Berger's ideas had influenced us, our own work over the years might have had some impact on the ways in which children, students and peers might see the world. Each of us in that group is now involved in the use of ICT in learning and teaching. Many of the questions and issues raised about visual literacy and ICT are not new, but are cast in a different light by the developments of digital media and tools. Some questions, however, do relate to the distinctive contribution that ICT makes to our experience of making meaning with visual forms. It is important, therefore, that as educators, whether trainees, newly qualified teachers (NQTs) or experienced teachers, we consider how to promote and extend children's critical awareness of their visual world.

The International Visual Literacy Association (IVLA) presents a definition of visual literacy from John Debes in 1969 as:

> Visual Literacy refers to a group of vision-competencies a human being can develop by seeing and at the same time having and integrating other sensory experiences. The development of these competencies is fundamental to normal human learning. When developed, they enable a visually literate person to discriminate and interpret the visible actions, objects, symbols, natural or man-made, that he (sic) encounters in his environment. Through the creative use of these competencies, he (sic) is able to communicate with others. Through the appreciative use of these competencies, he (sic) is able to comprehend and enjoy the masterworks of visual communication. (**http://ivla.org/org_ what_vis_lit.htm# definition**)

Despite the gender-specific language of the late 1960s, this definition is useful in highlighting the response of the 'visually literate person' in discrimination, interpretation, comprehension and communication. There is still, however, a sense of passivity in such looking, which does not describe the more dynamic aspects of visual literacy which enable the creative activities of composing, fashioning, communicating and evaluating visual representations of meaning for the maker and other observers.

There is an ongoing debate about the extent to which the visual is taking precedence over text in our society's communications and expressions. Kress and Leeuwen present an interesting discussion of this disconnection between visual and text in describing the visual component of a text as *an independently organized and structured message – connected with the verbal text, but in no way dependent on it: and similarly the other way around* (Kress and Leeuwen, 1996, p. 17). They argue that our media environments are increasingly visual, and that the images are perceived as consciously structured and independently meaningful. The world wide web is used as an example to illustrate this point, with the visual display of web browsers, navigation icons, screen designs and presentation of images as well as text.

Some would argue with this approach, however, by pointing out how much of the visual is still associated with text. Indeed, much of the world wide web is textual and many of the images are used for illustration, rather than independent, symbolic communication of ideas (Ellis, 2001; 2004). Whatever the balance between these descriptions of the communication 'landscape', our technologies for capturing, presenting, reproducing and sending visual images have developed, from pinhole cameras to mobile phones; and we need to address the challenges of visual literacy in our learning environments. Callow presents an interesting and useful overview of the theoretical frameworks which underpin our understandings of visual literacy. He places the latter within the wider context of new literacies and multi-literacies and highlights the key role that visual literacy plays in these developments in our technologies and communications (Callow, 2003).

There is a danger, when discussing the challenges of visual literacy in contemporary society, in regarding the ubiquity of visual images as a threat against which children and young people need to be 'inoculated' to withstand manipulation by those who present their messages, from advertisers to newspaper photo-editors. Although this view can be detected in some approaches to media studies, it is somewhat passive, and does not acknowledge the potential for children to have a more active engagement in both reading and creating their own visual images in a variety of media.

A quick, but somewhat glib, way to define 'visual literacy' would be to describe it as the capability of decoding and encoding meaning in visual forms. This implies processes of receiving or 'reading' visual images and representations, and then making or 'writing' visual images and representations to communicate meaning. Such a concise definition does not, however, convey the complexities of these processes. We don't 'just look' at images, such as paintings, posters, photographs, computer screens or films. We also bring our previous experiences, understandings, culture and sense of identity to that act of looking or gazing. Neither do we 'just make' images and visual representations, but draw upon our understandings of how pictures, diagrams, symbols, photographs and films work and communicate in our culture. In addressing these issues, some teachers approach the personal and political nature of visual literacy in the context of a struggle for social justice and democratic practices. Children can be actively empowered to express their own voices and perceptions, and ask questions about who constructs visual messages, and for what reason and with what benefit. They can become aware of their self, and how they and others are represented, situated within a social, cultural, historical and political framework (Muffoletto, 2001).

It should be no surprise that there is a degree of discussion, disagreement and dealing with a range of ideas as we consider our approaches to visual literacy. Rather, we should see these as healthy signs of critical thinking about the issues, and consider the implications they might have for teachers as they prepare their practice and design learning environments for their children.

Visual literacy and ICT

Why are these issues of particular importance in a book about the future of ICT in primary education? What role does ICT play in our discussions and development of visual literacy for young children? It can be argued that we, in the Western developed world, live in a society in which technology mediates and produces visual imagery to a far greater extent than that experienced by our grandparents and great-grandparents in the early twentieth century. We engage with visual representation and reproductions in photographs, TV, film, animation and computer graphics, as well as the use of icons in ICT, from simple drawing packages to the world wide web. Teachers in the early twenty-first century are therefore challenged to address questions about the similarities and differences in print-based literacies and more visual, screen-based literacies. What are the similarities between reading print and reading screens? What are the differences between writing stories and creating films and multimedia pieces? What experiences of visual forms in TV, games and hypertext do young children bring to the three Rs in their school lives?

Some years ago, the children in Glebe School participated in a project to investigate how they demonstrated visual literacy in using ICT to manipulate images to communicate meaning. The project was called '*The Big Breakfast*' and focused on the children's study of nutrition and the promotion of healthy eating. The children and teachers in this school had already had experience of working with photography, and had addressed many of the issues of developing visual literacy to interpret, conceptualise and communicate ideas. In using ICT to organise, manipulate and present their images, the children's work demonstrated nine interacting elements: narrative structure, content information, sense of audience, associations of colour, role of text, design format, the contribution of the technologies, the influence of affect and emotional engagement, and the interpersonal ways of working with each other. It was clear that the children were bringing their previous visual experiences and competences to the work in the project, yet the ICT resources – image manipulation software which enabled the children to select, move, scale, rotate, size and colour digital images captured with a scanner – allowed them to undertake activities and try out possibilities for visual representations that hadn't been as accessible to them previously (Loveless, 1997).

What were the ICT resources bringing to the project that offered new or distinctive contribution to the activities, processes and outcomes? I have discussed elsewhere the ways in which the interaction between the features of ICT and ICT capability can support learning and teaching. The distinctive features of interactivity, provisionality, capacity, range, speed and automatic functions afford opportunities for teachers to use digital technologies to make their work more efficient, or enhance their work in some way, or even to change the way in which they act and identify their role as teachers. When exploiting these qualities of ICT to enable pupils to find things out, develop ideas and make things happen, exchange and share information, and review, modify and evaluate their work, then ICT capability is being developed (DfEE, 1999b). This is expressed, not as competence in a set of ICT skills or techniques with particular hardware or software, but as higher order thinking within authentic and purposeful contexts (Loveless, 2003).

I would argue, therefore, that ICT plays a very important role in the development of visual literacy in contemporary society. It not only produces many of the images that surround us, from web page to film screen, but also enables us to capture, manipulate, create and share visual images in our own expression and communication of ideas. The use of ICT to access and create visual images also provokes us to reconsider our understanding of other curriculum areas: what role might visual literacy play in art, geography, science, mathematics, media studies, English? What contributions does the use of ICT in these curriculum areas make to our understandings of visual literacy? Long argues that art education needs to inform our use of digital technologies which afford us opportunities to move beyond digital scribbles and doodles to illustrate and express our ideas. He claims:

> the stimulus for making art has always been, and remains, the need to respond to the world around us and to communicate those responses both to ourselves and to others. Digital technologies can play a double role in this relationship, being both an increasingly important part of the visual world itself and possibly an increasingly important element in our visual responses to it. (Long, 2001, p. 214)

The challenge for trainees and practising teachers is to engage in approaches to visual literacy which enable children to look at, ask questions about and make connections between visual images. They must also be able to develop techniques and processes to capture, change, control and communicate visual images which express meanings and ideas. ICT can contribute to these experiences by making some of the activities more accessible and manageable, as well as affording opportunities to be involved in processes and concepts which are new and pushing at the boundaries of our under-standings of visual literacy in contemporary society.

Time to reflect

- *How do you think that ICT makes a contribution to visual literacy?*
- *How does ICT help us to interpret and create visual images in ways which are similar to other more traditional methods?*
- *How does ICT help us to interpret and create visual images in ways which are different and new?*

Looking, creating and thinking with images and ICT

This section will outline some of the ways in which ICT can be used to develop children's visual literacy through looking at images produced by others, and through capturing and creating their own visual images. It will also discuss some of the ways in which ICT can play a part in representing concepts and connections between ideas in visual forms. The range of technologies available in schools and in the children's lives beyond school changes quickly, and so this discussion will focus on types of technology, hardware and software rather than specific applications or products. A student teacher once commented to me that 'it's not learning how to operate the software that's difficult – we can go away and do that for ourselves; it's the ideas behind using it that are more difficult and that's what we need to get to grips with.'

Looking with ICT

In the late 1970s I laughed at my friend describing his work with a new prototype of computer called 'Lisa'. This machine used graphics to display a metaphor of a 'desktop' on which you could lay out your 'documents', organise them into folders or even throw them into the 'trash can' by using a pointer to click and drag on the area you wanted. I thought that it would never catch on. I could not have been more mistaken – it was the precursor of the Apple Mac. One of the first and most immediate visual encounters with ICT is the computer screen and the graphical user interface where windows, icons, mice and menus enable us to organise and navigate through files, applications and communications. The use of such an interface is not inherently 'intuitive', but because the icons often have a strong perceptual relationship with the applications or actions they represent, we quite quickly develop a shared understanding of what might happen if we click on particular icons. It is interesting to use an interactive whiteboard or large projected image to discuss with young children the icons that appear on their computer screens, what they think they represent, why they might have been chosen and how they as users go about finding out what the different icons mean and do.

The use of icons to represent items, actions and emotions has been developed much further in the special educational needs community. Visual symbols can represent complex concepts and symbol users have recognised the potential of ICT to display and manipulate graphical symbols in order to develop literacy activities and communications for individuals working independently and for groups working collaboratively. There are many different forms of symbols, but common sets are Rebus, Makaton and Bliss. Abbott (2000) describes a number of case studies in which symbol users are able to use software which enables them to identify, choose and sequence symbols not only to communicate basic wants, such as 'I'd like water', or 'I'm cold', but also to express more sophisticated and complex ideas, from instructions for a recipe to describing opinions and making choices. Indeed, as Abbott explains, *Symbols can also give a voice to those who may not otherwise be heard* (Abbott, 2002, p. 38).

Time to reflect

- *The use of symbols and icons has had a dramatic impact on literacy practices for symbol users. The wider community of ICT users has also witnessed a shift to visual representation in web pages, games, simulations and mobile technologies.*
- *Think about all the ways in which you encounter visual imagery in your work with ICT. What did you need to know and do to become familiar with using these icons and symbols?*
- *Ask the children in your class to identify the icons they use with ICT. How might they make a display to explain these familiar icons to a visitor from another planet who might not understand them?*

The access to visual images that the WWW affords is unprecedented. We can search and retrieve information from the web using icons for navigation and organisation, but when we download and look at many web pages, they contain visual images and icons themselves to illustrate and help us engage with their meaning and structure. We can consider three ways in which we can use the WWW to look at images: by providing access to collections of images; by using materials prepared for teachers' use; and by projecting images for performance and interactive group questions and discussion.

Many museums, galleries and archives make their images available through the WWW and open up the doors of the classroom to incorporate their collections. The Virtual Library Museums page (**http://vlmp.museophile.com/**) is a useful starting point for browsing through the hundreds of thousands of web pages of museums around the world. Children can visit the Tate Modern in London, the Musée D'Orsay in Paris and the National Museum in Tokyo in one morning (if that would be a useful thing to do!). The 24 Hour Museum (**www.24hourmuseum.org.uk/**) is a gateway to over 3,000 museums, galleries and heritage attractions in the UK, and the associated interactive Kids' Site, 'Show me' (**www.show.me.uk**) was nominated for the British Academy of Film and Television Awards (BAFTA). Similarly, the DARE site (Digital Arts Resource for Education – **www.dareonline.org**) provides access to a wide variety of work by contemporary artists.

It is not enough, however, for children to be given access to images. This would be similar to taking them to the door of the National Gallery, agreeing to pick them up in an hour and letting them wander around. They may well find and engage with a series of images during that time, but some may set off straight for the café and shop without benefiting from leading questions and guiding suggestions from their teacher. As teachers, we need to develop strategies to deepen our own knowledge and practise our skill in asking powerful questions. Pickford offers a useful site for trainees and teachers which presents exercises and images to help them in developing a repertoire of experiences and questions to support children's visual literacy. These range from listening to children's responses to pictures, to considering how we might challenge stereotypes through images and materials to guide teachers' questioning strategies. (**www.pickford.abelgratis.co.uk/vislit/**).

Some organisations have developed web-based resources to provide images, materials and suggestions for lesson activities for teachers to develop children's critical visual literacy. The Eye to Eye project, for example, is supported by the Save the Children Fund and offers a database of a library of photographs taken by young Palestinians recording their daily lives in refugee camps in Lebanon and the Occupied Palestinian Territories. These images can be searched, using keywords or themes, and different topics explored. The site uses photographs, short movie clips, sound, text and icons for navigation and provides different sections for pupils and teachers in primary and secondary schools. (**www.savethechildren.org.uk/eyetoeye**).

Learning to look with an informed, questioning and critical eye is not restricted to photographic images. The British Film Institute (BFI) also provides materials for teachers who wish to use film in their work, either to support other curriculum resources, or to develop children's visual literacy in the moving image (**www.bfi. org.uk/education**). The BECTa Digital Video (DV) Pilot Project gathered evidence of pupils' behaviours and engagements with digital video technology in 50 schools. The findings indicated that the highest quality work showed attention to the uniqueness of the 'language' of moving image and that understanding and control of this language, rather than simply of the technology, gives pupils access to expression through DV. Among other recommendations of the report, it was noted that teachers and pupils need to recognise the distinctiveness of the moving image as a unique mode of expression and communication (Reid, Burn and Parker, 2002).

Sharing and discussing images to be looked at can be brought alive by using projection onto screens, interactive whiteboards and even entire walls. An interesting development in such projection is the use of virtual reality (VR) resources which enable teachers and children to enter virtual spaces and 'look around'. There is a wide variety of such sites, from archaeological digs to a virtual tour of the Eden Project. Pickford's site, mentioned earlier, also includes a link to a QuickTime VR panoramic view of a Victorian classroom, which can be can be viewed dynamically through 360 degrees, and used as a very engaging starting point to ask children what they can see that is similar and different from their own classroom (see **www.pickford.abelgratis.- co.uk/vislit/images/Victorian.mov**).

Time to reflect

- *Which of these examples of ICT enable us to do things that we could do with other media and materials, but not as easily, quickly or efficiently?*
- *Which of these examples of ICT enable us to do things that we could not do without these technologies?*
- *Which aspects of visual literacy would you consider to be 'new' when we use ICT to look at images?*

Creating with ICT

Although the use of ICT certainly opens up interesting possibilities in learning to look at images, it is in the creation of visual images to communicate and express ideas that these technologies make a significant contribution to developing children's visual literacy. From making marks with simple painting packages to creating sophisticated multimedia pieces or editing digital video, children can engage in activities which are expressive, challenging and authentic, and which extend the boundaries of our understanding of visual literacy with digital technologies.

> *Children need a wealth of experiences in a variety of contexts to be able to draw together these elements of perception, media, knowledge, understanding and creativity. ICT provides a medium which can be compared with other media, such as paint or photography, but it also offers unique features which give opportunities for new techniques and expression.* (Loveless, 2003, p. 70)

Making marks and mimicry

Simple painting software enables children to 'make marks' by using the mouse, touch screen or interactive whiteboard to select icons which represent artists' tools, such as brushes, pens, rollers and buckets. These can be 'dipped' or 'filled' with colour or patterns which leave marks or trails on the 'canvas' as the pointer is dragged across the screen. These tools and techniques mimic the real tools of active painting, though the medium of paint is actually the range of colour values of the pixels on the screen and the tools of brushes and rollers are 'making the marks' with the mathematics of the software which plots the location and movement across the screen. Painting, filling and using selected icons as 'stamps' can be an enjoyable activity on a small computer screen or large IWB, but the direct control of the mouse or pointer pen is crude and does not compare well with the more kinaesthetic experience of working with real paint, brushes, papers, pens, inks and glue. It is important that children have the opportunity to work with a wide range of visual media and tools in order to discuss, compare and contrast their effects, and the techniques that have to be practised and developed in order to gain control in expressing visual ideas.

Martin Torjussen, while studying as a PGCE student at the University of Brighton, demonstrated how he used ICT to support the children's introduction to the work of the Spanish artist Joan Miró. After looking at a range of reproductions of Miró's works on postcards, in books and on posters, the children were encouraged to use a range of different paints to make a picture in the style of Miró. Small groups then worked with simple painting software to produce similar pictures. The class displayed all their pictures in the range of media and discussed the advantages and disadvantages of the different media and tools (Torjussen and Coppard, 2002).

These activities are interesting and worthwhile in drawing the children's attention to the possibilities of ICT drawing and painting tools, and how they might discuss the advantages, limitations and contrast with more traditional tools. I would argue, however, that using ICT to mimic other methods, or even copy and reproduce other artists' work, is not fully exploiting the features of ICT that enable us to manipulate, substitute and transform visual images to help us to develop and communicate more sophisticated visual ideas.

From manipulation to making meaning

If generating images directly onto the screen is clumsy, it is now possible to capture images with digital cameras and scanners and use them as the starting point for developing ideas further. Digital cameras are excellent devices for supporting visual literacy as children are able to view, compose, frame and capture pictures, and then immediately evaluate their results critically to consider whether they have indeed captured their idea, or need to have another go. The mobility and flexibility of digital cameras are well suited to the variety of activities in primary classrooms and the range of locations of resources for ideas! Scanners can also be used to capture images and children have demonstrated imagination and ingenuity in finding ways to arrange objects on a scanner bed — from fragments of pottery to sliced fruit.

Having captured and saved the visual images, the children can use these as starting points. Image manipulation software, from *Dazzle* to *Photoshop* can transform the visual image, altering or abstracting the different elements and the relationship between them. The provisionality of these ICT applications means that the children can be playful and exploratory with a range of effects, saving those that look promising, and discarding those that are not satisfactory. They can experiment with figure and ground, positive and negative, opacity and transparency, colour substitutions, blurring and blending, scaling, rotating, stretching and distorting until they feel that the image expresses their ideas. They might wish to change the emotional atmosphere of a scene, or place themselves into historical costume and location, or juxtapose several images to express a theme.

At the heart of such activities lies the opportunity for children to engage in authentic, expressive activities that echo the processes of contemporary artists who work with digital technologies. They are not constrained by any limitations of observational drawing, for example, in developing their personal themes, but can draw upon a wider range of images as starting points. Our work with artists and practitioners in a number of primary and secondary schools over the years has demonstrated this aspect of the children's experience in many different contexts (Loveless, 1997, 2000; Long, 2001; Creating Spaces, 2003). Long notes how pupils are able to place their own issues, themes and ideas at the centre of the activity, rather than their formal art skills and techniques, and that *students involved had felt that they were operating as artists with something unique and personal to communicate* (Long, 2001, p. 208).

'Fat pictures' – a new form of visual literacy?

It is in the making of multimedia that we encounter a new visual literacy concept which is uniquely demonstrated by digital technologies – 'fat pictures'. Multimedia challenges us to think about our understandings of literacies with screen-based technologies. Snyder argues that electronically mediated texts draw upon *multimodality*, that is modes including text, visual image, moving image, sound and hypertext. Multimodal texts require skills and conventions for meaning that are different from traditional print and paper, and preparing children and young people to be literate will not be easy when many of their teachers are not themselves confident in their own literacies with digital technologies (Snyder, 2002).

The creation of multimedia screens and web pages calls for elements of visual literacy in the design of screen layouts that clearly communicate information with text, images and sound. It is the use of *hypertext* that introduces the new challenge. The non-linear nature of the links between words, sentences and phrases within a written text raises interesting issues for both the designers and the readers of hypertextual, interactive work. (See, for example, two excellent accounts of developing multimedia in schools by Lachs (2000) and Atherton (2002)). When hyperlinks are associated with visual images, or parts of images, they are viewed and interpreted differently, as clicking on or rolling over these images can initiate actions – from pop-up boxes with additional information in other modes to navigation to new screens within the work or external sites on the WWW.

Vivi Lachs describes how children in a Year 5 class (9-10 years old) were drawing penguins to be used in a multimedia presentation about animals in their environment. They wanted the viewer to click onto different parts of the penguin to bring up text boxes with particular explanations of how the beak, flippers and webbed feet were adapted to the penguin's habitat. The children recognised the difference between a 'flat' picture of a penguin, and 'fat' picture of a penguin which was stuffed full of *knowledge waiting to be accessed giving it depth and meaning*. (Lachs, 2000, p. 63). She develops this description by explaining,

> In a 'fat' picture the image has become integrated with the text, making a word-enhanced-picture, or an information-image. The penguin in this particular case only links to pop-up text boxes of explanation, but it could also link to websites on penguins making the image a gateway to the outside world. (Lachs, 2000, p. 63)

In her work at Highwire, the Hackney City Learning Centre in London, Vivi Lachs challenges pupils to draw upon and develop their visual literacy to use ICT to help them grapple with, understand and express difficult ideas. The difficult ideas that they encounter in the curriculum might arise in science (Ethics and genetics), history (Points of view in the Cuban Missile Crisis), English (interpretations of *Twelfth Night*) or citizenship (Impacts of colonialism). Pupils address these areas by using a range of resources – from drama to digital technologies – to research, interrogate, evaluate, synthesise, analyse, critique and communicate their understanding. The final outcomes take the form of multimedia presentations, digital video and web pages in which the pupils give thought to the most appropriate medium for a particular message – text, image, video or sound – and how each relate to the others. The pupils are able to use their knowledge of visual literacy in their wider experience to make decisions about the presentation of their ideas, and they are able to develop this understanding by engaging with a wide range of digital technologies and making choices about media to communicate the complexities of their information.

Time to reflect

Look at the selected examples of websites below which celebrate children's visual multimedia work and think about the following questions:

- *How did you draw upon your own visual literacy to access and navigate through these sites?*
- *How is the children's visual literacy expressed in these works?*
- *How have the children's collaborations with teachers, artists, designers and external agencies supported their work?*

1. *The Chrisi Bailey Award – The National Award for Media Arts by under-10s – promotes media arts projects by children which explore photography, digital art, animation and video as creative visual media:* **www.thechrisibaileyaward. org.uk/**

2. *Highwire – Hackney City Learning Centre in North London:* **www.highwire.org.uk**

3. *Electric December – a project coordinated by Watershed, an Arts organisation in Bristol, in collaboration with Creative Partnerships and local arts, skills and news organisations:* **http://electricdecember.org/**

Thinking with ICT

The development of software applications for concept mapping and mind mapping has interesting implications for teachers promoting visual literacy in their practice. Concept maps, as described by Novak and Gowin (1984), are diagrammatic representations of internal processes in which concepts, or nodes, are linked by words and phrases – semantic units – that make propositions about the links between the nodes. Concept maps can therefore assist learners and teachers in externalising and expressing understanding or misconceptions in a topic. Mind maps, developed by Buzan (1993), are more focused on one idea or concept and represent the different connections and 'branches' in words, reflecting personal mental processes.

In the world of ICT in education, the Impact2 evaluation of the impact of ICT on school attainment in the UK used concept mapping techniques to explore children's self-reported experience of the use of ICT in their understanding of the complex nature of ICT (Somekh et al., 2002). This research activity was carried out using paper and pens, but established a useful approach to analysing concept maps and visual representations of understanding (Mavers, Somekh and Restorick, 2002). The approach was developed initially to inform the design of software to represent ideas in visual forms

(Pearson and Somekh, 2000) as the affordances of ICT seem suited to developing tools for visual, dynamic representation.

There are many commercial software tools designed to be 'graphic organisers' which are used in business contexts for 'brainstorming', planning and presentations. They allow the user to identify key concepts or themes as 'nodes', and then place links between them, indicating the nature or direction of the relationships. Some offer the facility to insert hyperlinks which make connections with other files, documents or web pages, setting up a series of 'threads' to organise material relating to the ideas being expressed. Such organisers offer users – both writers and readers – the opportunity to present ideas in a non-linear, web-related format that is immediate and visual, being more like a poster than a linear presentation.

One such application, developed in the USA, has been designed specifically for children and young people (see **www.inspiration.com**). Inspiration and Kidspiration offer the facilities of a graphic organiser, with a visual interface which is more appealing and appropriate for children. They can set up visual representations of ideas on the screen or handheld device by using symbols, connecting lines, integrated notes and links to text and audio files and live hyperlinks to the internet. Instructions and actions are controlled by icons and menus, and children can also design their own symbols to represent their key ideas. The commercial developers commissioned a research review of graphic organisers and claimed to demonstrate improvements in student learning and performance in comprehension, thinking and learning skills and retention of information (IARE, 2003). The studies reviewed focused on achievements in traditional curriculum areas, such as reading, writing and mathematics, rather than addressing issues of visual literacy with the digital concept mapping tool. It will be interesting to see how the use of such tools with technologies such as IWBs might have an impact on teaching strategies and approaches to visual literacy in classroom practices in the near future.

Visual literacy and ICT in the classroom – a case study

Jess Thacker was a PGCE student at the University of Brighton. She integrated the use of ICT in her classroom practice and drew upon her personal engagement with visual literacy to support her teaching in the literacy hour. The following case study is her account of her experience and reflections. Think about the following questions as you are reading about her work:

- **How did Jess draw upon her own interests and experiences in planning for her teaching?**
- **What connections did she make between text, image and film, and how did she bring these into the children's experience?**
- **How does Jess's experience in her teaching practice relate to, and draw together the issues raised in this chapter?**
- **What elements of your own experience of teaching literacy might you change, even a little, to incorporate such an approach to visual literacy?**

Using visual literacy to develop children's awareness of 'conventional' literacy

As a film-maker and a primary school teacher, I am interested in exploring how video and photography can be used to enrich the curriculum. I have observed that digital photography is used primarily in schools to produce a record of events. This, I feel, undervalues the potential of this technology. In this case study, I will describe how video and photography were used as learning tools to develop children's understanding of literacy. I also want to demonstrate that it is possible for all teachers to use these techniques. It is not just limited to those who have some specialism in using the technology.

Working with a high-attaining set of Year 6 children during literacy, I noticed that they tended to respond very well to visual explanations of grammatical ideas. For instance, when explaining passive and active sentence constructions, I found that the best way to communicate the difference in meaning was to show the children two different photos. To illustrate this, Figure 7.1 shows the active construction, 'The girl stroked the cat.' The focus of the shot is on the girl, and her feelings about the cat.

Figure 7.1: 'The girl stroked the cat'

In Figure 7.2, the focus is on the cat, and his view of being stroked. This shows the passive construction, 'The cat was stroked by the girl.' The photos show that each sentence construction implies a different point of view, which can be used to influence the reader's response to the characters.

Figure 7.2: 'The cat was stroked by the girl'

My experience in using visual images in this way showed me something very interesting: the children were often much more comfortable with 'reading' and understanding visual images than they were with 'reading' written text. It seemed to me that it was possible that children's exposure to TV, film and computer games meant that they had at least an equal amount of practice (and interest) in developing their 'visual literacy' skills as in their conventional reading skills.

I decided to capitalise on this interest. I had noticed that the children found it hard to identify the writing techniques that authors use. This was having an effect on the children's own writing, as it limited the mental model of writing they had to work from. Realising that there are similarities between the 'language' of books and the 'language' of films, I decided to engage the children on a project that linked the two. I asked the children to adapt an extract of text into a storyboard for a film. In doing this, the children had to identify their responses to the written text and then draw on their existing knowledge of film to find ways of communicating their responses to their audience. Through this process, the children moved from being readers of the text to being writers of the film.

To initially focus the children on the author's techniques, I began by asking the children to identify the characters, narrator, and relationships between them. I asked them to try to justify their ideas using the text. We considered the use of dialogue, slang, body language and the narrator's 'voice-over'.

We then moved on to creating the storyboard. A storyboard is a means of planning the shots used in a film without having to actually film it (Figure 7.3). By thinking about the relationship and positioning of the characters in each shot, the children had to explore ways of communicating their feelings about the characters from the original written text.

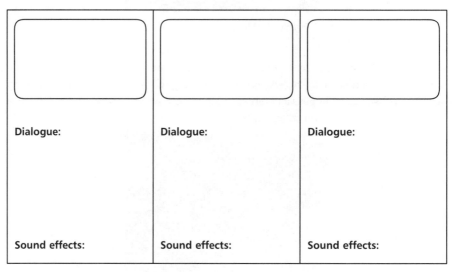

Figure 7.3: Example of a blank storyboard
A storyboard contains a series of images, which show the position of the camera
in relation to the actors. Underneath each image can be listed the dialogue and any
actions, as well as details of any extra sound effects, voice-overs and camera movements.

In order to aid this process, I asked some children to take digital photos of each shot. This enabled the children to try out different ideas, and reflect back on whether they were working. Unlike cameras that use chemical films, digital cameras allow the photographer to view the photo they have taken immediately. This has two key benefits. Firstly, the photographer is able to take more shots, and compare them in quick succession. The photographer becomes in effect his or her own audience, and can experience which techniques have most impact on him or her. Secondly, the immediacy of the technology means that the actors are able to get round behind the camera and become directors themselves.

I found that the children's use of the digital camera was very impressive. I had demonstrated to the children how placing the camera below the eye line of a character makes him or her look imposing, while putting it above the eye line makes him or her look diminutive (Figure 7.4).

Figure 7.4: The children have used low camera angle
to make 'Nana Flowers' look imposing

The children quickly took on board these ideas, and used them to convey their ideas about the relationships between the characters. They also used their ideas about narrative techniques from the original text and included the narrator as a character, using his responses to 'Nana Flowers' to emphasise her scariness to their audience (Figure 7.5).

Figure 7.5: This response shot emphasises the scariness of 'Nana Flowers'
by showing how the narrator reacts to her

Finally, they experimented with using close ups to emphasise the tension of the argument (Figure 7.6).

Figure 7.6: The tension of the scene is communicated
through the use of a close-up

The children's understanding of the techniques used by the author (and themselves as directors/authors) was shown when they went to see Niki Caro's adaptation of *The Whale Rider* at the cinema. Her version was very different to the children's, and they were outraged! I was very pleased to see their engagement. They were able to identify which techniques the director had used, and how they had a different impact on the audience.

After this experience, I decided that I wanted to use Visual Literacy to develop the children's written work directly. I therefore taught a series of lessons in which I asked the children to adapt a scene from a novel into a playscript. We began in a similar way, identifying the characters and relationships between them. This time I asked the children to video their performances of different drafts of their scripts. We kept the technical skills needed to a minimum, using a single take on a static camera. The children had to plan to make the most of this camera, and made decisions about putting the most important character nearest the lens, while using body language, movement and expression to communicate effectively. Through this activity, the children used the immediate feedback from the technology. Again, the children were able to become their own audiences. This enabled the children to identify what needed changing in their scripts; self-assessing their work according to their wide-ranging experiences as TV and film viewers. The fact that the performances recorded themselves at different stages of the drafting process meant that the children were able to see their progress, which acted as a source of motivation.

In these experiments, the children used their existing knowledge of 'reading' and 'writing' photos and video to explore the relationship between the author and the audience, and were able to relate this understanding to their writing. Visual Literacy can therefore supply a 'way in' to comprehending more conventional forms of literacy. Digital photography and video are useful tools in that they allow children the freedom to experiment until they find something that looks and 'feels' right; from this they can work backwards to explore why it works, and what they are trying to say.

Credits

With thanks to the children of 6JS at Buckingham Middle School, Shoreham, in particular Nicola Ramshaw, Tom Bell, Sophie Winder and James Ashley, whose digital photos have been used in this chapter.

Texts and films used in the projects

Ihimaero, W. (2003) *The Whale Rider* (novel) London: Robson Books.

Caro, N. (2002) *Whale Rider* (film).

Morpurgo, M. (1995) *The Wreck of the Zanzibar* (novel). London: Heinemann Young/Mammoth.

8 ICT AND CREATIVITY
STEVE WHEELER

There are no problems – only opportunities to be creative.
Dorye Roettger

There are two ways of being creative. One can sing and dance.
Or one can create an environment in which singers and dancers
flourish.
Warren G. Bennis

This chapter will enable you to:

- **explore notions of creativity;**
- **link creative thinking and action to the use of ICT;**
- **consider ways of using ICT to stimulate creativity in the classroom.**

What is creativity?

How can we begin to define creativity? This is an almost impossible question to answer, and a subject that has occupied the minds of philosophers, scientists and artists for centuries. Let's try: creativity might be defined as that 'spark of something' that, given the right circumstances, compels us to produce something that is surprising, new, or useful. This is a definition originally offered by psychologist Margaret Boden, who argued that creativity is *the ability to come up with new ideas that are surprising yet intelligible, and also valuable in some way* (Boden, 2001). It is no doubt this same creativity that caused Archimedes to shout 'Eureka!' while sitting in his bath. It is the same spark of originality that caused the artists Van Gogh and Picasso to challenge contemporary art paradigms. It is the same rush of inspiration that compelled the Beatles to write such memorable and enduring tunes. Whether it is scientific thought, artistic expression, musical virtuosity or something else entirely different, there is an essence of creativity residing in each of us. The American psychologist Howard Gardner (1993) has made a strong case for at least eight different types of creative intelligence, including interpersonal intelligence (our ability to communicate with each other), kinaesthetic intelligence (the kind of movement and balance used by gymnasts and dancers) and visual-spatial intelligence (sculptors and fashion designers make use of this). Gardner claims that the capabilities of each intelligence reside in each of us – we simply don't make use of them all, and specialise in one or two. If Gardner is correct, then it appears we are not limited to one kind of expression of our imagination, but have the potential to be creative in many ways. One of the most important roles a teacher can play in the life of children may be to devise environments and circumstances in which this potential for such creativity can be drawn out and unleashed to enable them to express themselves fully.

Imagine this ...

Children are naturally imaginative in their play. You simply have to stand and observe them during their break time to know the truth of this. Games of make-believe and role-playing are normal activities for younger children, and any item can be (and usually is) turned into a fantastic play thing. A cardboard box can become a beautiful palace or a pirate ship, and an old stick can become a silver sword or a wizard's magic wand.

Teachers don't normally need to work too hard to encourage young children to let their imagination run riot. There are some children however, who express their creativity better when encouraged and supported, while others may be at their most creative when they are under pressure or have a difficult problem to solve. Part of the art of good teaching is to know under which conditions children can best use their imagination and how to turn these ideas into creative action for learning. What I am trying to suggest here is that while imagination is usually spontaneous, the art of creative thinking may at times need a little professional nurturing.

Children are also naturally curious. They ask questions all the time, and they don't stop at the 'why?' questions. They also ask the 'what if?' questions – a sure sign of an inventive mind. Digital video for example, is an ideal medium to test 'what if' questions. Film-makers claim that they learn more about a subject by making a film of it. It is the process of researching, planning and editing that draws out the creativity within the film-maker's art and enhances knowledge about the topic (TES, 14 May, 2004a). A group of children using a digital video camera to make a film will learn several important transferable skills during the process, including negotiation skills, decision-making, working in a team, problem-solving, leadership and visualisation.

The computer is another ideal medium for creativity. On a computer screen, nothing is permanent unless you wish it to be, and things can be changed as many times as children have new ideas. Think of the editing potential of a word processor – this chapter was revised and polished many times before we were happy with it. Now it sits on a page in a book in your hands – the most complete version of our thoughts after it has been through a long process of creative revision.

Thinking creatively

Children need to develop creative thinking skills in their early years. Creative thinking can be applied to many learning contexts to enrich and enliven the acquisition of knowledge and skills. Without the ability to think creatively, children would be unimaginative, lacking in the necessary transferable skills to engage in personal and professional life in later years (Wheeler, Waite and Bromfield, 2002). In this chapter I am going to argue that ICT can be used to help children to think and act creatively, by tapping into their natural imagination, and transforming the learning experience. I will present several ideas to help you to think about how you might use ICT to scaffold this process.

The quote by Bennis at the beginning of this chapter is particularly appropriate for this topic – teachers can be creative in their approaches to developing stimulating learning environments, and if used imaginatively, ICT can play a vital role in this process. How do we know when teaching transforms into creative teaching? One possible answer comes courtesy of a school featured in a recent *Times Education Supplement* article. One teacher declared that teaching is shown to promote creativity when *children start going off in directions you would not expect them to go in and start to do things that you have not taught them* (*TES*, September 2004c). ICT is an ideal tool to facilitate the 'going off in new directions' approach to teaching. Pupils can explore for themselves, test out their own ideas and discover new experiences through the use of interactive technologies. The remainder of this chapter focuses on ways in which ICT can be used to unleash the explorer in children and enable them to think in new and creative ways.

ICT as a creative tool

'That's ingenious!' is an expression we use when we see something that is so useful, yet so unusual, that in some way it takes us by surprise. It is often a response seen when teachers use a videoconference link or interactive whiteboard for the first time. The general idea is familiar, but the means through which it is accomplished can appear to be quite magical. *Technology that is sufficiently advanced*, Arthur C. Clarke once declared, *is indistinguishable from magic.* Children can very quickly engage with computers. They have grown up with this technology, and although at first it can appear to be 'magical' to them, they often quickly see past its novelty and begin to use it as a creative tool.

It is often the teacher that acts as the catalyst to this process, however. Teachers need to use ICT creatively to ensure that children have the opportunities to express themselves in a creative manner using the same technology. Lim argues that teachers must move away from being the exclusive source of expertise and authority, towards exploring the opportunities and limitations of ICT, organising activities to take up its opportunities and address its limitations, reflecting upon the activities and re-adapting them accordingly (Lim, 2001).

Activity

How do you know when a child is being creative? List some of the important signs of creativity (either thought or action).

Barriers to creativity

Sadly, creative thinking can sometimes be stifled in the classroom. Teachers who always insist on a 'correct answer' can cause children to disengage from lessons. Sometimes there *is* only one correct answer, say in numeracy or science. Yet there can be many ways of arriving at that answer, and teachers can encourage their pupils to think 'around' the question and enable children to come up with some novel approaches to solving the problems presented to them. When I was nine years old I asked my teacher a question in class. She misconstrued my question, told me it was a 'silly question', and the class laughed at me. I don't think I ever asked another question throughout the rest of my time in primary school.

Time to reflect

How can ICT be used to stimulate creativity? Think of a class you currently teach and imagine some new uses of ICT which will tap into the creative potential of your pupils.

The time constraints teachers work against to deliver the National Curriculum may also militate against 'time for play' and exploration that is often needed if children are to foster new ways of doing. Curriculum and assessment, however, can also be used by teachers to their advantage as frameworks in which creativity can be supported and nurtured. It is possible to apply ICT in a way that maximises available time and provides space for children to explore and discover for themselves. If used effectively, ICT can also liberate teachers from many of their mundane tasks and can enhance and transform curriculum delivery. The final section of this chapter deals with this topic in a little more depth.

Considering the above statement, you may wish to test out for yourself where and how you could use aspects of ICT to transform your own teaching practice. Think about the questions in the box below, and then read on, where I provide a few examples of creative approaches to the use of ICT in teaching that I have witnessed in primary classrooms.

Time to reflect

- *What areas of your own teaching practice are difficult to perform with the resources you already have?*
- *Can you think of ways in which your teaching could be transformed or enhanced if an ICT application was applied?*
- *What would be creative about it?*
- *What might be the limitations of using this ICT application?*

Creative use of ICT in numeracy teaching

I recently witnessed a teacher working with children in a numeracy lesson and using an interactive whiteboard very creatively. She was working on number bonds with a group of 32 children in a Year 5 lesson. Such a lesson can be tedious if handled ineffectively, and engaging 32 children for almost an hour can be quite a struggle for some. The teacher I observed went about her task creatively and imaginatively – she showed a series of previously prepared random number pairs on the interactive white board, and then gave the children a series of target numbers to calculate.

The teacher asked them to work initially in small groups to find the number pairs from the whiteboard that made up the target numbers. Each group elected a member who in turn was then asked to approach the whiteboard and to use their fingers to grab and move two numbers together to create the number bond, while explaining their choice. A variation on this theme was to ask each child to draw a red line between their two numbers on the interactive whiteboard or to circle their choices in matching colours. This simple but effective use of the interactive whiteboard was a joy to watch. The children were enthusiastic and engaged throughout the entire lesson, and it was obvious that they were having fun.

The session was successful for other reasons too. The children were involved in collaborative work, using their cognitive skills to reason through the problems, and were required to apply verbal and tactile skills to demonstrate their understanding of the principles underlying the number bonds. This was observed to reinforce the learning. The teacher was creative in her approach to what could have been a dull and tedious lesson, and what we observed was a wonderful example of a creative application of ICT. She was enthusiastic and had also taken time to prepare her lesson and accompanying resources well. The teacher created a stimulating learning environment and encouraged the children to work together, collaborating creatively with each other, using a visually appealing stimulus to enliven a potentially mundane subject.

You don't even have to have ICT to use it to teach creatively. As we have already seen, children can use their imagination very effectively. Ted Wragg relates a story where he used imaginary telephones to teach a reception class some numeracy principles. Each child was assigned a number which was their personal telephone number, and they were encouraged to 'phone each other up' and have conversations, by calling out each other's numbers. Wragg claimed that several important principles were learned during that session, including the use of number combinations, language and junior citizenship – a useful cross-curricular outcome using merely the notion of ICT (Wragg, 2001).

Problem-solving as a creative strategy

The teaching scene above was an example of problem-based learning. The children were given a problem and some tools, and then asked to work through it to arrive at their solutions. There are many ways to use problem based learning in the primary classroom, and many creative learning outcomes can result from these kinds of focused activities. You don't necessarily need ICT to facilitate problem-based learning, but ICT can certainly add a creative dimension.

Each of us faces problems every day. Some are small and take a few seconds to negotiate, while others can be quite daunting, and may take weeks, months or even years to solve. Presenting children with problems to tackle not only engages them deeply within the context of the problem. It also enables them to develop creative skills for tackling similar problems later in their lives. Have a look at the problem below and then have a go at trying to solve it:

Activity

With a pencil, and using only four straight lines, and without the pencil leaving the paper, connect all nine dots together. You are not allowed to go back over lines twice.

The problem can be quite difficult on first examination. There are rules that need to be obeyed. Some people tackle the problem by trying to break (or bend) the rules, using curved lines, or attempting to go back over the lines they have already drawn, trying to create a 'Union Jack' effect. Generally, people experience difficulty because they see a 'box' created by the nine dots, and this constrains them to think 'within the box'. To solve the problem, you need to deviate outside of this imaginary box, at the risk of 'breaking a rule' that isn't actually there. We are fixed in our thinking, and it is this 'fixity' that constrains us from being more creative. Fixity refers to our unconscious unwillingness to go beyond what we perceive are the limits of the problem. The answer to the problem is provided in the box below (start at the top left and go right, then draw diagonally back across, following the arrows).

Solution

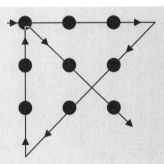

We need to think 'outside of the box' if we are going to find creative solutions to some of the problems we encounter in life. ICT is an ideal medium to encourage children to think around problems and to tap into their imagination reservoirs. Before I describe some of the creative approaches to ICT I have seen, let's examine a useful set of guidelines for using ICT in teaching.

Creative use of ICT in literacy teaching

Allyson Tyldesley, a literacy consultant to Derbyshire Local Education Authority, has offered the following guidelines for those wishing to make effective use of ICT in the literacy hour:

- **ICT should be used as a resource to teach the NLS objectives for literacy, not the objectives for IT capability.**
- **ICT should only be selected as a resource if it is more effective than alternatives.**
- **Planning will need to take into account a broad range of ICT tools including portables, multimedia desktops, simple word processors, programmable toys and spellcheckers.**
- **Activities with ICT need to be based on clear learning objectives from the Framework at word, sentence or text level.**
- **Feedback and assessment should not be left out of the equation.**

Tyldesley's second point is arguably the most important point she makes – teachers should reflect on their use of resources at all times. Which are the most appropriate tools to use? Can a computer be used to greater effect than, say, a textbook? It is here that creative thinking can lead to creative use of a resource and transformation of the learning experience. The important question should be: What attributes of a computer can be used to support pupils' learning that a textbook could not achieve?

These sentiments are echoed by Twining (2001) who argues that where long texts need to be imparted, paper is a better medium than a computer, whereas enabling pupils to experience another culture can better be facilitated using a video (if a visit is out of the question). The task of the teacher is to select media and technologies that are the best for the job.

Time to reflect

Can you think of topics within literacy teaching that would benefit from the following ICTs?

- *internet access;*
- *interactive resources;*
- *multimedia;*
- *sound;*
- *video;*
- *interaction with others through e-mail.*

Are there other resources that could be better used to teach the topics you have in mind?

The above exercise can be used to think about how ICT can be applied creatively to any subject, but for the moment let's concentrate on literacy. A simple feature of a word processor, such as a spellchecker, may stimulate pupils to work harder to improve their spelling. The words they have typed into the word processor will be as permanent as the children want them to be. Spelling errors will often be automatically highlighted by the spellchecker software, and it is a simple task for the pupil to right-click the mouse to adjust text appropriately and quickly. For creative writing, spell-checkers are a boon, as they free up the mind for imaginative expression and children are able to free-flow with their ideas.

The equivalent paper-based resource is a dictionary. The dictionary would be a less immediate resource — the pupil would have to locate a dictionary, search through it, open it to the correct page and then apply the correct spelling to the text — but it might be more accurate than a computer spellchecker in certain instances. Most spell-checkers still tend to ignore words if they are spelled correctly but in the wrong context. Read through the humorous poem entitled *Candidate for a Pullet Surprise* below and you will see some of the dangers in relying too much on the spellchecker in your computer!

Candidate for a Pullet Surprise

I have a spelling checker,
It came with my pea sea.
It plane lee marks four my revue
Miss steaks aye can knot sea.
Eye ran this poem threw it,
Your sure reel glad two no,
Its vary polished in its weigh
My checker tolled me sew.
A checker is a bless sing,
It freeze yew lodes of thyme.
It helps me right awl stiles two reed,
And aides me when I rime.

Each frays come posed up on my screen
eye trussed too bee a joule.
The checker pours o'er every word
To cheque sum spelling rule.
Bee fore a veiling checker's
Hour spelling mite decline,
And if we're lacks oar have a laps,
We wood bee maid too wine.
Butt now bee cause my spelling
Is checked with such grate flair,
Their are no fault's with in my cite,
Of nun eye am a ware.

Now spelling does knot phase me,
It does knot bring a tier.
My pay purrs awl due glad den

With wrapped word's fare as hear.
To rite with care is quite a feet
Of witch won should bee proud,
And wee mussed dew the best wee can,
Sew floors are knot aloud.
Sow ewe can sea why aye dew prays,
Such soft wear four pea seas,
And why eye brake in two averse
Buy righting wont too pleas.

(Sauce Unknown)

Once you have deciphered it, I am sure you appreciated that this is a very creative poem, with an amusing yet clear message for all PC users. It should be evident that all learning resources, including ICT-based teaching aids, should be evaluated for their usefulness, taking benefits and limitations into consideration, and that the best option should be chosen to optimise children's learning. Teachers simply need to be more imaginative in the manner in which the chosen resource or most available ICT is used, so that children can be motivated and encouraged to think creatively for themselves.

Musical expression through ICT

One of the best ways children can express themselves is through music. It is an internationally understood language, and all children sing to themselves and their friends. Learning a musical instrument is the next logical step for many, and in primary education music has always been a key creative outlet for children. Chapter 4 provides clearer clues about how ICT can be used to transform music education, but for the present purpose here is a useful, extra-curricular example of how children in one small primary school were seen to tap into the huge power and potential of ICT as a means of creative musical expression.

In one corner of the small classroom a number of items of ICT-based equipment were located. Taking centre stage was a polyphonic Musical Instrument Digital Interface (MIDI) keyboard, attached to a personal computer. Also attached to the PC were other items such as a CD burner, microphone, small mixing desk and a set of headphones. During the lunch-time breaks, children would come into the room and compose, record and mix their own pop songs. Lyric writing was considered important, as was the tempo and 'beat' or rhythm of the songs they created. They took great care to mix sounds and words that would optimise their messages, while at the same time creating pleasurable audio effects and rhythms. The children were very proud of their finished products and when we listened to the CDs, we found them very impressive. It was difficult in some instances for us to discern the qualitative differences between the compositions these children had created and some of the tracks we heard on Radio One. Can ICTs be used as a truly creative mode of expression? This is certainly clear evidence that they can.

The science of ICT

In the teaching of primary science, ICT can be used very effectively to encourage creative thinking. In geography, for example, pupils can explore local, national and international issues through the exploration of sites on the internet. Children can work with 'live' maps on interactive whiteboards, or navigate their way across a cityscape using interactive media. Active engagement of this kind enables children to apply knowledge as action, developing for themselves a sense of 'praxis', thereby bridging the gap between what they *know* and what they can *do*. This is often difficult to achieve with paper-based resources alone.

BECTa has entire pages of resources related to the use of ICT to supplement the teaching of the QCA's primary science and ICT schemes of work. Many offer a combined approach, utilising computers and peripheral devices to enhance the delivery of the science lessons. These resources can be found online at: **http:// curriculum.becta.org.uk**. Collecting data, referred to as 'datalogging', is one area in which ICT can become an extremely useful and transformative science teaching resource. Children love to experiment, so teachers can tap into their natural curiosity by involving them, asking them to measure temperatures, light or sound levels, the pulse rate in the human body, or humidity in the atmosphere. By directly engaging with the measurement of such data using logging devices connected to a personal computer, the children can see graphs or charts created in real time, and can see the changes that occur when they act directly upon the environment. The teacher's task then should be to decide how to use such sensing and logging devices in a creative and imaginative way to enhance and transform the learning experience for the children.

Activity

Can you think of creative ways in which the following data logging devices might be used in science teaching?

- *light sensor*
- *thermometer*
- *pH meter.*

Here are a few of my own ideas. The first device – the light sensor – was used by teachers to show pupils that different coloured gels would let in different levels of natural light. Pupils were given several pairs of large, Elton John style sunglasses which had a variety of coloured gels inserted into them. In small groups, the children were asked to measure the light levels coming through each lens, using sensors attached to their personal computer. They were then required to create a bar chart in *Excel* which represented the coloured gels and their respective light filtering values. Some children created bar charts with colours corresponding to the coloured gels to illustrate the results of their research.

Thermometers measure temperature and so can be useful in teaching human biology, while pH meters measure acidity and may be useful in the teaching of plant biology.

How could these be employed creatively, to catch the children's imagination? Use your own imagination!

In this chapter I have tried to offer a flavour of some of the innovative approaches I have witnessed in primary teaching, but of course space is limited and these are merely a taste of what can be achieved if ICT is used imaginatively and without boundaries.

Creative engineering of teacher roles

Finally, we turn our attention to the creative use of ICT by teachers to support their own teaching roles. Wheeler (2001) argued that many of the traditional roles of teachers were likely to change as a result of the introduction of ICT in schools, so creativity is likely to emerge naturally. He suggested that traditional tasks such as record-keeping and assessment were likely to be transformed because ICT could liberate teachers from time-consuming and mundane tasks because computers and specialised software would perform much of the 'donkey work'. Four years on, many schools now attest to this kind of re-engineering, with many teacher roles increasingly transformed as ICTs become more accessible, usable and integrative.

For example, the ways teachers communicate with each other, parents and local education authorities (LEAs) are starting to change through the utility of e-mail. Electronic record-keeping is fast replacing paper-based records, and the use of spreadsheets and databases can provide rapid access to pupil records and efficient reporting of assessment scores. Presentational tools are becoming more effective. Teachers are discovering that interactive whiteboards working in combination with *PowerPoint* slides provide a visually appealing, interactive and easy to update set of resources. The list is endless, and space prohibits other examples. ICT is transforming primary teaching and learning, and it is doing so in new ways, and through creative methods. The trend is set to increase, and the only barrier to a creative transformation of education through the use of ICT will be … our imaginations.

Conclusion

In this chapter we have examined the notion of creativity and explored a variety of ways in which information and communication technologies can be used to support creative teaching and encourage children to think creatively. Problem-solving was proposed as a useful means to unleash creativity and several scenarios were described where ICTs were a central component of the process. Several examples of creative uses of ICT were offered, and we counsel that ICTs should be evaluated prior to their use to gauge their appropriateness, and the benefits and limitations they bring to the child's learning experience. Teachers can use ICT in imaginative ways to create stimulating learning environments. Children can use ICT in creative ways if they are set loose to explore and devise their own ways of thinking and doing.

From each according to his abilities, to each according to his needs.
Karl Marx (1818–1883)

This chapter will enable you to:

- **consider possible sources of individual differences in children's use of ICT;**
- **plan for ways to address these differences;**
- **develop strategies for maximising the potential for each child's use of ICT.**

Introduction

The tremendous potential of ICT to motivate and support children's learning has been discussed elsewhere in this book. This chapter draws upon longitudinal research conducted in a school in which every child had a PC on their desk all day and every day and considers the differences observed in their use of ICT. In your own classroom you may have noticed different levels of engagement when using ICT – this chapter aims to help teachers develop a language for talking about these differences and how pedagogy might influence them.

ICT and individual differences

Much of the research which has been discussed elsewhere in the book does not comment on the *differential* use of ICT by individual students, except in terms of their experience through home computer ownership (e.g. Hayward *et al.*, 2003) or their gender (e.g. Joiner *et al.*, 1996).

The relationship between ICT and attainment is focused principally on the effect of ICT on attainment (Cox *et al.*, 2003), where ICT is seen to support learning. The converse has rarely been examined: how higher attainment or ability levels may affect students' use of ICT. Harrison *et al.* (2002), for example, found no evidence that pupils at any one ability level were advantaged or disadvantaged by high use of ICT. This would seem to suggest that ICT might offer a level playing field for all pupils. If ICT is increasingly seen as becoming a mediator of learning, it may be that ICT proficiency may impede development of other learning in a similar way to how a lack of literacy skills can hinder access to other areas of the curriculum. ICT acts as a conduit for learning and might therefore be expected to have moderating effects on attainment. The expectation of greater personalisation of learning (DfES, 2004d) makes it especially important to begin to unpack some of the factors at an individual level which may impact on students' optimal use of ICT for learning.

Sources of individual differences

Every day we can observe individual differences in the way people react to the same set of circumstances. Reflecting on our own behaviour, we can usually pick out certain familiar patterns of behaviour, preferences for ways to approach tasks and typical reactions to certain situations. Some of these responses are fairly habitual and some are much more variable, dependent on mood and context. The source of these differences and the responses they engender, whether they remain stable over time and how they contribute to differences in performance, are somewhat difficult to determine. Research has been carried out for many years in terms of intelligence, cognitive styles, learning approaches and personality types as some of the psychological constructs that have been associated with the study of individual differences and their influence upon patterns of behaviour. However, a major obstacle to fuller understanding of the differences is that as most studies focus on one of them, this reduces complexity at the expense of appreciation of the interactive nature of many factors.

In addition to internal constructs, past experience of individuals is clearly an additional source of individual differences and combines with internal factors to evoke different responses. The following sections briefly discuss some of these principal factors of individual difference.

Cognitive style

This has been defined as *an individual's preferred and habitual approach to organising and representing information* (Riding and Rayner, 1998, p. 8). Cassidy (2004), in a comprehensive review of cognitive and learning styles and preferences, distinguishes between *traits,* which are relatively stable and fixed (cognitive and learning styles) and *states,* which are more responsive and fluid (learning strategies). For teachers, these states represent the area within which fundamental approaches to learning can be supported to develop alternative strategies appropriate to different learning contexts.

While there are tests of cognitive and learning style, their practical application in the classroom is the subject of some debate. There is some evidence to suggest that the reliability, validity and usefulness of some tests of cognitive and learning style is limited (Coffield et al., 2004; Smith, 2002; Leutner and Plass, 1998). Furthermore, some tests are not appropriate for primary age children. Many young children might struggle to complete tests based on self-report which requires a level of self-awareness of learning preferences which they do not all possess. Gardner's Theory of Multiple Intelligences (1983), Riding's Cognitive Styles Analysis approach (1991) and Dunn, Dunn and Price's Learning Styles Inventory (1989) are probably the most commonly used with primary aged learners. The models on which these tests are based, however, may offer alternative frameworks for factors accounting for differential use of ICT by young children. Both Dunn and Riding are frequently cited and used but Dunn, Dunn and Price (1989) have been criticised because of a lack of independent evidence of their test's effectiveness, both as a reliable psychometric measure and as a useful tool for tailoring pedagogy for individuals. Riding and Rayner's (1998) test content validity has been questioned for dealing only with cognitive and not affective and behavioural aspects of learning (Coffield *et al.*, 2004). The use of these tests can only be expected to give a partial view of the individual differences influencing the student's learning at best, although their use may serve to focus and interpret observed habitual responses to learning.

Visual, auditory and kinaesthetic learning

This system of talking about learning styles has gained a lot of currency in schools and most teachers are able to assign their pupils to one or other of these groups. However, it is important to remember that these are not fixed and that we can all learn outside of our dominant form of learning style. Indeed it could be argued that it is advantageous to develop the capacity to do so since we are not always able to learn in our preferred way because of practical constraints. Nevertheless, this does mean that a range of different learning experiences is likely to benefit a group of children. Multimedia offers appeal to both visual and auditory learning styles. Children may benefit from text being read to them as well as being on screen. It would be interesting to explore whether predominantly kinaesthetic learners find sitting at a computer frustrating. Opportunities to break from such work and be active may help some pupils sustain concentration.

Personality

The field of learning styles and cognitive styles is Byzantine in its complexity with different labels and concepts overlapping (Cassidy, 2004). Some researchers believe them to be correlated with personality traits (Jackson and Lawty-Jones, 1996), while others claim that personality only has a moderating indirect effect on learning style (Riding and Wigley, 1997). Personality may, however, have a direct impact on the differential use of ICT (Benyon, n.d.) in its own right. For example, you might expect extravert personalities would be drawn to the communicative and multimedia possibilities of ICT, which offer high levels of stimulation. On the other hand, the potential of ICT to reduce classroom noise and distraction through the use of electronic communication and by independent computer assisted study might be more attractive to introverts. These personality characteristics may determine what features of ICT are most used by individuals. High levels of anxiety may also impede children's capacity to remember and hence their ability to process information (Elliman *et al.*, 1997) and this may create an especially poor learning environment for pupils anxious about the medium of ICT. In such cases open-ended tasks may increase anxiety, whereas a sequenced set of steps could support learning through the task and reduce anxiety. Another possible application to reduce anxiety might be drill and practice tests where failure to get the right answer is between the pupil and machine and does not involve embarrassment in front of others if they get a wrong answer. This could be extended to groups and gradually build up willingness in pupils to take risks with answering. Children who like high levels of stimulation or who are easily distracted may enjoy and benefit from wearing headphones with music while doing work on the computer.

Deep and surface approaches to learning

Another way to think about the individual differences which impinge on students' use of ICT is their approach to learning (Marton, Hounsell and Entwistle, 1994). Those students motivated to understand the material they are learning will tend to adopt a deeper approach to learning and look beyond the surface features required to satisfactorily complete tasks. An emphasis on presentational features of ICT may suggest a more surface approach. Other research (Waite, 2004) has suggested that sometimes pupils are still using word processing programs for low-level typing of rough drafts. This tends then to exclude the computer from the 'loop' of cognitive processing of the text and lose the benefits of easy rewriting to improve writing. Use in this way may demand good ICT skills, but also perhaps an intrinsic interest in the subject matter. Freedom to research areas that are of personal interest might therefore help students to develop skills and sustain interest.

Valle *et al.* (2003) suggest many pupils have multiple goals, including learning and performance goals (similar to deep and surface approaches), which offer more flexibility to adapt in different learning situations. They distinguish between approach–avoidance tendencies to either promote favourable judgements of competence or avoid negative assessment of competence. An anxiety to *appear* to be doing well may encourage more surface approaches and a narrower focus on requirements for task completion. For those pupils dominantly motivated by performance goals, clear use of criteria which include exploration as well as outcome may support different uses of programs and thereby their developing capacity to choose appropriate tools. Lower levels of ability may affect students' tendency to adopt deep or surface learning approaches, whether because of anxiety about their competence or a lack of understanding of broader learning opportunities within tasks. Selecting appropriate websites and providing frameworks to help extract information rather than simply cutting and pasting might also support more *active* use and understanding. A balance of structure and freedom is necessary to respond to different individual needs.

Time to reflect

You may wish to read some of the referenced texts to support your reflection.

Consider a class you have been teaching.

- *How might you categorise them? Explore with different frames, e.g. cognitive style, learning approach, personality characteristics.*
- *What do you notice about your categories and how do they relate to your own preferred mode of learning?*
- *Does your teaching appeal to all the different types of learners you have identified?*
- *How might you change your ICT use in class to respond to these individual differences?*

Looking more closely

Steve Wheeler, Carolyn Bromfield and I investigated the impact of ICT on learning in a primary school classroom over several years. We took baseline measures through interviews and observations in Year 5 (children aged 9 and 10) in a classroom with three personal computers. In Year 6 (children aged 10 and 11) in the school we studied, every child had access to his or her own personal networked computer all day and every day. We wanted to look at the implications of this for teaching and learning from both staff and pupil's points of view. We followed individual case studies through from Year 5 to Year 8 (second year of secondary school) to explore the impact of ICT in differing educational environments.

We looked at the detail of what was going on in the small space between the child and the computer while monitoring the context of the classroom from a seat by the pupil. We noted the teacher's interventions, the presence of different staff and the social interaction of the children. We recorded their individual activity and use of computer programs. We wanted to get this detail to help us understand how these factors interacted to create unique learning experiences for the children in our study. In interviews and 'on the hoof', we listened to the ideas of the children and staff about what they thought had been happening in their classroom, keeping field notes as well as taping more formal interviews. This follows an ecological approach to research, which Kemmis, Atkin and Wright (1977) recommend as acknowledging the importance of the environment within which learning takes place.

We selected six children as 'representatives' to explore the effect of gender and attainment levels. We anticipated gender might explain the differential uptake of ICT (Clegg, 2001; Joiner et al., 1996). Joiner (1998) compared performance on software that was structurally identical but either male or female stereotyped and found that girls performed worse than boys on both versions of the software even taking into account computer experience. Passey et al. (2003) have suggested that ICT has a more positive effect on boys through extending their interest span. On the other hand, Harrison et al. (2002) found that this did not translate into an advantage with their learning over girls.

We also thought attainment might be a major factor (DfES, 2001b), so we included one male and female to represent high, medium and low attaining children, as assessed by their class teacher, in our observational target group. The head teacher also added a seventh, high-attaining female pupil.

Activity

- **Make lists of the pupils in a class you are teaching in terms of gender and attainment.**
- **While you are with them, note beside the names any particular issues you have noticed regarding their use of ICT.**
- **Are the issues grouped by gender or attainment?**
- **How might this affect your practice for groupings to use ICT?**

The characteristics and attitudes of teachers are clearly influential on students' development. We thought it important to note what sort of interaction pupils had with staff. As there were also two teaching assistants present, it was considered vital to keep observational records and field notes of the overall picture in the classroom. We also noted in the observation schedule when there were visitors. Field notes and observation records therefore enabled us to take account of some background characteristics of the learning environment.

We found from a pilot study that it was impossible to tell how individuals were working from a single vantage point in the layout of the room and groups working together and geographically co-located to enable group observation were rarely occurring (Wheeler, Waite and Bromfield, 2002). In any case, we would argue that being this close to the individuals allowed us to experience more of what it was like to be that person within the particular social and learning context than if we had sat at a remove. We decided to observe the target group children for periods of 16 minutes each, noting their actions every minute, and then moving on to another child to repeat the process. The observations included a running record of activity, which was coded under the following categories:

- date;
- time;
- whether the child was in the main classroom or annexe;
- what curriculum area was being covered;
- what principal software was used;
- the nature of the activity the child was engaged in;
- whether they were on or off task, quiet or talking;
- what sort of contribution the teacher or teaching assistants were making at that point;
- what staff were present in the room.

We tried to ensure balance in the number and timing of the observations so that each child was observed for approximately the same length of time and at different times of the day and week. We took over 200 individual records of each child during 22 visits to the school throughout the school year and at different times of the day. We interviewed and observed the target children in the summer term before they joined the Year 6 class to get a baseline measurement for how they worked and an insight into their attitudes towards computers. They were then observed on an almost weekly basis, varying the day of observation, for the whole of their final year in primary school. They were interviewed at the end of this final year, after a term at secondary school and again after a year and a term at secondary school. They also completed the NFER-Nelson non-verbal reasoning tests 10 and 11. This is a measure of the ability to recognise similarities and patterns in unfamiliar designs. It is believed to be related to the ability to understand and assimilate new ideas and information (Smith and Hagues, 1993) and we thought that it might distinguish which of them were more 'suited' to the discovery way of learning through exploration which this class used. The school operated a computer-based assessment system whereby children were assessed annually as high, medium or low within National Curriculum levels. (Peter Hicks and Jonathan Bishop provide a detailed account of this school in Chapter 10.) Learning gain was derived from these assessments.

We analysed our data using SPSS. We had set out to look at attainment and gender as factors influencing the use of ICT but as our data collection and analysis progressed, we realised that there was finer level of detail in the different uses of ICT by the children studied. We were interested in what the source of these individual differences might be.

We had limited opportunities to observe the children in music or art and so would be unable to infer ability in these areas, so it did not seem appropriate for us to use Gardner's multiple intelligences model of learning styles (1983). Art and music rarely featured as part of the regular school day in the class we studied. Subjects were mostly taught through topic and project work for the majority of the year, with a period focused on practice papers as SATS preparation.

Using theoretical models without tests

Coffield et al. (2004, pp. 25 and 33) have criticised Dunn, Dunn and Price (1989) for the theoretical underpinning of their model and suggest that the simplicity and potential value of Riding's model is undermined by its measurement tool, the CSA. It may be that the categories, without relying on tests may help consideration of individual differences in a more exploratory way. Riding's (2002) categorisation offered a means of exploring cognitive style as a possible source of the individual differences observed, by inferring from observation and interviews where the individual children lay within his schema. Observation may be particularly helpful as a tool for assessing learning style when children are unaware of their preferences. It also has the advantage of being grounded in real learning as it occurs in a classroom situation rather than being assessed through testing. However, a note of caution needs to be raised in that it is their behaviour which places them in a construct defined by those very behaviours rather than as a result of an independent pre-test.

Riding (2002, pp. 25–8) describes two cognitive style dimensions:

- *wholist* (tendency to see material as a whole, have overarching view and appreciate context) to *analytic* (tendency to see elements of material and be good at comparing and contrasting parts but may struggle to see bigger picture);
- *verbaliser* (tendency to consider material as words and more externally, socially oriented) to *imager* (tendency to consider material in pictures and more internally oriented).

The interaction of these dimensions may complement and moderate or intensify these features. We inferred where the target children lay in Riding's framework with two researchers categorising the pupils on the basis of questionnaires about their computer use, interviews and observation into these descriptions. This process is illustrated by quotations in Table 9.1.

Table 9.1: Inferred cognitive styles

Target child	Inferred cognitive style	Illustrative quotations
1	AI	You can get Clipart to put in your work and you can change colours. You can get pictures of the car and make your own pictures of the car and that. And take pictures of your group.
2	AI	The internet, making my web page, looking at pictures. I look for golden retrievers and other kinds of dogs. I look at wrestling pages. Ive written Pokemon dessert and put the pictures on. I need to still do the writing part.
3	WV	The best thing is the technology really and the information you can get from them. At home, I probably spend about 25% on games, 25% on work and another 50% on other whatever, like e-mail, something like that. I can read the documents … and then use it for work, I want to be an individual, so I do my own thing.
4	WI	We did do quite a bit of art on my home computer. Its just a lot more fun than a book and sitting on a chair and writing in your book. I dont do a lot of e-mailing. If I get bored I can sometimes put a sound on … and then go back to my work and it can help me keep awake for a lot longer.
5	AI	You dont know which program does what and youve got to find it out, work it out which program does what by playing around with things. I like writing stories, just to let your imagination go wild, you can make up anything you want.
6	AV	Write work down, go on internet, send e-mails. At home for writing invitations and thank you letters and to play games.
7	AB	I'm making internet pages … there are special drawing programs. Theres all sorts of things, like I can make sounds … the way you can change the computer … I can design my own background if I wanted to. Weve discussed it in our groups and I understand it a lot more now … writing in your books is boring but if you do it on the computer on Textease you can … just put a few pictures on them and change the writing, colours and things.

Key: AI = Analytic imager; AB = Analytic bimodal; AV = Analytic verbaliser; WI = Wholist imager; WV = Wholist verbaliser

Caution is necessary as other aspects of individual difference were also operating, such as experience of computers outside of the school environment. However, you may find it useful to consider how these dimensions relate to children within your own class.

Our findings

Gender

Girls were observed as having nearly twice the number of socially interactive activities (asking questions, helping others with work, seeking help, discussion, answering questions, instant messaging) in comparison to the boys. Although male and female were equally represented in the top users of programs, the sorts of programs they favoured differed. Typically, boys engaged in *Starspell*, databases, file manipulation, CD ROMs and internet, while girls used *Media Player*, *Photoshop*, communication software, *Publisher*, *PowerPoint* and the intranet to a greater extent. This echoes Clegg's findings (2001) about more social uses of computers by females.

Attainment

The programs they were seen to use to a greater extent tended to be directed towards an end product, such as *Word*, *PowerPoint*, *Photoshop* and databases. The medium-attainment group were observed using process programs, such as the intranet and file manipulation, to a greater extent, as were the low-attainment group favouring CD ROMs, communication software and *Media Player*. This process/product divide is reinforced by the sorts of activities engaged in; writing was more common in the high attainment group and socially interactive activities in the lower attainment groups. This mirrors findings by Passey *et al*. (2003) that *communication* through ICT was more important to those with learning difficulties, while *information* through ICT was more important to gifted and talented pupils.

Levels of communication

Another individual difference that you may often be aware of in your class is differing levels of communication. We found some individuals had very low levels of interaction with adults in the class, for example target child 6 and target child 2 especially, regardless of whether they were on or off task. The observations also showed that target child 6 (a high attainer) was the quietest, least off task and had least interaction with adults. Target child 4 (a low attainer) was the most off task and talked a lot to peers. This might seem to suggest that talking was disruptive to attainment but, of all the children, target child 7 spoke the most to peers. However, a high proportion of her talk was task-related. Target child 1 was the least quiet but spoke least to peers and most to adults.

These social observations helped to fill out the pictures of how the children tended to approach learning and to provide insight into how independent in their learning the pupils are and the extent to which they seek peer or adult support. Frank, Reich and Humphreys (2003) reported how pupils of this age seek personal contact, although we found that, for some pupils, the distancing of electronic communication removed interpersonal conflict and thereby supported group learning (Bromfield, Waite and Wheeler, 2003). Being sensitive to these different amounts of talk to aid learning might help to provide appropriate learning experiences. The Primary National Strategy advocates peer talking to support self-esteem, social skills, learning and achievement (DfES, 2004e, p. 24). Riding (2002, p. 29) suggests that in addition to being more reliant on text for learning, verbalisers tend to use more talk in their learning and that wholists prefer to learn in groups (Riding and Read, 1986). Personality characteristics such as introversion might also explain this difference.

Time to reflect

Do you know which children in your class enjoy talking about their work? What opportunities are there at present for children to talk in different contexts in the class, e.g. talk pairs, group projects, hot-seating, explaining, presenting? What other ways might you introduce to provide a range of contexts for children to talk about their work?

What guidelines might you want to put in place to ensure on-task talk?

Program appeal

In our study, we also found that the *use of programs* varied between individuals, as different programs might be more compatible with their preferred way of learning (Riding and Grimley, 1999). The pupils were not told which program to use. Instead their teacher gave the pupils in our study a great deal of freedom about how and when they did their work. They would have a number of tasks to complete, which the teacher usually sent to them via e-mail, having initially introduced each new topic in a whole-class session.

Those who sought more social contact took up the *communication* opportunities of e-mail and instant messaging (amalgamated under 'Outlook' in Figure 9.1).

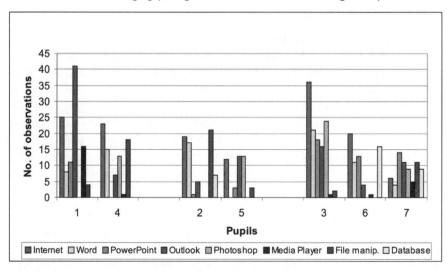

Figure 9.1: Individual variation in use of program types

The advantage of this was that whether the child was on or off task, communication was less disruptive to others working independently around him. However, it was also more difficult for the staff to detect if the communication was off task.

As differentiation was by outcome, the potential to find suitable learning activities and to stretch children was in each child's own hands rather than controlled by the teacher and this suited some but not all students. The teacher would sometimes require pupils to stay in at break if they had not achieved certain amounts of work within sessions due to a perceived lack of effort. It may be that pupils keeping a log of the programs used and evaluating them for their own learning would increase their meta-cognitive awareness of the best support for their learning. Another possible support for learning might be the directed use of programs for certain tasks.

One of the interesting individual differences in activity in our study was in 'file manip-ulation', where the pupil was moving *between* programs. This could be interpreted as familiarity with the programs and a facility for ICT. In fact, it often seemed a new tech-nological equivalent of unnecessary sharpening of pencils, a time-wasting activity, perhaps to afford 'down time' from work and indicating an uncertainty about how to approach a task. One way this might be circumvented is by tasks being broken down into small achievable steps with timed sections, which would support the child in how to approach a task and increase the pace of their work. Of course, we have to remember that it is important to factor in thinking time too!

Do all children love computers?

In the classroom study, four of the children used their computers for around 40 per cent of the time but target child 5 used the computer much less than this (21.8 per cent) and target children 1 and 3 used it much more (68.3 per cent and 75 per cent). This would seem to indicate that for target child 5, the class reliance on the computer as her main tool for learning may have had detrimental effects on her learning. Her use of the computer was largely a result of direct instruction rather than choice.

How do you accommodate a dislike of ICT when it is an increasingly important part of the curriculum, not only as a subject but running throughout the whole?

All the students had at least one home computer but there is an interesting difference in the reported sort of use pupils made of the computers that suggests the home use of computers could be influential in how they are used in the classroom. Home computers are rapidly becoming a mainstream household item. The BECTa 'Young People and ICT' survey (2002) found 81 per cent of households had access to a compu-ter in the home, up from 78 per cent in the 2001 survey and that 98 per cent of 5–18 year olds used computers at home, school or elsewhere, with 92 per cent using them at school and 75 per cent using them at home. The 'digital gap' appears to be in how these computers are used (Facer, 2002). In our small study we found those children who were using the computer for homework alone made less learning gains than those who used it for multiple purposes. It may be that the children are less confident with the computer, feel less attracted to its use, or merely use it as they might use a fountain pen to 'copy up in neat' or a book to 'find out facts'.

Mumtaz (2001) and Comber et al. (2002), cited in Coffield et al. (2003, p. 13), suggest a lack of congruence between children's home and school experience of computing which fails to blend out-of-school and within-school use constructively. However, it does not seem to be enough to just bring the *opportunity* to 'play' into school since the class teacher in our study allowed this at times within school in contrast to the very focused and skills-based teaching of ICT in many primary schools. A more exploratory approach might be fostered by scaffolded use of ICT, where pathways of exploration are signposted for children or children are paired with more exploratory partners.

The way in which the computers are used may also depend on the pupil's innate approach and the 'meaning' they attach to the tasks. The more narrowly instrumental pupils are in their use, the less computers may offer a scaffold to learning. It may be that it is *understanding* computers as one tool among others and the matching of this to tasks and learning style that is important, rather than skills in using the capacity of the computer for improved presentation. To increase this understanding, children need to practise ways of thinking and talking about what they need to do in order to approach various tasks and what different programs might offer to support this. This will develop their metacognitive ability. Modelling and paired work can be helpful in this context. The Primary National Strategy website has many examples of how ICT can be used through the curriculum (see **www.ictadvice.org.uk/index.php? section =ae&page=about&theme=73**).

Support is crucial as we found some evidence that the higher-attaining pupils seemed to be widening the gap between themselves and low-attaining students in the ICT-rich and open-ended task environment of our study. There did not seem to be an association between particular programs or activities and learning gain; for example, target pupil 7 has an even spread of use across the available software as does pupil 4 who makes far less progress.

Providing different contexts for learning

Kemmis, Atkin and Wright (1977) set out three different curriculum paradigms: Instructional (drill and practice), Revelatory (discovery, playing) and Conjectural (solving problems). They also postulated a fourth, Emancipatory, associated with each of the above, which essentially took away the tedious elements of work. All these paradigms have a place in the classroom and providing a range of different tasks will appeal to different learning styles. The Revelatory paradigm may be especially important if our finding about playful home computer use being associated with greater learning gain is valid. The entitlement to ICT in English is detailed in a BECTa ICT website (see **www.ictadvice.org.uk/downloads/entitlement_doc/entitle_ eng_prim.doc**). Try reading this advice with these paradigms in mind.

In our classroom study, the children were set tasks by the teacher which fell within these categories. They were expected to begin the afternoon session with *Starspell Plus*, a drill and practice spelling program. They also had Eggy day challenges where they designed and built a parachute and a car to convey an egg safely, which built up their group problem-solving skills. They were given a free hand to use and explore the possibilities of software for research and presentation in Revelatory mode. Some of the children clearly enjoyed the playing and exploratory nature of their access to ICT; others were using it principally as an information source for personal or educational purposes. All the children commented in interview how the computers freed them from the tedium of writing and rewriting, echoing the Emancipatory dimension. They also valued the presentational improvement in their work, although they did not always seem to be using redrafting possibilities. Sample work taken from first draft through to the final version often had few improvements. Indeed new errors were sometimes introduced. Furthermore, spelling mistakes often remained in spite of the children's lauding the computers' spellchecking facilities. However, time was freed up for reading work:

> I'm reading it through now, because I never used to read it through. I used to do my work but I never used to read it through after but now I do. I find I've got time to read it now.'
> (Target child 1)

Support in the form of guidelines for redrafting, then, might help pupils make better use of this opportunity.

Time to reflect

Think about the different activities you might offer involving ICT. Where do they fall in terms of these curricular paradigms? Make a list with these headings. Are you satisfied with the balance in the list? Can you devise some more Revelatory activities to stimulate exploration and creativity?

A further source of variation in individuals' learning may be attributable to them not finding the tasks set easy to understand or structure, as this introduced an additional layer to their work. If they worked more slowly than others did too, this would then mean they were unlikely to achieve the entire task within the time frame allowed. Skills to work within Revelatory and Conjectural curricular paradigms need to be supported by effective explanations and support. The repeated experience of non-completion of tasks could lead to lower levels of self-esteem and incomplete learning. This might then lead to anxiety about competence. In its turn this could make pupils adopt more avoidance tendencies, i.e. strategies to hide their 'incompetence' and a surface approach, i.e. concentrating on the superficial requirements of tasks rather than the learning that underpins them (Valle et al., 2003). Self-esteem and attainment both appear to contribute to successful use of ICT.

The higher attainers seemed to be able to adapt their learning preferences and turn their hand to most tasks. They also saw tasks to completion more than the low attainers did. The individual effect of ICT may therefore have been masked by an overall effect of attainment. It is likely that where students are unable to adapt their learning approach, they will be disadvantaged, unless the task is adapted for them. It is therefore important that tasks set appeal to a range of learning styles and that scaffolding is provided in the form of frameworks or stepped tasks to support children where they are working outside their preferred learning style.

Where pupils are unable to complete tasks, they can however find alternative activities on the computer, which do not interfere with others' learning. There is a danger with this; because the ICT makes off-task behaviour less visible and disruptive, it is less likely to be detected and redirected by the teacher. Are your tasks using ICT differentiated to support children who either do not easily break down tasks or do not readily explore the possibilities of ICT? How can you monitor how individuals are working when they are at the screen?

One size fits all?

While the use of computers may mediate a 'one size fits all' teaching approach to some extent (McDonald and Ingvarson, 1997), we suggest that further progress might be made by a more differentiated use of them. Pittard, Bannister and Dunn (2003) suggest spontaneity and flexibility are important forms of ICT use in their summary of large-scale studies of the impact of ICT on attainment, motivation and learning. They also suggest that:

> using ICT in the right ways can help personalise pupil learning, develop pupil-centred and collaborative approaches to learning and offer new ways of supporting and enhancing pupil's conceptual learning. (Pittard et al., 2003, p. 14)

Attention to the differences in pupil response to ICT may help to direct how these 'right ways' can be addressed practically.

If the availability of ICT does not directly liberate some pupils' learning, then some other means of making it more appropriate to individual learning needs to take place. This might involve creating more structure in open-ended tasks (Hoyles and Noss, 1992, cited in Cox et al., 2003, p. 17). The teacher in our study verbally outlined ways to approach tasks such as 'Who, What, Where, Why, How' and, on some occasions, this was sent through the interactive white screen to each pupil's computer, but wholists and some low attainers may have benefited from this guidance being available as permanent writing frameworks. This would then have freed them from an initial stage in the task of trying to create a structure for their exploration. They might also have benefited from more paired work where a different approach to ICT use would allow them to experience beyond their own capabilities or inclination.

On the other hand, proficiency in ICT offered a source of self-esteem for some low academic attainers and anxious personality types. Choosing work partners with either strength in subject knowledge or ICT skills would enable teachers to combine pupils to give both partners a zone of proximal development to encourage their learning and opportunities to build their self-esteem. Collaboration which builds on responsive and flexible learning *strategies* rather than styles might also help to scaffold learning (Cassidy, 2004).

Analytics and anxious personality types may find difficulty in navigating programs, being unable to retain the overall picture of how it works. On the other hand, they may be helped by activities such as writing a leaflet about how to use programs, as this allows them to sequentially organise the material. Verbalisers and extraverts may also be enabled to learn socially through the extended means of communication and through joint work projects, perhaps culminating in a *PowerPoint* presentation. A variety of tasks would support this broader appeal of ICT for different cognitive styles.

Labels

We need to be careful when using the labelling we have explored in this chapter as it may diminish attention to the complexity of interrelationships through oversimplification. It is likely that each individual will have several, possibly conflicting, individual differences, and that these will tend to dominate and interact in different contexts. Our study suggests that use of a single learning style inventory might yield little of practical value to personalise teaching. Since it is the *interaction* of individual characteristics, tasks and programs which is fundamental to the successful use of the ICT for learning, it is important to become aware of individual preferences and differences at an early point. For example, this might mean staff working alongside individuals to observe their approach.

Staff sensitivity to individual learning differences may usefully be enhanced by having a language with which to conceptualise them (Rosenfeld and Rosenfeld, 2004). Coffield *et al.*, (2004, p. 39) refer to a 'lexicon of learning' which allows teachers to discuss their own and other learning preferences without labelling and praise the practical value of Jackson's Learning Styles Profiler (2002 cited in Coffield *et al.,* 2004) as a self-development tool. We have used labels in this chapter, but only in the sense that they are symbols to help us discuss difference. In the reflective activities we have tried to provide several ways to think about how pupils differ and how you might develop your teaching strategies to meet these differences and personalise the curriculum.

Activity

Have a go at conducting your own mini research project. You, a teaching assistant or a parent volunteer should sit by children when they are using the computer. Use the observation schedule in Figure 9.2 to note how it is being used by that pupil.

First of all fill in the name of the child, where they are working and the date and time. There is a section for a description of the task. The observation schedule has four columns: the first to note what program is being used; the second to note what the child is doing, e.g. writing, maths; the third to note any social interaction; and the fourth to make a note of any teacher or teaching assistant contributions. You may wish to adapt the schedule to focus on a particular skill. Notes are taken every minute for 6 minutes.

Collate these to see what types of programs and approaches are being used. How much choice has the child had in deciding what to use? How did individual children differ in their use? How might you use this information to adapt your teaching to draw on these strengths and preferences?

Using pairs of children to observe and then feedback will help them to become more self aware of the processes of learning. It could even form the basis of a pupil research project.

OBSERVATION SCHEDULE

Name:	Location:	Time/Date:

Description of general context of task:

Program in use	What child is doing	Social interaction with others	Teacher/TA contribution
1			
2			
3			
4			
5			
6			

Any other observations:

Figure 9.2: Observation schedule

Conclusion

Research has indicated that ICT can be a powerful motivator (Bromfield, Waite and Wheeler, 2003; Passey et al., 2003) and an impetus for creative thinking (Wheeler, Waite and Bromfield, 2002). This creativity and motivational aspect is supported by a movement away from drill and practice software or 'copying up' handwritten drafts (Waite, 2004) and the increased use of open-ended tasks, which allow some pupils to match the execution of tasks and selection of programs more to their preferred style and which introduce more flexibility. But this is not the case for all pupils: some children appear to be unable to direct their use of ICT to the goal of learning without further structure.

Moseley et al. (1999 cited in Cox et al., 2003, p. 11) found that effective explanations were important to good practice in pedagogy using ICT, where pupils were involved and examples and counter-examples demonstrated. Modelling may help here, and the increase of interactive whiteboards in classrooms makes this easier to do. There may also be a correlation with attainment level. If pupils are very able, they appear capable of adapting the ICT to their own purpose more than if they have lower ability, so that benefits of ICT in terms of improved attainment are further reinforced by high-attaining pupils' more flexible use of ICT.

Further research is needed to explore whether this circular relationship holds true in other contexts and whether the indications from our small-scale study are widely applicable. However, methods to prevent this apparent gap ever-widening may include developing pupils' awareness and understanding of the potential of ICT for learning and creating structures and activities that encourage exploration. By establishing these metacognitive strategies as a habit in the process of learning, understanding is likely to be enhanced. We suggest that class based research into individual differences and preferences may provide vital and practical insights into how teaching can support a productive and personalised approach to using ICT throughout the curriculum.

Teaching tips

- *Set open-ended projects and get children to detail in a timesheet how they went about achieving their goals (metacognitive awareness development).*
- *Involve children in real-life problems, set up by them, and planned and logged by computer.*
- *Allow free play – this seemed to have a beneficial effect. Support free play for those not naturally inclined to explore by pairing children so they can complement each other with skills.*
- *Have a range of frameworks for different sorts of writing available on the computer for children to choose whether to use them or not. Ask children why they have chosen or not to help develop their awareness of what helps them to learn.*
- *Break tasks into several shorter stages to support children who find planning difficult – a project or task timeline template might help.*

- *Use the different skills of the children to group them to maximise benefit from collaborative work, e.g. pairing a lower attaining pupil with computer expertise with a higher attaining pupil in the subject area. Both will contribute and support each other's learning.*
- *Go to the BECTa and Primary National Strategy websites or look in the Excellence and Enjoyment: Learning and teaching in the primary years continuing professional development materials for more ideas. (Use www.google.co.uk to search for latest links to these sites, as these do change).*

PART 3: CASE STUDIES

10 SCHOOLS OF THE FUTURE
GEORGE MUIRHEAD, PETER HICKS AND JONATHAN BISHOP

The significant problems we face cannot be solved at the same level of thinking we were at when we created them.

Albert Einstein (1879–1955)

The future and all that

Many technology philosophers have tried to predict the future, often with humorous results:

- **On seeing moving images (cinematography) for the first time, the celebrated inventor Thomas Edison predicted that it would replace written text within ten years. For once he was hopelessly wrong.**

- **One of the most ironic quotes came from Thomas J. Watson, head of IBM, who declared** *I think there is a world market for maybe five computers.* **Fortunately for the stock value of 'Big Blue', its CEO was also wide of the mark.**

An inadvertently humorous statement about technology came from a mayor in a small town in America, who had just witnessed the demonstration of Alexander Graham Bell's fabulous new invention – the telephone. The mayor proclaimed with prophetic fervour that *one day every town in America will have a telephone!* He was of course right – every town in America *does* have a telephone. In fact every town in America has many, and the people who live in these towns also walk around with personal telephone systems in their pockets. We can try to predict the future, but where technology is concerned, we run the danger of being either inaccurate in our predictions or hopelessly off target. While the future is uncertain and making predictions is hazardous, we can nevertheless detect trends in the use of new technologies in the short term and begin to plan for what might be highly probable scenarios.

Strategic planning is normally undertaken by the managers and leaders of schools, and good leadership is a vital part of successful ICT implementation in primary education. Without visionary leadership, new technologies are unlikely to be widely promoted among teachers, but with insightful and creative head teachers adopting and championing ICT, success is more probable. In this chapter, we hear from the head teachers of two Devon primary schools and glimpse their visions for the role of ICT in transforming schools into the schools of the future.

The first part of this chapter on 'Schools of the Future' is written by George Muirhead, whose school Woodfield Primary was the first in Plymouth to adopt a completely wireless strategy for its ICT deployment. As a head teacher, he has dealt with issues that reflect his own particular concerns in leadership. In *Why Wireless? Why Laptop?* he makes the case for wireless schools, and expresses strong opinions, based on extensive experience of the day-to-day running of an inner-city school and the management of all its attendant problems.

The second half of the chapter offers another perspective on how schools will use ICT to transform their working life in the future. Again, it is written by a head teacher, Peter Hicks, with added experience provided by the school's deputy head, Jonathan Bishop. Situated in a rural part of Devon, Broadclyst Junior School is one of a small cluster of innovative primary schools in the UK, providing a personal desktop networked computer for each of its Year 6 pupils. Hicks and Bishop offer you their own personal vision for *'Schools without Walls'*.

Steve Wheeler

Why Wireless? – Why Laptop?
The case for wireless laptops
in primary schools

George Muirhead

If the automobile had followed the same development cycle as the computer, a Rolls-Royce would today cost $100, get a million miles per gallon, and explode once a year, killing everyone inside.

Robert X. Cringely, *InfoWorld*

This first part of Chapter 10 explores a range of issues related to the use of wireless technologies and laptop computers in primary education and points the direction in which some schools are already heading. How much will wireless technology enhance the teaching and learning environment? What new practices will emerge as a result? What are the health issues? What resourcing is required? What expertise is necessary to achieve success? These and other questions are addressed in this chapter. The author is head teacher at Plymouth's first all wireless school, and shares his experiences and insight into how this innovation can be applied to primary education. The case study was conducted in conjunction with the University of Plymouth.

The section will enable you to:

- **evaluate the uses of wireless technologies in primary education;**
- **examine some of the key issues related to the use of laptops in primary teaching;**
- **begin to develop ideas for their use in your own professional practice.**

Weathering the storm

As you are starting out on a career in education it is necessary for you to understand one important thing about governments. They act like the weather, blowing hot and cold over initiatives, blustering around like the wind, often with no real direction until finally they tend to blow themselves out. Where governments are most like the weather however, is in our inability to predict how they are going to affect us in the future. This is mainly because just like the weather they don't really know themselves what they want or what the future will look like. You may be familiar with the use of 'chaos theory' to predict the weather. Think the same for anticipating our political masters. There are limited policy areas politicians can affect these days, so the areas of social policy still in their control they find impossible to leave alone. This makes planning in education extremely difficult and points to the need for leaders to set their own agenda and hold tight through the troughs, depressions and highs of any new initiative.

Nowhere is this truer than in ICT. Since 1990 there has been a requirement within the National Curriculum to teach ICT in schools. This spawned the development of the National Grid for Learning (NGfL) and the New Opportunities Funding (NOF) to provide resources and guidelines on how to implement this strategy. However, as Kirkman points out:

> Whilst the ICT National Curriculum has made a useful contribution to the development of ICT in schools, the original vision of delivering ICT across the curriculum has not been realised in the majority of schools. (Kirkman, 2000)

Teachers have a great ability to subvert initiatives if they do not fit in with their own philosophy of education. The chance to impact on practice within classrooms, once doors are shut, has always been the biggest challenge to managing change in our schools. This problem has been compounded with the government's promotion of ICT suites as the preferred solution for the deployment of ICT over the last ten years. DfES new school builds still have an ICT suite as a key area within the design of the building. This has resulted in ICT being compartmentalised so that it is failing to achieve its intended outcomes.

If you make a mistake in geography and buy the wrong textbooks they can stay out of sight in the back of a cupboard. The same is true in all areas of the curriculum except ICT. It is expensive, visual, and easy to get wrong, complexly interrelated, requires a lot of commitment and training and for many of our ageing teaching force this can become somewhat of an embarrassment in terms of teacher–pupil relationships. Teachers know how to handle and manipulate books and other audio-visual aids (AVA) but many find it difficult to discover that their pupils know more about computers than they do. This is an area where new entrants to the profession tend to have fewer problems with the pupils, but this can lead to problems within the internal politics of the staffroom where the 'new boy' or 'new girl' clearly knows more than the 'seasoned campaigner'.

It is no wonder then that most school leaders stick to a tried and limiting path, which the majority of their workforce feel comfortable with, when it comes to this major investment. This usually means row upon row of gleaming, well protected stack (desktop) systems linked by a wired network and safely contained within a box called the ICT suite. Too many schools see ICT as an end, a box to tick rather than a means of researching, collating, presenting and sharing the building blocks of information, knowledge. Huge amounts of research point to the disillusionment young people feel with this approach and the need to be more dynamic and flexible in supporting pupils in their use of ICT.

A report from Cardiff University School of Social Sciences found that children have a very different experience of using computers at home to that in school. Their study looked at 855 children aged 9–14, 60 per cent of whom had computers at home. The survey asked them about the full range of use of computers and the Internet, everything from mobile phones to TV and consoles. Sixteen families were chosen for an in-depth analysis which included interviews with the whole family and video observations of the children using computers.

The pupils were not difficult but all shared one common view of the communication technology at school, it was not meeting their needs and did not reflect the way they used computers in their 'out of school' life. The contrast between home and school was quite stark. They were surrounded by a range of resources at home with parents, friends and software a constant source of guidance and support. At school they never felt that they 'owned' the technology and most guidance from teachers was verbal. Their disappointment led to dissatisfaction which led to them being turned off their provision in school.

The research pointed to the need to re-engage these youngsters and make them feel part of the process rather than just a recipient of a system. The Government initiative of Anytime, Anywhere computers is a potentially positive move in this direction.

In order to engage youngsters we need to do more than take the exciting developments of the last twenty years and reduce them to little more than moving textbooks. The implementation of ICT through NGFL did not start with a philosophy and craft the technology to meet it, rather it started with the technology and left the philosophy to discover itself. This has led us down the path of over-concentrating on its use to administer remedial practice, record pupil progress and centre a philosophy in a room, the ICT suite. Bryson and De Castell (1998) reflected that it is the equivalent of using a high-end, multi-capacity server for little more than typing practice. Many teachers have argued against this development of hardware before philosophy and have frequently been portrayed as semi-Luddite. Bryson and De Castell argue that maybe these teachers are actually the only people brave and honest enough to say when they see the nakedness of the emperor.

This rush for appearance rather than reality is evidenced in the creation of the ICT suite. It has a status and an investment which says, 'I am important', but a delivery system which works completely against its potential. This is not a new idea as research projects in the past have pointed to the increased effect that laptops have on learning when set against computer suites. Saul Rockman conducted research (1997; 2000) involving 150 teachers and more than 450 pupils from 20 schools where children have 24-hour access to laptops and they are fully integrated into their class work. He used a combination of interviews, simulated problem solving, surveys and observations to find the following results.

- **Laptops helped students in problem solving and critical thinking skills. Eighty-five per cent of the teachers reported that students with this type of facility used a far greater variety of information sources, developing better defined critical thinking skills than their contemporaries.**
- **Laptops had a huge impact on writing where the work was of a much higher quality according to 87 per cent of the teachers surveyed.**
- **Laptops extend the length of the school day as students using them spent 10 times as much time out of school on their work as their peers who had desktop computers at home.**

Although sponsored by Microsoft, the independence of which can be questioned, it does nonetheless reinforce the need for a dynamic, relevant approach to ICT provision in our schools.

A case study

I also carried out some extensive research in 2002 into children's perceptions of the two most common platforms for the delivery of ICT: the stack system (desktop PC) and the laptop. I felt it important to carry out some research into what young people wanted as a part of their future. I chose this simple divide as one system clearly lends itself to the development of ICT suites, due to the cabling/networking issues, whereas the other lends itself to flexible deployment due to the portability of the system. Our current group of children in schools are the first digital generation. They view ICT not as a technological innovation but as a natural part of their lives, a view supported by their regular use of mobile phones. I wanted the research to question the nature and concept of the immovable stack system and its most common current deployment within ICT suites.

The research involved returns from 1,432 Year 6 pupils in Plymouth primary schools during the summer of 2002. The aim of the study was to ask a series of fairly simplistic questions about this age group's perceptions of a laptop set when compared to a stack system. I followed the protocol recommended by the TEL 598 Survey Questionnaire Construction for constructing the questionnaire. If carrying out research in your future career with children it is important to embed it within clear criteria. The basic rules of my questions followed the guidelines that the questionnaire and questions should:

- **ensure relevance to the research problem;**
- **be as short and simple as possible;**
- **avoid ambiguity, confusing or vague questions;**

- avoid prestige bias (this is where a question relates to a prestigious person or group so the respondent may reply relating their response to their feelings towards this person or group rather than to the question);
- avoid double-barrelled questions, two questions in one;
- avoid leading questions (those that start with statements like 'don't you agree that');
- do not ask questions that are beyond the respondent's capabilities, particularly important when researching with young people;
- do not ask questions that are irrelevant to the respondent's experience.

I deliberately chose very simple, unambiguous questions which attempted to ascertain perceptions of value. In order to ensure as honest a response as possible I flagged the point at the top of the questionnaire that there were no right or wrong answers, just what the respondent thought. The tick box approach also limited the likelihood of error as did the instruction for the survey to be carried out by a teacher reading the questions, if reading was a problem for the pupil. Given all these safeguards, there were of course variables outside of my control, like the way in which the survey was conducted and the enthusiasm or bias put in by the teacher controlling the survey. The returns are shown in Table 10.1

Table 10.1: Questionnaire responses from Plymouth schools (n = 1432)

Question	Laptop	Stack
1. Which costs more?	64%	36%
2. Which is better?	76%	24%
3. Which would you want to own?	77%	23%
4. Which would make you work harder?	60%	40%
5. Which would you like to see in your school?	75%	25%
6. In the future which will be a greater part of your life?	78%	22%
7. Which would be more fun to use?	75%	25%
8. Which would be more valuable in helping you succeed in life?	73%	27%
9. Which would you be prouder to show a friend?	80%	20%
10 Which of these do you have at home?	26%	70%

Six per cent of the children crossed both boxes or put neither underneath, but the results are quite clear. One set of 10–11-year-olds in the summer of 2002 in Plymouth viewed the laptop as an intrinsic part of their future. They see the stack system as less desirable in every question and do not view it as particularly relevant. Interestingly all the schools surveyed had to a larger or lesser degree gone down the stack system route and have computer suites. Although included in the overall table, I have also tabulated my school results separately in order to contrast the results of all these schools with a school which has no computer suite.

We have developed an entirely wireless method of working with laptops where even the mouse has been removed. This system operates with children as young as five working the touchpad and select keys on the laptops. They quite naturally accept that this technology is wireless, portable and available in any room. The children come together for one discrete ICT lesson per week, or anywhere in the school as we are able to redistribute 30 laptops to meet particular combinations of teaching needs as they arise. Table 10.2 shows the results from my own school to the same questions as in the large survey.

Table 10.2: Questionnaire responses from wireless school (n = 27)

Question	Laptop	Stack
1. Which costs more?	91%	9%
2. Which is better?	96%	4%
3. Which would you want to own?	100%	0%
4. Which would make you work harder?	75%	25%
5. Which would you like to see in your school?	89%	11%
6. In the future which will be a greater part of your life?	87%	13%
7. Which would be more fun to use?	89%	11%
8. Which would be more valuable in helping you succeed in life?	93%	7%
9. Which would you be prouder to show a friend?	93%	7%
10 Which of these do you have at home?	14%	77%

Nine per cent of the children crossed both boxes or put neither underneath. This is of course based on a very small sample of just 27 children; however, there are significant differences between the perceptions of this group for whom laptops and no computer suite are the norm and the rest of the sample.

The challenge

The challenge therefore is for our country to develop a policy which takes on board the aspirations of the digital generation and presents opportunities for them to learn in a flexible, interactive and meaningful way. I contend that the creation of computer suites and the enshrining of ICT as a special area subject with hard-wiring are entirely counterproductive to realising the aspirations of our young people.

So the problem has been stated and teachers now need to discover the solution. The media-driven world of politics encourages the sound-bite approach to policy communication. The government has a new buzzword it has been developing over the last two years – *creativity*. Its previous favourite buzzword was *conformity* and this was illustrated by the resources, time and impetus given to seeing the literacy and numeracy strategies delivered across the land from 1998 and Ofsted expectations to comment on it in practice.

For most teachers creativity is a far more interesting and productive word and is to be welcomed. Chapter 8 deals with the subject of creative use of ICT in greater detail. Many young teachers raised on a diet duet of the literacy and numeracy strategies are finding the concept difficult to grasp, as they are used to being told what to do, but given time they also will realise the huge window of opportunity that the government has opened. This philosophical shift has two main driving forces, the new primary strategy 'Excellence and Enjoyment' and Creative Partnerships. Creativity in the curriculum is seen as essential in order to move on pupil's progress as the document states in its executive summary:

> Develop the distinctive character ... take ownership of the curriculum ... be creative and innovative. (DfES, 2003c, p. 4)

Combine this with the impact that Creative Partnerships is having. Funded by the Department for Culture, Media and Sport and delivered through the Arts Council, it sets the learning agenda on a course of combining creative providers in the community with schools in a wide range of settings across the country. The government has now clearly grasped what Tobin and Shrubshall (2002) describe as the 'downward focus' of the public sector. The effect of centrist government policy-making and Ofsted has been to emphasise the risk of failure rather than the potential of success. Tobin and Shrubshall make the point that:

> Employees within any organisation develop an innate understanding as to what treatment is dispensed if ideas are initiated that subsequently fail. In organisations that display downward focus, failure tolerance is low and the repercussions punitive. (Tobin and Shrubshall, 2002, p. 18)

The gauntlet has been thrown down by central government to schools and their leaders. The role of the new teacher and their contribution of enthusiasm combined with energy could be critical in driving this forward: come up with creative solutions to old problems and don't feel constrained by many of the old barriers. This approach, however, is new to some leaders within education but has always been the solution to local problems in each school – a one-size-fits-all approach has never worked and never will. Leadership and management of any problem in schools have always been solved by senior leaders having vision. BECTa point to a raft of research from Evans (2002), Yee (2000), Sheppard (2000) and others which makes the simple point that:

> Senior leaders need to communicate and share a clear vision of ICT with all levels of staff ... . (they) will have different leadership styles, but they all need to have a vision of learning transformed by ICT. (BECTa, 2003c)

Key questions they believe to be vital for schools and practitioners to consider are:

- **What barriers do teachers in your school think affect their use of ICT?**
- **Is the whole school involved in and supportive of the process of integrating ICT?**
- **Are ICT resources deployed so as to enable teachers to access them easily and integrate them effectively?**
- **Is your ICT training provision focused on pedagogy, differentiated by skill level and arranged with sensitivity to teachers' workloads? (BECTa, 2003, p. 3)**

So the current scene is one of opportunity where the government has accepted the irony that its policy of centrist control has had a level of success but that success is now limited by the longer-term effects of the policy. Therefore never has there been a better time for schools, and new entrants, to consider how to plot the way forward for their future success. Nowhere is this more important than in ICT as all the research points to a very clear correlation between a successful dynamic use of ICT and the future academic success of their pupils. Ofsted and BECTa have both produced reports supporting this relationship. One quote summarises the effect:

> There is a strong relationship between pupil's attainment, effort and independence in ICT and the quality of ICT resources, their strategic use and the teacher's understanding of ICT. (BECTa, 2003b, p. 1)

It is necessary therefore to put ICT at the heart of future developments in our schools. I believe my introduction to this chapter has pointed to the lack of returns of the traditional ICT approach and intend demonstrating the impact and balance of gains in adopting a future development based around a wireless networked laptop solution.

Justifying the investment and risk

So risk-taking is officially OK – as long as you get it right of course, and there's the rub for educational leaders as, of course, no one wants to fall on the wrong side of their risk assessment. All risk assessment is based on two elements:

- **the likelihood of something happening;**
- **the consequence if it does.**

Placed into the ICT context this raises two important questions for school leaders to address:

- **How difficult will it be to develop a solution that everyone can use and fits into the skill levels and abilities of the staff while providing a future proof, interoperable system which will match needs? – set against ...**
- **What will staff, the governors, audit and Ofsted think? What will be the economic impact on learning with the poor return on such a high investment if we get it wrong?**

There is a management maxim that states you can usually achieve 80 per cent of change in 20 per cent of the time while the last 20 per cent of a change will take the remaining 80 per cent of your time. (This is the Pareto principle, more properly referred to as 'Juran's assumption'.) I translate this to the effectiveness of any initiative and believe that if you can achieve 80 per cent of what you hoped at the beginning of an initiative then you will have a lot of time to get the rest right. Teachers are professional critics and no matter what initiative you introduce there is always a downside. However, it is also worth remembering that schools, like all institutions, are always changing – they are either getting better or getting worse. Calculated risk-taking and managing change are the two most important elements of ensuring that a school performs better.

The future will not be the same as the past yet many schools plan for their ICT deployment as if this were the case. There is a risk in changing and a risk in doing nothing. Here are some of the thoughts of some of the leading thinkers in the field as reported in *Newsweek* on 25 October 2001 when they were asked what a school will look like in 2025:

The drive over the next 20 years is to integrate these multimedia tools to the point where people become authors in the medium of their day … when students are creating themselves, learning is taking place. And teachers will be at the epicenter of this. (Steve Jobs, CEO Apple)

All of our students will have personal laptops connected to the world with wireless networks … teachers will be more of a coaching role.. a guide on the side helping students find answers online rather than a sage on the stage. (Linda Hammond, Darling Professor of Education at Stanford University)

Assume that the wireless network is there … high speed connection … students have a personal use tablet PC … it's for collaboration, communication, creativity; it's along the lines of what the PC is today. (Bill Gates, CEO Microsoft)

There won't be desks bolted to the floor facing the dispenser of knowledge at the front of the room. Assignments and lessons will be printed on demand in some rich interactive media. (John Doerr, Technology Investor)

Wireless laptop solutions

The challenge is to prepare our young people for the world of the future not the issues of the past. This can only be achieved when school leaders develop solutions which are based on future needs not past problems. Let us therefore examine some of the disadvantages and advantages of a wireless laptop solution as opposed to the traditional rows upon rows of computers bolted to a desk and hard wired into a very limited network.

The lows

BATTERY LIFE AND CHARGING ROUTINES/NEEDS
This is essential and is becoming increasingly difficult to get right. Modern batteries have a memory which responds to charging cycles, which means the more you charge it the less it holds a charge. If you have a mobile phone you will understand the principle. This is a real issue for schools as most children and staff automatically want to plug in an electrical item. We have detached the leads from the base unit so that a laptop has to be taken to a charging area when its battery has run out of charge. They do have audio warning devices which activate when the battery is running down to warn users to save any data to their file in time. I have put this first on the list as getting this right is essential, but this in turn leads to another problem.

LOSING PARTS
There are problems when laptop accessory parts are left in classes so it is important that the school keeps track of the location of all equipment. There is a great deal more safety and security for equipment in an ICT suite as it doesn't tend to move around. Portability means that items of equipment with local area network (LAN) cards have the potential to become lost. Schools are like most organisations whereby if someone can get away with not owning up to losing something then they won't. We call this the Atlas 'sloping shoulders' approach to resource management – you may remember he was left holding the world and all its responsibilities, while his

colleague disappeared. The same can happen with lost equipment and is an issue that you will need to think through. As a solution to this problem, we label each item of equipment and allocate it to a class, but this is not a completely foolproof solution.

PORTABILITY, DAMAGE AND ACCOUNTABILITY

Accidents will happen and usually do. When kit moves around this possibility can increase. Our experience as a school over four years of this approach is that generally we have not had any more damage than we would have expected. Portability means the ability to take laptops home. We have identified lead ICT children in each class and they have taken the laptops home to work through programs. Unfortunately problems now arise with pupils' potential internet use and all the pitfalls currently inherent within an uncontrolled environment. Chapter 5 deals with the potential dangers of the internet in a more general context. In our school, we are exploring removal of the capability of some laptops to be linked to the internet before allowing these to be taken home by pupils, but this is only a partial solution. The school's insurance arrangement is not adversely affected by this portable solution as it allows for the removal of resources from school which if identified are still covered by our premium.

WIRELESS CAPABILITY

This is an extremely important issue to resolve prior to any decision on laptop deployment being made. The Victorians built many schools which long ago served their purpose, but are still with us. The Victorian architects did not envisage the need to transmit electronic signals through walls: in fact quite the opposite – they designed their buildings so that noise would not pass from one room to another. Similarly in the 1950s and 1960s another post-war boom in building was witnessed in which a lot of steel was used within the beams of the buildings. This is an issue for whoever manages your site to look into before a decision is made. Important questions to ask are:

- **Can wireless signals be transmitted through the walls of your school?**
- **Is there interoperability between the base station and wireless cards?**
- **When you upgrade or replace the signal transmitters, often called 'ears', will your LAN cards be compatible?**
- **How many people at one time do you anticipate will need to simultaneously download multimedia through the wireless network and how large is its bandwidth? Will the available bandwidth cope with the demand?**
- **How secure will your data be due to the increased possible risk of hackers accessing it?**

Teaching tip

- *Find out if your placement school has wireless technology installed and if so how it is being used.*
- *What do you understand by the term 'bandwidth'?*
- *What are the issues that need to be addressed?*
- *Are these issues similar to the ones above?*

HEALTH AND SAFETY

A question that is of increasing concern to parents is: is there a significant health risk to the children? How safe is the technology when there is so much controversy about mobile phones and radio waves? What about carrying laptops – are they too heavy for children, particularly if they take them home in bags filled with books? The impact of health and safety and all its associated legal pitfalls is increasingly concentrating the minds of school leaders.

The Australians have led the field in mobile solutions to ICT problems and a very good source of information can be found at: **http://members.ozemail.com.au/~cumulus/ wireless.htm#Health**. This very useful website gives a lot of information about wireless solutions in schools but its author Keith Lightbody points out that research in Australia shows this solution to be far less dangerous than mobile phones. Wireless solutions have been used in children's hospitals from Perth in Australia, to Sheffield in the UK, where mobile phone technology is banned. However, he also points to Oak Park elementary school in Illinois, USA where parents have launched a class action lawsuit over concerns about wireless radiation. In early 2005 the UK government's advisory group on radiation safety – the National Radiological Protection Board – has recommended that children under the age of 12 should avoid regular and prolonged use of wireless technologies such as mobile phones (*BBC News*, 18 January, 2005).

Activity

Ask your friends, family and colleagues what they think about children using wireless technologies.

Do they express any concerns about health issues?

Do people's views differ depending on:

- *age?*
- *gender?*
- *their professional background?*

The highs

MATCHING PUPILS' EXPECTATIONS AND NEEDS

Without any doubt for me the most important point in this debate is that the favoured solution is educational, whereas the only problems, or 'Lows' are practical issues. Research around the world points to the advantages of using laptops for learning.

When visiting other primary schools I frequently ask head teachers that if their ICT suite is where they keep their computers then which room do they give over to the use of pencils and is there a room set aside for writing in books? This seemingly absurd line of questioning illustrates the entire point as fixed systems and ICT suites give young people the message that communications technology, which they know is wireless and portable in the real world, is not organised like this in school where it is static and fixed. The digital generation are prepared to put up with this, but when asked simply express disappointment that the way in which they need to use ICT is not reflected in the way schools are set up. This is just another step along the road to disenchantment and viewing schools as irrelevant to their futures. However, let's move from the philosophical to the practical.

INCLUSION AND BEHAVIOUR MANAGEMENT

Currently an overriding issue for many schools concerns the impact and management of disaffected children. Through non-attendance or exclusion these young people have often missed some of the vital building blocks of their learning. We all know that to succeed they are often in need of being supported with time-consuming repetitive self-correcting work and that computers can achieve this task well. However, the advantage we have found with laptops relates to some of the more subliminal messages. The technology can be taken to them wherever in the school they end up being supervised and, just as importantly, they know that they are being trusted with an expensive piece of equipment. Good behaviour policies are born from trust and respect, so laptops can help in a very practical way to reinforce this approach.

Time to reflect

Can you think of any other ways in which ICT tools might possibly be used to foster a sense of trust and responsibility in primary school children?

- *Reflect on your knowledge of young people and the way they interact with technology.*
- *Consider the effect of trusting a disaffected youngster with a laptop.*
- *Think of the benefits that constant repetition within a computer format can have for motivation.*
- *Decide whether you would prefer to listen to a teacher or do self-directed study in cyberspace.*

SPACE SAVING

One of the biggest issues in schools is the availability of space. This issue has been exacerbated in recent years with the introduction of a raft of support programmes like Early Learning Support (ELS), Additional Learning Support (ALS) and Springboard, all of which need a space for small groups to work in.

A wireless laptop solution enables teachers to bring all the children to one place for discrete ICT teaching, which in our school takes place over one and half days a week. These activities are conducted in a teaching area and, because there are no wires and plug-in problems, as soon as the children leave the room, it is available for other activity. We have converted part of the room into a children's kitchen area which also doubles as our breakfast club space. The room is also available for small-group work, other learning activities or perhaps a space for music and drama or special events/visitors. Such a situation could never have been achieved with a standard ICT suite. It enables school managers to tick the Ofsted box saying 'effective use of available space has been achieved'.

FLEXIBILITY, DEPLOYMENT AND CROSS-CURRICULAR USE

The biggest single problem with a fixed network, stack solution is the issue of taking the person to the solution rather than using the solution where it is needed. I have already referred to the increasing need young people have for portability. Within my school the children can work in their classrooms, the playground, the library or anywhere in the school that they need to access their files, server or the internet. This is rather like carrying a pencil around with them rather than going back to their class base, or 'pencil room', to fulfil their task. In our school we do not use a mouse either, this makes the system like a notebook – all children are able to do this, even infants, as it is all they know and therefore they have developed this skill naturally. Laptops combined with wireless technology can be configured in any way your teachers need. A group of two, four, six etc., a whole class, one child on their own, all these are options when you have the flexibility to move the kit to the problem in hand. This makes the use of ICT in learning a more natural and relevant activity, rather than learning bolted onto ICT in a special room.

The spin-off from this is that it is far more likely to be used in a cross-curricular way as the teachers and children can and do access all the benefits of the internet, their files and the server from wherever they need to be. The increasing emphasis on embedding ICT in the curriculum is easily achieved with a portable laptop solution. I see many ICT suites empty for large parts of the day owing to the literacy and numeracy strategies and the staffing issue relating to small groups needing to work at a separate base if they want to access ICT. How much more sensible to simply have the solution on hand so that the teacher and any support staff can work with the children in the same way they would if the child needed information from a book or help with their writing. This of course can extend to laptops going home. We have an ICT initiative in the school where individual children in classes are targeted as lead ICT pupils and get additional training so they can help staff in lesson time as well as move on their own learning. Because of our flexibility there is the option of allowing them to take home a laptop to develop their learning at home.

Time to reflect

- *How can you embed ICT in a cross-curricular approach from one room?*
- *In a world of mobile communications will young people of this and future generations want to come to school?*
- *Consider the layout of your placement school and the provision of the ICT suite – how well does it work?*
- *List three things that would need to be changed to improve it.*

Conclusion

So this is the challenge for our schools of the future: how can we ensure, in a creative, relevant and future-proof way, that ICT is embedded in the curriculum? How can we make sure that it reflects young people's expectations and ensures that we prepare the next generation for a world where significant information is being created without human involvement? Virtual worlds can be created and people are starting to make links with automated personalities to achieve their working goals. I feel that the flexible, portable solution of wireless laptop computing is the way ahead and best prepares the pupils in my school for this future. Are you able to say the same for your school?

SCHOOLS WITHOUT WALLS

Peter Hicks and Jonathan Bishop

Without the freedom to develop, we will simply cling on to the security of the past. Delivering an outdated curriculum, in an outmoded manner and confirming its 'success' by irrelevant assessment and inspection procedures.

Jim Smith

For this country to be able to compete successfully within the new order defined as globalisation securing our economic prosperity as well as the social cohesion necessary, schools have to do far more than simply improve literacy and numeracy skills; schools must develop and sustain a curriculum that is both broad, flexible and genuinely motivating; a curriculum that recognises the different talents of everyone.

Excellence for All, DfES White Paper

The challenge

There is a challenge facing all of us today. It is a challenge similar in magnitude to that which faced the education service at the beginning of the twentieth century. It is firstly to recognise the very particular and different circumstances that exist at the beginning of the twenty-first century and, secondly, to seize this opportunity to both recognise and value the obvious strengths that are to be found in the cultural, creative and human diversity of the people living in this country. In so doing, we shall promote the quality of our national life.

New technologies are providing unprecedented access to ideas, information, people and organisations throughout the world as well as to cultural exchange and under-standing, new ways of personal expression, new ways of getting things done and the removal of national boundaries. For the first time in human existence, the sum of human knowledge is but a key press away!

So do we really want our schools to go forward seeking to reflect the needs of our future and our pupils' futures still so grossly attached to a bygone time?

The importance of human capital

It is now recognised by all stakeholders that the key ingredient for success in this century in a globalising world is human capital – the relationship between one's perso-nal qualities and one's personal capabilities. Without human capital no other kind of capital is able to be productive. The positive and successful engagement of an indivi-dual's human capital with that of those around him is the sole factor that determines the greatness of a country. Our own futures, if they are to be secure, depend upon developing the personal qualities and capabilities of the pupils of today and it will be the sum of their human capital that will determine whether this country is one that is worth belonging to. Getting the most out of human capital means giving people access to genuine education – an education that:

- **reflects tomorrow's world rather than the hangover of the world of yesterday;**
- **is inclusive of all and presents all with success;**
- **empowers all pupils to develop aspirations for themselves and for others;**
- **enables schools to develop genuinely effective partnerships with a wide range of individuals and agencies to enrich the schools' provision.**

Developing the skills to uplift and support human capital is now fundamental to ensur-ing the success of our pupils. Without these skills, pupils will be placed at a great risk of being unable to participate, even at a low level, within the new order demanded of human capital. If a school limits the reinforcement, development and extension of these skills then teachers will actually educate out of pupils those key aspects of human capital that are necessary for developing the growth of opportunity for all.

Further, pupils will be entering a world that is very different from that which we entered. Not only must they be able to apply the skills from the 4 Rs (reading, 'riting, 'rithmetic and reasoning) in a variety of situations that demand their use but they also need to have developed those personal qualities – creativity, social adeptness, adaptability and empathy – that will make certain that they are able to work colla-boratively and successfully with all others in a 'target oriented' culture and in so doing, be of genuine value to themselves and to others. Academic ability alone is not able to guarantee success or, for that matter, personal achievement.

These critical demands require equally critical changes in the purposes of our schools and the roles of our teachers. Firstly, schools can no longer be seen as institutions – this is far too limiting and limited – schools are resources and very valuable resources at that. Schools are key resources for pupils and for their communities, responding to their learning needs, engaging as influencers of change, ensuring that individuals and communities adapt and move forward. It means that the school's 'footprint' is no longer limited by its physical boundaries but by its ability to respond to the needs of the school community and the wider community. Secondly, the role of teachers has changed – teachers are required now to be mediators and facilitators implementing a 'needs led' curriculum, one that is matched to the needs of the learner. In such a curriculum teachers have to devise and employ far more interesting and novel ways to encourage the pupil's active learning and involve the pupil's active participation.

Children bring with them a natural curiosity and a willingness to explore the new and unfamiliar. Sadly these qualities can so easily be suppressed in many classrooms and, when that has happened, learning ceases to be anything other than a series of disjointed and unenjoyable experiences that lack extension and rigour and have little bearing on 'real life'. Computers and ICT are essential elements of real life … now. ICT skills are essential core skills having parity of esteem within the 4Rs. Anyone who has a thought that these skills might be grafted on at a later date because pupils need to be taught the fundamentals is seriously missing the point. ICT skills are already now fundamental to an individual's success and in particular the success of all pupils in order that they can be assured of continuing educational progress. ICT is not a discrete subject but an all-pervasive core skill that should not be limited to a timetabled slot once or twice a week.

The reality for all schools is that the core skills – the 4Rs with ICT – are the means through which access to all other subjects is made possible, practicable and successful and through which a broad and balanced curriculum flourishes. What is increasingly becoming important is that the school curriculum must be broad, balanced and, most importantly, responsive to the individual needs of each child. Assessment to facilitate individualised learning is the key factor.

Individualised learning is at the heart of an ICT strategy. Such a strategy will use technology as an integral part of both teaching and learning not only within the school but within the pupil's home too. Schools need to be determined to put the very latest technology at the disposal of learners employing robust networked systems providing children with the use of a PC on a day-to-day basis in almost all activities.

Activity

Find out how ICT is being used in your own placement school. Questions you ask might include:

- *If you have a networked system what kind is it?*
- *Who looks after the computer network?*
- *Is whole-group teaching performed with ICT as a resource?*
- *How interactive are the ICT-based lessons?*

Schools without walls

There are already those which we describe here as 'schools without walls'. Although there are not many when seen as a proportion of the total number of schools in England and Wales, they do however hold an influential position, for they are setting out a new model for education – one that is exciting and dynamic, one that employs successfully the medium of the age and one that delivers excellence for all. They are transforming the way that schools operate; they are seeking to develop and extend opportunities for everyone in embracing the development of human capital and, in so doing, they are creating new models of teaching and learning. These schools understand how necessary it is to move forward from the traditional ways of doing things to new ways that are being made possible by employing ICT in order that a future for our pupils, for us and for this country can be secured. These schools already appreciate the need for their communities to become e-confident, the need to integrate teachers, pupils, parents and the community into a truly connected learning environment with the school at its heart. What we describe below is one such school. This school is a primary school with a roll of 350 pupils and a genuinely fully comprehensive intake.

This 'school without walls' has learners, teachers and teaching assistants. It is a truly dynamic place where natural curiosity abounds and learning is an enjoyable and valued experience involving intellectual rigour and extension. This learning has a real bearing on real life and is centred on bringing about opportunities for each and every child, whatever their innate capabilities, to reach out and to aspire to the highest ideals with the professional support and determination of teachers.

The teaching staff in this 'school without walls' are respected and recognised not because of their position but by their substance, how they are able to lift up their pupils, by the capabilities that abound within and around them ... their energy, their excitement about learning and their genuine engagement with their pupils.

Assessment cannot be separated from teaching and learning

All assessment work, planning, target setting and measurement completed by staff in the 'schools without walls' is done online at **www.online-assessments.co.uk** which is described as 'the defining outcome of QCA's NC (National Curriculum) in Action website (**www.ncaction.org.uk**)'. This key assessment site provides every pupil with an individual learning plan (ILP) and enables staff to know the learning gains of each pupil within each aspect of each core subject. Staff are able to track individual pupils' performances as well as their achievement and are able to do so in a professional, immediate and obvious way without having to extend the teachers' workload. In fact each teacher knows with precision where each pupil is with respect to their performance and achievement, where they have to be at the end of three terms and importantly, how to get them there. This aspect of the professional work of the teacher within the 'school without walls' has given back to teachers the time to do what they do best – teach.

'Schools without walls' employ an educational process that uses the acquisition, development and extension of ICT skills in an all pervasive way throughout the whole of the school's curriculum. This process does not rely on the make of PC but on sound educational philosophy and practice. The 'school without walls' does not have ICT lessons since ICT is a generic skill just like reading and writing and is seen simply as a tool and not as a discrete subject. It is understood and practised as being inclusive; bringing all people irrespective of their colour, creed, gender, learning needs or socio-economic classification together in task-orientated educative scenarios working purposely and collaboratively towards agreed and established educational goals. This process is inclusive of all and should we as teachers deny the actuality of inclusion within our schools we shall be seen and rightly so, as lacking that level of humanity that we are required daily to demonstrate in order that our society may be a decent society, one that is just, caring, compassionate, cohesive and committed to giving every pupil whatever their background the chance to be successful and to be the very best that they can be.

All children within the 'schools without walls' have their own e-mail addresses, their own web pages and their own file space and every one of them accesses the world wide web throughout the day. All pupils have direct and immediate access to a personal computer and are taught in a fully interactive, multimedia environment complete with image projection and theatre-style surround sound. In these 'schools without walls', ICT skills are one of the many ways in which reading and writing are reinforced, developed and extended. Within such an educative environment a broad and balanced curriculum flourishes well meeting the demands of today and the needs of tomorrow.

Activity

Talk to the senior staff in your placement school and find out what they consider to be:

- *the demands of society;*
- *the needs of tomorrow.*

How do they think the current curriculum meets these demands and needs? Do they think that ICT plays an important role?

'Schools without walls' provide:

- **individualised learning programmes (ILPs);**
- **a curriculum planned and managed to meet the needs of the individual;**
- **each learner and teacher with their own web space to share and collaborate;**
- **a range of communication and organisational tools;**
- **team collaboration;**
- **document sharing and document tracking;**
- **a teacher as both mediator and facilitator;**

- **extensive open-ended activities matched to the individual's learning needs – a needs-led curriculum;**
- **effective group work set within task-oriented situations.**

Teachers assess learning as a part of professional practice (see Figure 10.1) and ILPs play a central role in the process. ILPs are needed for a number of reasons: for the teacher to know where each pupil is with respect to their performance and achievement; for the teacher to know where each pupil must be at the end of three terms; for the teacher to know how to get them there – in fact an individual learning plan for each and every child. For everyone would agree that the performance and achievement of learners are, by definition, going to be along a continuum (see Figure 10.2).

Figure 10.1: A teacher makes an assessment as part of her daily professional work

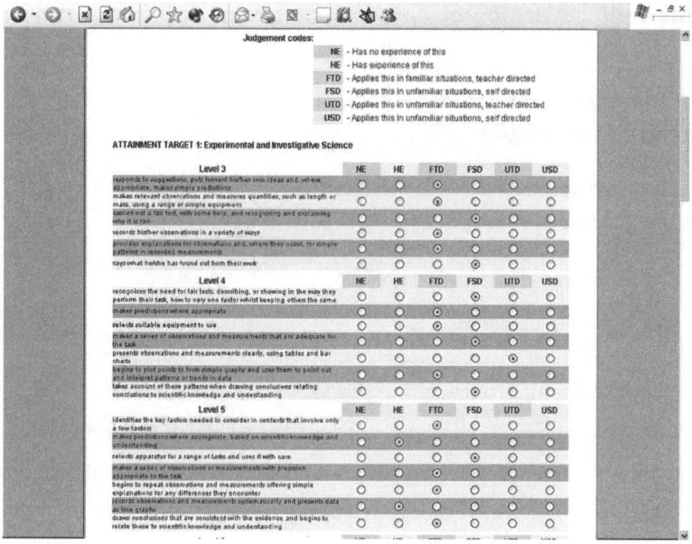

Figure 10.2: Making an assessment using online assessments (**www.online-assessments.co.uk**)
Note that the quality of a pupil's performance is professionally judged against the criteria
from 'no experience' to 'is able to apply in an unfamiliar situation self directed'.

Assessment linked directly to planning

To be able to assess a pupil's performance matched to each aspect of the intended learning outcome (the curriculum) and for that assessment to be linked directly to planning is one of the critical elements of good professional practice. In such a way, each learner will have an ILP – see Figure 10.3 – which becomes a component in the process of the individual learning cycle (see Figure 10.4).

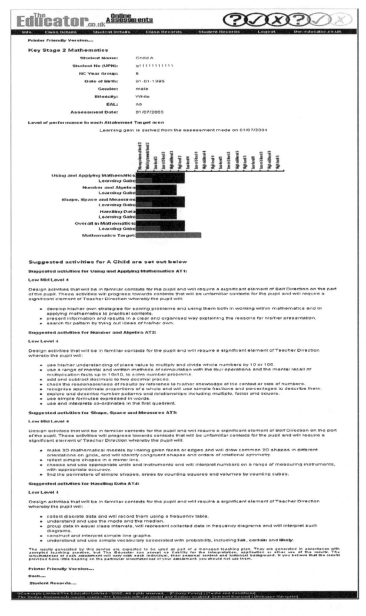

Figure 10.3: A pupil's ILP – this is returned to the teacher immediately after he or she has made an assessment

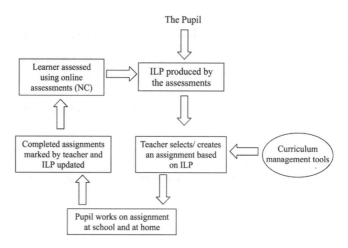

Figure 10.4: Individual learning cycle

Effective assessment practice in these 'schools without walls' is linked to both clarity about its purpose and 'standardisation' of the teachers' professional judgements. This 'standardisation' or professional understanding is founded upon the consistent inter-pretation of clear and agreed criteria. The quality of assessment quite naturally will depend upon the quality of evidence upon which it is based. In turn this evidence will depend upon the knowledge and the skills of the teacher. Assessment forms the basis for determining both future teaching and learning and therefore must link directly to planning. Integration of assessment and planning requires knowledge of the pupil and knowledge of aspects of the curriculum upon which evidence about the child's capabil-ities is sought. When this is done the educative opportunities to uplift, develop and support human capital are ensured as is the success of each pupil.

The analysis of data specific to the performance and achievement of the pupil is central and a key aspect of assessment. The analysis must be immediate − how else is one able to ensure professionally the continuing and progressive success of the learner? It is especially important that the school is able to note trends and patterns early. In this way, the teacher is able to develop both teaching strategies and curriculum inten-tions that will genuinely be in support of each pupil's learning. Further, by having such essential analysis at hand, the school is able to respond directly to parents in a much more informed way.

The 'school without walls' − the e-learning environment

E-learning has the power to transform the way we learn, bringing high quality, accessi-ble learning to everyone − ensuring that every learner is more likely to achieve his or her full potential, not merely gaining a proficiency. Young people quite rightly now expect to use leading-edge technologies at school as well as at home. These are the skills we increasingly need for everyday life and work. E-competence is an essential element of real life.

The school uses ICT in the following contexts:

- 'Schools without walls' are at the centre of e-confident communities where classrooms are without boundaries, where learning is truly valued and ripples out from these key centres through the community. Where pupils continue with their schoolwork even when away from the school, computers at home are connected to the school's extranet system.
- Pupils have access to their e-mails, communication tools and files from home.
- Pupils have access to all the teaching staff and their expertise from outside school.
- Work is assigned and resources are made available.
- Other agencies are readily accessible (extended schools).

The curriculum of the future:

- reflects tomorrow's world;
- ensures that all pupils are included;
- ensures that all children are empowered and become independent learners;
- enables schools to develop effective partnerships;
- requires more than academic ability on the part of all pupils.

What technology does a 'school without walls' need (managing the technology)?

- The school needs to set up a Learning Gateway.

In order to do this:

- the school requires a Windows 2003 file server;
- the school requires an Exchange mail server 2003;
- the school requires access to secure online teacher assessment services;
- the school needs to create an e-learning environment;
- the school requires a Microsoft ISA server;
- the school requires SharePoint portal services;
- the school requires a live communications server;
- ideally the school requires a media streaming capability.

This means that:

- the school can create a curriculum that is planned and managed to meet the pupil's individual needs;
- each child and teacher can have their own web space to share and collaborate;
- the school will now have a range of communication and organisational tools;
- team collaboration will be possible;
- document sharing and document tracking is an available service;
- online discussion forums can take place.

Using ICT to develop creative thinkers requires:

- **the teacher to be both a mediator and facilitator;**
- **the use of extensive open-ended activities matched to individual needs;**
- **effective group work in task-oriented situations.**

The real beauty of the 'school without walls' system is the way in which all pupils are encouraged to collaborate and structure their learning within the e-learning environment. This is made possible through the software the teachers use. Schoolwork is assigned using Microsoft *Class Server*, distributed and collected automatically. This software enables pupils and parents to view all the year's submitted work at a glance along with current projects. The work can then be displayed on the whiteboard and discussed with the whole class. It allows teachers to manage the vast amount of innovative content aligned to the National Curriculum plus interactive content including clips and video, web material and material from an ever-increasing number of educational publishers, and combines the child's ongoing school work as web-based activities, linked directly to online teacher assessment provided at **www.online-assessments.co.uk**. This secure online teacher assessment tool gives an accurate indication (NC level) of the pupil's performance, their achievement and provides assessment data and data analysis as well as those critical targets.

The learning gain of every pupil is known and an individual education plan for that pupil is produced, allowing both school and parent to monitor their child's progress through the National Curriculum. Microsoft *Class Server* enables each pupil to be working on a different subject at their own pace. Microsoft's *Class Server* along with Microsoft's SharePoint Services create the key elements for the Learning Gateway which, with the online assessment service, provide pupils with ownership of their own learning, actively encourages collaborative working and provides the opportunity to be successful regardless of learning ability. By utilising modern technology in this way, our pupil's learning is not only stimulated but we are now truly a 'school without walls'.

All pupils within this 'school without walls' environment have a personal e-mail address and access to the internet throughout the school day. The vision and the actuality is one of complete inclusion – in particular ensuring that all pupils and families benefit from the technology and learning revolution, regardless of family income. This has helped pupils of all ability ranges, including those classified as having severe emotional and behavioural difficulties (EBD), to develop their communication skills, and has impacted on motivation.

Activity

Find out how the e-mail system works in your own placement school.

- *Are children given their own personal e-mail accounts?*
- *What is the teaching staff's attitude to this idea?*
- *What policies and rules are in place?*
- *What constraints are there to the school's e-mail system?*

Home school learning

The 'school without walls' established the first genuine Home School Learning link. This meant that it became the first school in England to link together learning in schools and learning in homes. Parents can gain access to their child's assignments including upcoming work and teachers manage homework, projects and the National Curriculum in a secure online environment. The Home School Learning environment or portal was developed to promote, among other things, greater home–school collaboration. Home and school learning brings home and school together enabling parents to be directly involved with their son or daughter's learning in a genuine partnership that provides learners with continuing and progressive success. Each child accesses their work, e-mail and organisational tools from home and taps into resources that are made available by the school at any time of the day or night. Consequently, children are more directly involved in their own learning and, with the support and direct involvement of parents, 'schools without walls' is providing successful schooling for the twenty-first century and beyond.

Home School Learning is a national pilot for similar schemes around the country (see Figure 10.5 for the project's home page). When children are ill, on holiday or they just want to touch base with their everyday tools available at school, it's all there at the click of a button from anywhere in the world, including library access. As well as making it easier for the pupils to access information and to work collaboratively with others, it contributes enormously to parents' opportunities to add to the life of the school. All the family can now be directly involved in their child's learning, enabling them to continue to play a truly valuable part in the education process.

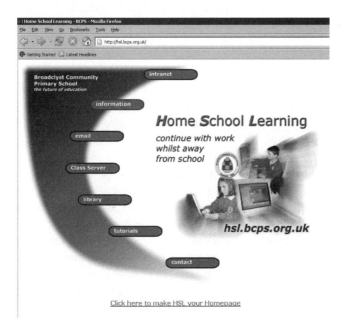

Figure 10.5: The front page of the Home School Learning link

Creative action

We all learn best when the learning situation is novel, interesting, highly motivational, open-ended, collaborative, and related directly to real life. These learning situations abound within the 'school without walls' and in such situations we are fully engaged, excited by the learning taking place, willing to 'have a go', able to apply knowledge and skill from different areas of endeavour and positive in our outlook. In fact, in such an environment children become very successful learners.

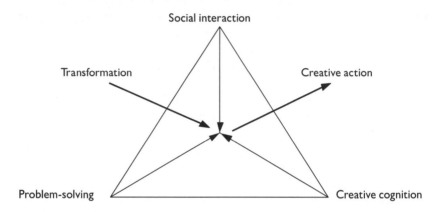

Figure 10.6: Creative Cognition Model (Wheeler, Waite & Bromfield, 2002)

A lot of this success will depend upon the transformative power of creativity in learning – creative action which, according to the model offered by Wheeler, Waite and Bromfield (2001), derives from a combination of social interaction, problem-solving and creative thinking (Figure 10.6).

Wheeler *et al.* state that this does not necessarily occur naturally, but that *encouraging creativity in the classroom is primarily the task of the teacher. Harnessing the power of divergent thought and marrying this with the power of ICT will be the aim of many teachers who espouse the use of computers in the classroom.* (Wheeler, Waite and Bromfield, 2001)

In a 'school without walls' neither learning nor success is rationed. At the start of this new millennium, our attention was drawn to what a decent society should be. Teachers have a prime responsibility to focus upon, support and lead in developing those attributes and qualities that ensure that a society and, in particular our society, is just, caring, compassionate, cohesive and committed to giving every pupil, whatever their background, the chance to be successful. This wholesome support and positive development of human capital brings with it a release of tension and distress because people become of genuine value to themselves and therefore to each other and a country's hopes and aspirations are able to openly prosper.

11 ICT IN THE GLOBAL CLASSROOM
MICHELLE SELINGER

> *From the standpoint of the child, the great waste in school comes from his inability to utilise the experience he gets outside while on the other hand he is unable to apply in daily life what he is learning in school. That is the isolation of the school — its isolation from life.*
>
> John Dewey (1916)

Introduction and background

Many schools are increasingly becoming divorced from the reality of life in the Information Age in which technology has become ubiquitous. The quotation above from John Dewey was written in 1916 and in 2005 it is even truer than it was then.

A colleague and I were writing a paper about the disconnect between pupils' lives in and out of school. It was never completed but it started like this:

My 16-year-old daughter lives in a networked, digitised collaborative world. She takes it for granted and feels comfortable in it. Before she enters and from the moment she leaves the school gates she is connected by SMS and mobile voice to her network of friends and family. From the moment she arrives home (or, more often, somebody else's home) she is *googling*, instant messaging, chatting and e-mailing her way through a worldwide network of friends and information. Her immediate group of friends have designed their own portal where they share homework tips, poems, pictures, thoughts and worries as well as apparently endless chat. If she needs someone to join her in the portal, she texts them. If she needs pictures she goes into her personal photo portal. If she needs information she goes on the web. She and her friends live in their own autonomous, ever-changing, connected republic.

From the moment she walks through the gates of her excellent London state school, all this stops. She attends a school where her teachers live in a paper-based, repetitive, task-based individualistic world. They write things on a board and hand out bits of paper. They send me letters all the time. They do not have e-mail addresses except for one or two individual hotmail addresses. They do not reproduce or share lesson plans and outlines. They do not give access to information, homework, tips, references, timetables on line. They do not collaborate with each other or encourage their students to collaborate. They do not give help and guidance in navigating the digital information world. They do not enrich their lessons with multimedia. They have a few computers in the school library where students are allowed to use *PowerPoint*. This break in the learning day allows them to catch up on the apparently endless flow of paper-based administrative tasks, pointless marking, register reconciliation, scheduling, budgeting and so on ad infinitum. If they are particularly good at teaching they are promoted into positions where they are allowed to do less of it so they can focus more on timetables and budgets. They live in a disconnected autocracy that has remained virtually unchanged since the nineteenth century.

Children in the UK are increasingly asked to leave their lives outside the school gates and enter a society where access to technology is piecemeal at best and almost non-existent at its worst. Yet the power of ICT has the ability to bring the world closer to the school and for learners to engage in real communication with a world that includes but goes far beyond their local community. We have at our fingertips the tools that unlock the potential to communicate immediately with parents, the local community, the rest of the UK and the world at the drop of a hat. Every classroom can have a telephone and video conferencing at little or no extra cost providing there is comprehensive broadband coverage in the school and the community at large.

This chapter aims to encourage you to think about the world as a global classroom. You will:

- **learn about how other countries use ICT in primary education;**
- **learn about and explore the benefits of school twinning and collaboration across the world;**
- **learn how cultural traditions have implications for the way children learn and how they respond to you as a teacher;**
- **become more aware of the cultural differences between children in the classes you will teach;**
- **discover how ICT can celebrate differences and allow you to plan relevant learning experiences for each child;**
- **consider the range of learning resources available from international websites and how they might be exploited to provide a rich source of teaching and learning materials.**

Teaching and learning with ICT across Europe and Australia

In this book you will have explored ICT policies and practice in the UK, but how do these compare to policies in other countries? The developed world is technology-rich and the ratio of pupils to computers is low. In all EU countries, one or more national or public bodies are responsible for implementing or promoting official ICT-related initiatives. Their tasks include:

- **defining the objectives to be pursued;**
- **organising continuous professional development for teachers;**

- developing new software and multimedia support;

- monitoring and coordinating the various ICT and education initiatives;

- responsibility for the application of the decisions taken and the agreements concluded.

This role is usually assigned to a Ministry of Education or the highest decision-making authority in education matters. However, in over half of the EU countries there is at least one additional official body which takes co-responsibility. In most cases, this is either a body for coordinating educational activities in general terms or specifically put in place for ICT or a higher education institution. In the UK this is the role of the British Educational and Communications Technology Agency (BECTa). Sweden is the only country where there is an official body to manage all ICT-related matters independent of the ministry (Eurydice, 2004, p. 19).

ICT is part of the compulsory minimum curriculum for primary education in most European countries, except in Italy, Bulgaria, the Czech Republic, Latvia, Lithuania, Hungary and Slovakia. When ICT is included in the core curriculum, two main approaches can be distinguished. It may be taught as a separate subject in its own right or used as a tool for other subjects – in some cases both. The most widespread approach is the use of ICT as a tool. Apart from the UK (with the exception of Northern Ireland), ICT is a separate compulsory subject in the Netherlands, Iceland and Poland. In Romania, it is included in the curriculum solely as a subject in its own right (Eurydice, 2004, p. 20).

Whatever the approach advocated, the teaching and use of ICT in primary schools tends to cover these five areas:

1. The use of software
2. Information searches
3. Communication via a network
4. The use of ICT to enhance subject knowledge
5. The development of basic programming skills.

With the exception of Belgium (the Flemish community), Spain and Luxembourg in which no objective is clearly specified, the recommendations generally cover the first four areas. Only a few countries (Germany, Greece, the UK and Romania) include the development of programming ability in the primary curriculum (Eurydice, 2004, p. 23).

The central authorities are rarely solely responsible for the purchase and maintenance of hardware. In most European countries, these responsibilities are either assumed solely at the local level and/or by the school, or they are shared by different authorities, depending on the level of education (Austria and Portugal) or type of expenditure concerned (purchase of hardware or software, or equipment maintenance) (Eurydice, 2004, p. 29).

In the majority of countries there are no central recommendations specifying the number of pupils per computer or the number of computers per school. Schools or local authorities decide on their own investment scheme based on their priorities and specific needs. Hungary and Poland have specified that there should be at least one computer lab in each school, irrespective of the number of pupils enrolled. The situation is changing though. For example, Greece, Portugal and Lithuania have established official objectives for reducing the number of pupils per computer. Most countries have higher pupil-to-computer ratios in primary schools than in secondary schools, while Nordic countries have more computers for school children than the rest of Europe.

In the rest of the world the situation is similar, gross domestic product being a significant factor in the uptake of computers in schools and in the home. In Australia at the federal level, the government seeks to achieve two school education goals for the information economy:

1. All pupils will leave school as 'confident, creative and productive users of new technologies, particularly information and communications technologies, and understand the impact of those technologies on society.' (MCEETYA, 2002, ch. 9).

2. All schools will seek to integrate ICT into their operations, to improve pupil learning, to offer flexible learning opportunities and to improve the efficiency of their business applications.

The Victoria government in Australia has a *Curriculum and Standards Framework*, developed by the Victorian Curriculum and Assessment Authority (**www.vcaa.vic. edu.au**) which identifies what children should know and be able to do in the eight key learning areas from Preparatory Year to Year 10. Within these key learning areas, the major knowledge and skills are arranged into strands: within the Technology Key Learning Area there are three strands – Information, Materials and Systems.

At each level for each strand, the major content is identified in the curriculum focus, and the standards that children are expected to demonstrate are identified in the learning outcomes, for which indicators are provided to inform teachers of the evidence they should look for in learner performance.

You might like to compare these standards with the UK National Curriculum Standards for ICT and think about the similarities and differences and what you can learn from making such comparisons and how they develop your ideas about teaching and learning with technology.

Learning from others

A number of organisations like UNESCO and the OECD encourage the sharing of practice between countries. They organise seminars and publish papers, reports and guidance for all aspects of education, including the use of ICT, which can be referenced from their websites (**www.unesco.org**, **www.oecd.org**). Imfundo: Partnership for IT in Education, based at the UK Department for International Development

(DFID), focused in particular on ICT for educational development in developing countries (**www.imfundo.org**). The Global eSchools and Communities Initiative (GeSCI) is a new organisation whose aim is to 'attempt to transform today's pilot efforts for ICT education into a comprehensive and efficient model carried out by strong partnerships'. GeSCI believes that, by employing such models, ICT solutions could be delivered at costs that are potentially five to ten times less expensive than current approaches. This new global initiative is an independent organisation created to stimulate and support national and regional e-school initiatives. It was created by the United Nations ICT Task Force, whose founding members are Sweden, Ireland, Canada and Switzerland.

The distinctive feature of GeSCI is that it does not limit its impact to improving education through the use of ICT. It goes further and aims to use the strengthened education infrastructure to empower local communities, by facilitating their access to global and local information and knowledge.

One of the models that GeSCI is basing its developments on is the Jordan Education Initiative (see Cubeisy and Cox, 2004). Under the auspices of the World Economic Forum, the Jordan Education Initiative brings together the IT and telecoms industries with local IT companies and the Government of Jordan with the intention of accelerating education reform in the Kingdom. Jordan has already committed to reforming its education system. Under the government's Educational Reform for a Knowledge Economy (ERfKE), the Ministry of Education is following as part of its learning development agenda a programme of curriculum reform, teacher training, the use of ICT as an enabler to learning and the upgrading of schools' IT infrastructure. The Jordan Education Initiative is an attempt to complement and accelerate the implementation of the Ministry of Education's current reform strategy. The project also provides an opportunity for the sustainable development of Jordan's emerging information technology industry.

The Jordan Education Initiative is designed to serve as a model of effective ICT-enabled learning that can be replicated and implemented across Jordan, as well as in other countries in the region. The programme is built around three areas of focus or 'tracks'. Each track is further subdivided into multiple work streams.

Track One focuses on the 100 Discovery Schools and falls under the larger theme of 'enabling the act of discovering' for pupils and teachers alike. Track One aims to introduce new approaches to learning that are conducive to acquiring the skills necessary for the twenty-first-century knowledge economy. It will also demonstrate how the partnering firms work together and share in each other's experiences to develop strategies and solutions that contribute to a cooperative environment. There are three strands in this track: the development of e-curricula; the implementation of in-classroom technology; and teacher training. The aim of the e-curricula development is to support the integration of ICT into teaching and learning and to use the teaching notes embedded in the content to help teachers develop an understanding of the need for greater learner engagement and autonomy in learning and to change their pedagogy to support this approach. Track Two focuses on lifelong learning and Track Three on the development of the IT industry.

After the first 18 months of this Initiative 13 schools are equipped with a maths lab, teachers have been given the exclusive use of a laptop and data projector, and they are teaching Mathematics Online, the first of several e-curricula in development or planned, each funded by one of the partners. Mathematics Online is funded by Cisco and developed in collaboration between the Cisco Learning Institute Rubicon, a local Jordanian company and 30 teachers who were released from their duties by the Ministry of Education for a period of one year. They were trained by Jordanian, US and British experts in the development of e-content and in new teaching approaches consistent with equipping children with the skills needed in a Knowledge Society. The resulting curriculum provides a whole course of study for grades 1 to 12 in Jordanian primary and secondary schools and includes teacher notes, media, worksheets, independent study materials and media to be worked in whole-class situations. The professional development materials are closely linked to the curriculum resources and support teachers in engaging learners more actively in their learning.

By using the skills of the developed world, Jordanian curriculum development and pedagogical change has been accelerated while the partnership with local teachers and media development experts ensures that it has been able to maintain the norms and practices and led change through the appropriate cultural channels. The importance of cultural relevance cannot be underestimated and we shall return to this theme later in the chapter.

The model that GeSCI is planning is to take the products and knowledge about education partnerships acquired in Jordan and find ways to use them in other countries. The e-curricula being developed have global relevance (mathematics, science, ICT, Arabic, English as a second language) and therefore the Jordanian resources can be adapted at a relatively lower cost by local experts in each country to ensure their relevance and to fit them to their country's requirements. The expertise gained around educational reform processes can also be used to ensure that the reform can be achieved more efficiently and effectively as the lessons learned from hindsight are applied.

The UK did not have such benefits as it was a pioneer in ICT for education which in turn has brought its own successes and failures. It may be the fact that the use of ICT in the 1980s and 1990s was fraught with problems and the teacher training needs were not adequately addressed that led Ulf Lundin to comment that UK teachers are the most reluctant across Europe to use ICT in their teaching (Lundin, 2004, p. 137).

European Schoolnet

Ulf Lundin is the Director of the European Schoolnet (EUN) which is an international partnership of more than 26 European Ministries of Education developing learning for schools, teachers and pupils across Europe. EUN provides insights into the use of ICT in Europe for policy-makers and teachers. EUN offers communication and information exchange across primary and secondary schools and acts as a gateway to national and regional school networks.

The EUN is reached through the European portal (**www.eun.org**). Through eSchoolnet, the portal offers teachers resources, discussions, news, classroom activities, collaborative tools, practice examples and training opportunities.

Teachers can also benefit from European Schoolnet's numerous pan-European communities and networks. These include:

- **Virtual School which provides online learning resources, tips and activities in curriculum subjects;**
- **myEUROPE which organises regular activities for schools with an interest in European citizenship, mobility, cultural diversity and trans-European collaboration;**
- **Comenius Space which supports thousands of schools involved in the EU's COMENIUS programme;**
- **School Managers Centre which encourages sharing experience in school leadership;**
- **eSchola which celebrates use of ICT and recognises outstanding examples of practice via the eLearning awards;**
- **ENIS – the European Network of Innovative Schools – which links front-running establishments to share practice and test new learning technologies.**

The European Schoolnet Community Environment enables anyone to create online communities via a rich set of tools including chat, bulletin boards, file-sharing and web publishing.

EUN has recently launched the new myEUROPE website. This website is a practical tool for teachers to better support European citizenship and to raise children's awareness of European issues, by sharing knowledge within the teacher network. The website hosts a wealth of educational projects, activities and resources, providing features such as activity contributions, photographs, practice ideas and the partner finding tool, which offer the best opportunity to bring Europe alive to the young citizens of today and engender a community spirit (see **http://myeurope.eun. org/ ww/en/pub/myeurope/home.htm**).

Since its launch by EUN in May 2000, this project has focused on European citizenship and intercultural education through online activities and classroom practice examples. myEUROPE has become one of the largest school networks in Europe and has encouraged contacts between schools, teachers and pupils from European member states and beyond, by involving children in collaborative educational projects.

E-twinning: learning with and about others

Collaboration between schools has become far more common as the technology has facilitated speedy communications. Early twinning programs relied on letters, photographs and faxes. The post took time and continuity and relevance was difficult, if not impossible, to maintain. The advent of ICT with the possibilities of instant messaging, e-mail, video and telephone conferencing, digital images and websites has meant that the timescale between exchanges can be negligible and whole schemes of work can be built around such exchanges. This has become known as e-twinning.

Elizabeth Holmes (2003) offers this advice about e-twinning:

> Basically, you can make as much or as little as you want to out of twinning. The essential thing is to keep an eye on the opportunities it provides for covering elements of the curriculum, and the more you look into this, the more that opportunities reveal themselves. Over time, your school may even get into holiday exchanges (perhaps even home swaps between teachers as an inexpensive holiday) and much more ...

What can you hope to achieve?

The list of benefits of twinning is endless; the most common are included below:

- **It allows for an easy route for exchanging ideas, research and teaching techniques.**
- **Teachers can share best practice and trends in teaching pedagogy in their home countries.**
- **Pupils and staff can exchange experiences, culture and heritage. This can give them a more intense understanding of the needs of others as well as a wider perspective on global issues.**
- **Communication between pupils can enhance the use of communications technology.**
- **Teachers themselves could take part in teacher exchanges, therefore being able to enrich their work in the classroom by drawing on the learning programmes and curricula in partner schools.**
- **It may be possible to facilitate language development.**
- **It may be possible to work simultaneously on the same project so that children can learn together and even discuss what they have learned through video conferencing**
- **Jointly recognised festivals and events can be celebrated together. Pupils can teach each other about those which are not mutually celebrated.**
- **If you are twinning with a school in a developing area, you can use it as a focus for fundraising or other such support.**
- **Twinning with more than one school can facilitate multilateral interaction between all schools involved. (Holmes, 2003).**

The ICT tools for e-twinning can be synchronous like video and audio conferencing and instant messaging or asynchronous like e-mail, discussion boards and project environments. Additionally schools can develop web pages where they can post digital images of themselves using password-protected sites to more open sites where they can post and share images of their society and culture. None of these solutions need be expensive since as long as bandwidth is available there are a number of free resources such as Skype and video conferencing using tools such as iSight and MSN Messenger instant messaging. Of course these open environments can cause concerns about inappropriate people joining the conversations, but as long as pupils are supervised and made aware of the potential dangers, then there is no reason why they should not use these tools. After all they will be using them at home and often unsupervised. We have to allow children to bring their culture into the classroom, as discussed at the beginning of this chapter, if we are going to ensure schools remain meaningful and relevant learning places.

The EU has a fund called COMENIUS aimed at promoting partnerships between European schools. I interviewed a teacher who has been involved in such a project between three schools – one in the UK, one in Germany and one in Norway. Apart from a teacher exchange, where a greater understanding of differences and similarities between schools and education systems was gained, the schools encouraged children to collaborate in story writing. Each of the teachers involved got their pupils to write the beginning of a story. These beginnings were then e-mailed to a school in another country who wrote the middle and then forwarded the stories for completion by the third. The finished stories, each composed by the children of three countries, were published in a book on the internet.

There are several global e-twinning projects you can join. In January 2005 the EUN launched a new e-twinning project to develop and reinforce networking and learning among schools, to nurture a multilingual and multicultural society (**www.etwinning. net**).

iEARN (**www.iearn.org**) is the world's largest non-profit global network that enables young people to use the internet and other new technologies to engage in collaborative educational projects that both enhance learning and make a difference in the world. Its most famous project is the Teddy Bear project whose aim is to foster tolerance and understanding of other cultures. After teachers register, the facilitator matches the class with a partner. The classes send each other a Teddy Bear or other soft toy by airmail through the normal postal system. The bear sends home diary messages by e-mail at least once a week. The children write the diary messages as if they are the visiting bear describing its experiences in the new culture. This project provides opportunities for authentic writing by providing the children with a real audience and a reason to write.

Authentic writing has many merits. Selinger *et al*. (1998) found that when students used e-mail to write to other students in their own country or internationally they took far more care composing their messages, checking their grammar, spelling and meaning before sending their e-mail key. Primary teachers reported that the quality of pupils' writing was far superior to their normal class work when they wrote for their teacher. Authentic activity like this encourages learners to make more effort and take more care.

World Links (**www.world-links.org**) is a US-based teacher training programme focused on teaching teachers how to use ICT in education with a focus on the use of the internet in developing countries. Once teachers are trained they encourage them to twin with schools in the developed world.

Science Across the World (SAW) is a subject-specific site offering children and teachers in primary and secondary schools the opportunity to exchange information, opinions and ideas on a variety of science topics (**www.scienceacross.org**). The topics selected are well researched for their global relevance and significance and encourage scientific enquiry. SAW aims to go beyond fact finding: *it explicitly explores science in its social context and that makes for interesting exchanges of information, ideas and opinions between students from different countries.* (Cutler, 2004, p. 33).

Two of SAW's topics cover the primary age range from the age of 8 – Eating and Drinking and Renewable Energy, and a third, Road Safety, is aimed at the ages of 10 plus. For the Eating and Drinking topic, younger children, *survey the food they eat during a typical school day, investigate the role of labelling from foods in their kitchen cupboards and analyse different advertisements for food.* (Cutler, 2004, p. 35). After background research pupils are encouraged to discuss and debate their findings and are further encouraged to take positive action as a result of their research. Once the initial research has been undertaken schools each complete an Exchange Form and post it on the website. They can then select schools from an online database working on the same topic and with similar age students. They have their research findings as the basis for discussion so providing a real purpose for exchange, and the website itself suggests further ideas for discussion.

Links to UK education policy

E-twinning contributes to the citizenship agenda at Key Stage 1 and 2, Unit 5 'Living in a diverse world', which currently states:

> *In this unit, children learn about their identities and communities and about different places in the world. Through a range of activities, they explore sameness, difference and diversity. They learn that, as humans, we are all equal, have basic needs and rights, and belong to a range of groups and communities, including school and family. Children learn about the importance of respecting each other, and that it is wrong to abuse people for any reason, including their race. Through a theme such as toys or clothes, they explore what other places are like and how we are connected with different countries in the world (interdependence). At the end of the unit, children have the opportunity to reflect on what they have learnt and to share their ideas with others in the school community. (DfES, 2004f)*

The DfES are very keen to promote international understanding and to prepare young people and adults for life in a global society and work in a global economy (DfES, 2004g). The first two goals are relevant to primary education:

1. To instil a strong global dimension into the learning experience of all children and young people.

2. To transform our capability to speak and use other languages.   (para. 7)

Another goal is to instil a global dimension into the learning experience of all children and young people. The view is that as we live in a global society we need an understanding of eight key concepts:

1. *Citizenship* – gaining the knowledge, skills and understanding of concepts and institutions necessary to become informed, active, responsible global citizens.

2. *Social Justice* – the importance of social justice as an element in both sustainable development and the improved welfare of all people.

3. *Sustainable development* – understanding the need to maintain and improve the quality of life now without damaging the planet for future generations.

4. *Diversity* – understanding and respecting differences, and relating these to our common humanity.

5. *Values and perceptions* – developing a critical evaluation of images of other parts of the world and an appreciation of the effect these have on people's attitudes and values.

6. *Interdependence* – understanding how people, places, economies and environments are all inextricably interrelated, and that events have repercussions on a global scale.

7. *Conflict resolution* – understanding how conflicts are a barrier to development and why there is a need for their resolution and the promotion of harmony.

8. *Human rights* – knowing about human rights and, in particular, the UN Convention on the Rights of the Child.

(DfES, 2004g, para. 8)

Not all these concepts will be appropriate at primary level but it is not too soon to start promoting others. The ability to use ICT makes it so much easier to search for information about other cultures, to hold conversations through video conferencing or audio conferencing, and to engage in basic conversations in another language with real pupils as well as receiving e-mails so as to get answers from authentic sources.

Technology dissonance

Pupils (and teachers) need to understand that not everyone in the world or indeed a country has access to the internet; when they do have access, it may be very expensive and very slow. Video conferencing or audio conferencing become impossible and websites using reduced pixels and smaller images may be the only way pupils can gain a graphic image of what people look like and what their house, schools, community and their living conditions are like. Recognition and understanding of the digital divide can be achieved through the partnerships that develop between schools.

Technology dissonance (Selinger and Gibson, 2004) is the term coined to refer to situations where the availability of ICT varies wildly and where different culturally relevant learning models predominate. But technology dissonance and indeed pedagogical dissonance do not only exist in virtual exchanges: next time you are on school experience find out just how many pupils in the schools were born in the UK or started their schooling there. How will your teaching to the pupils from overseas appear to them? What are their experiences of ICT?

Educational systems in different countries tend towards a dominant field psychology and although there has been some change over the last twenty years, Woodrow (2001) argues that there has been little fundamental movement. He compares the dominant psychology in three education systems to illustrate just what he means:

> British education has been dominated by Piagetian developmental psychology; American education dominated by the notions of behaviourist psychology; European education underwritten by Gestaltian traditions in which grand ideas are the object and end points rather than particular skills. (Woodrow, 2001, p. 7)

Picture again the children in a classroom in which you recently taught or observed. How many different nationalities were represented? How many were first language English speakers? How many are second-generation British? The UK is now a truly multicultural society and there are very few classrooms in which all children's parents were born in the UK and even fewer where their grandparents were. Each set of children will therefore come with a strong cultural heritage that can provide a challenge for your particular teaching style. Maybe you yourself are from another country and you may have found that how you are expected to act in a classroom, how you are meant to respond to the pupils, and how you expect them to respond to you may differ from what you are familiar with from your own school experience and what your tutors in your teaching training course and your mentors in school espouse.

Perhaps there is an opportunity for you to share your understanding of teaching and learning based on your experiences with other beginning teachers. It can help you all to focus on and challenge aspects of pedagogy that will make you think about the role of the teacher and the role of the learner in the classroom and think about the need to personalise the learning experience of each child so that they feel comfortable in their learning environment.

Multicultural classrooms can provide the basis for a rich debate. I was first sensitised to this as a mathematics teacher studying for my Masters degree. One of the teaching sessions focused on the range of different counting systems from the ancient civilisations of the Babylonians and the Mayans to tribes living today in Papua New Guinea. Back in school this research prompted me to ask my Year 7 pupils to explain how they used their fingers to perform calculations. Every child had a slightly different method for at least one of the four rules of arithmetic, and I vividly remember that between us we learned from each other new rules for multiplying by 3, 6, 9 and 11. I also noticed that children's self-esteem began to improve as they saw their cultural origins being valued, and they talked proudly about the methods their parents and their wider family had taught them to help them remember how to perform certain calculations. Nowadays this lesson can be enriched and extended by searching for information about counting systems on the internet and whole mathematics projects constructed around the findings that will improve pupil number sense and provide them with a rich sense of the history of mathematics.

ICT to support the range of languages, cultures and learning styles in the classroom

There is a wealth of global learning resources available from the internet that can be an excellent source of support for your teaching. How often do you surf the internet for resources that go beyond the UK? Or do you just rely on the ideas for using ICT in the National Curriculum schemes of work and the resources catalogued on the Curriculum Online website? If you do go beyond UK boundaries and find teaching resources that look as though they could be useful, do you check them for National Curriculum relevance, and do you reject them if it seems that the approach they take seems wrong? Or do you look at them to see the approaches that other countries and cultures take to a topic, the relevance to the range of children in your class and think about using that approach with your pupils? The geography curriculum is rich with opportunities to use the internet. Take the example given for Unit 3, an island home, which focuses on an imaginary island called Struay in Scotland. Why not compare the features of this imaginary island with one of the myriad of islands across the world whose details can easily be found on the internet?

The sites from the countries of origin of your pupils may well take an approach that the children feel comfortable with, but if they are in a language that you do not have, it can prove problematic as you will be unable to assess the relevance, reading level and usability of the content. However, many websites often have an English translation and you can assess their relevance before allowing a child to work from the information or activity presented there. Allowing older primary children to gather information from a site from their own culture can increase their self-esteem and potentially increase their learning. They can present the results of their search and resulting work to the rest of the class.

The adaptation of ideas from one country to another is illustrated in the following example from the Netherlands. They have adopted an idea developed in the UK in the early 1990s and developed on laser disks. This is a project that explores in depth one square kilometre of the country. The children map the area and find out about the culture, the community and the people. This is all posted to one website with a clickable map of the Netherlands. Clicking on an area takes you to a web page rich with information about that part of the country. The website is at **www.ictholland.nl/diane/indexen.html**.

Summary

After reading this chapter you will have come to a greater realisation that not only is the world a global classroom but also the children you teach may be a multicultural subset of that world. The children you teach are increasingly exposed to the world at large through the media and the internet. These children are learning in a world that is becoming smaller and smaller as ICT enables us to reach people living on the other side of the planet faster than the time it takes them to walk to school. Not only can they reach them, they can speak to them through text, phone or video and learn from first hand accounts about their lives and their countries. Take, for example, the recent earthquake disaster in Asia – hours can be spent surfing the web, reading first-hand accounts from ordinary people and seeing images that bring the full horror to the desktop. Such experiences bring empathy and understanding in a way that television and books are unable to do.

Now look at each curriculum subject you teach and think about how it can be enhanced by global access to others or by access to a wealth of multicultural online resources that are not found in textbooks.

At the beginning of this chapter it was argued that schools do not harness the full power of technology and certainly do not allow learners to make full (if any) use of the artefacts they use outside school. Yet this chapter has shown the potential that ICT has to help children learn about life in other countries.

By using ICT in primary education, pupils can learn about the tools they will use at home and in their future lives in ways that can promote and further their knowledge and understanding not only of the subjects they study but of other cultures and other ways of life.

As a teacher you can promote global citizenship, cultural understanding and tolerance by exploring the benefits of collaboration across the world through school twinning programmes that are either subject-specific or cross-curricular. You should also be more aware about cultural traditions and how they have implications for the way children learn and how they respond to you as a teacher. You should also become more aware of and think about ways to celebrate the cultural differences between children in the classes you will teach. To this end you can also use ICT to personalise learning experiences for your pupils.

Consider going beyond the range of learning resources available from the UK and exploring international websites that might be exploited to provide a rich source of teaching and learning materials suitable for the global citizen of tomorrow.

Abbott, C (2000) *ICT: Changing Education*. London: RoutledgeFalmer.

Abbott, C (2002) Writing the visual: the use of graphic symbols in onscreen texts, in Snyder I (ed), *Silicon Literacies: Education, Communication and New Technologies*. London: Routledge.

Ager, R (2000) *The Art of Information and Communications Technology for Teachers*. London: David Fulton.

Ajzen, I and Madden, T (1986) Prediction of goal-directed behavior: attitudes, intentions, and perceived behavioral control, *Journal of Experimental Social Psychology*, 22: 453–74.

Alexander, R (2001) *Culture and Pedagogy*. Oxford: Blackwell.

Assessment Reform Group (1999) *Assessment for learning: beyond the black box*. University of Cambridge School of Education. Online at: **www.assessment-reform-group.org.uk** (retrieved 10 January 2005).

Atherton, T (2002) Developing ideas with multimedia in the classroom, in Loveless A and Dore B (eds), *ICT in the Primary School*. Buckingham: Open University Press.

BECTa (2000) *ICT in inclusion and SEN*. Online at: **www.becta.org.uk/teachers/display.cfm?section=1** (retrieved 12 January 2004). [6]

BECTa (2001) *The Digital Divide*. Online at: **www.becta.org.uk/page_documents/research/digitaldivide.pdf** (retrieved 22 July 2004). [1]

BECTa (2002) *Young People and ICT*. London: BECTa. [9]

BECTa (2003a) *An Exploration of the Use of ICT at the Millennium Primary School, Greenwich*. [1]

BECTa (2003b) *Primary Schools, ICT and Standards: An Analysis of National Data from Ofsted and QCA*. Online at: **www.becta.org.uk/research/research.cfm?section=1&id=538** (retrieved 24 January 2005). [10]

BECTa (2003c) *What the Research Says about Strategic Leadership and Management of ICT in Schools*. Online at: **www.becta.org.uk/page_documents/research/wtrs_stratleaders.pdf** (retrieved 24 January 2005). [10]

BECTa (2004a) *How to Use ICT across the Curriculum*, ICT Advice. Online at: **www.ictadvice.org.uk/** (retrieved 10 June 2004). [1]

BECTa (2004b) *How to Support Children Using ICT*. Online at: **www.ictadvice.org.uk/** (retrieved 26 January 2005). [4]

BECTa (n.d.) *ICT advice: Timesaver Checklist for Recording ICT-based Activity*. Online at: **www.ictadvice.org.uk/downloads/timesaver/timesaver2/Scotinspect2_lessonictform.doc** (retrieved 12 January 2004).

BECTa Evidence and Research Team (2002) *ICT and Pupil Motivation*. December.

Beeland, W D (2002) Student engagement, visual learning and technology: can interactive whiteboards help? *Action Research Exchange*, 1(1). Online at: **http://chiron.valdosta.edu/are/** (retrieved 30 September 2004).

Benyon, D R (n.d.) *Accommodating Individual Differences through an Adaptive User Interface.* Online at: **www.dcs.napier.ac.uk/~dbenyon/inddiff.pdf** (retrieved 15 July 2004).

Berger, J (1972) *Ways of Seeing.* London: BBC and Penguin Books.

Blamires, M (1999) What is enabling technology? in Blamires M (ed), *Enabling Technology for Inclusion.* London: Paul Chapman.

Bloom, B S *et al.* (1956) *Taxonomy of Educational Objectives. Handbook 1: Cognitive Domain.* London: David McKay.

Boden, M (2001) Creativity and knowledge, in Craft A, Jeffrey B and Leibling M (eds), *Creativity in Education.* London: Continuum.

Brackett, G (2003) Commentary on Westreich, J, High-tech kids: trailblazers or guinea pigs, in Gordon D (ed), *The Digital Classroom: How Technology Is Changing the Way We Teach and Learn.* Cambridge, MA: Harvard Education Letter.

Bromfield, C, Waite, S J and Wheeler, S (2003) *Can ICT Switch Children on to Learning? Indications from a Longitudinal Observational Study,* Paper presented at the European Association for Research into Learning and Instruction Conference, Padua, Italy, 26–30 August.

Brosnan, M J (1998) *Technophobia: The Psychological Impact of Information Technology.* London: Routledge.

Bryson, M and De Castell, S (1998) New technologies and the cultural ecology of public schooling: imagining teachers as Luddites indeed, *Educational Policy*, 12(5), 542–62

Burgin, V (1982) Photography, phantasy, function, in Burgin V (ed), *Thinking Photography.* London: Methuen, pp. 177–216.

Bush, N, Priest, J and Coe, R (2004) *An Exploration of the Use of ICT at the Millennium Primary School, Greenwich.*

Buzan, T (1993) *The Mind Map Book: Radiant Thinking – The Major Evolution in Human Thought.* London: BBC Books.

Byers, R and Rose, R (1996) *Planning the Curriculum for Pupils with Special Educational Needs: A Practical Guide.* London: David Fulton.

Callow, J (2003) Talking about visual texts with students, *Reading Online*, 6(8). Online at: **www.readingonline.org/articles/art_index.asp?HREF=callow/index.html** (retrieved 12 December 2004).

Cassidy, S (2004) Learning styles: an overview of theories, models, and measures, *Educational Psychology*, 24(4): 419–44.

CFS Technologies. Online at: **www.cfs-technologies.com/home/?id=1.4** (retrieved 15 January 2005).

Chu, M (1995) Reader response to interactive computer books: examining literary responses in a non-traditional reading setting, *Reading Research and Instruction*, 34: 352–66.

Clark, R E (1994) Media will never influence learning, *Educational Technology Research and Development*, 42(2): 21–9.

Clegg, S (2001) Theorising the machine: gender, education and computing, *Gender and Education*, 13(3): 307–24.

Coffield, F, Moseley, D, Hall, E and Ecclestone, K (2004) *Should We Be Using Learning Styles? What Research Has to Say to Practice.* London: Learning Skills Research Centre.

Cope, B and Kalantzis, M (ed) (2000) *Multiliteracies: Literacy Learning and the Design of Social Futures*. London: Routledge.

Cox, B (1991) *Cox on Cox*. London: Hodder & Stoughton.

Cox, M J, Preston, C and Cox, K (1999) *What Factors Support or Prevent Teachers from Using ICT in Their Classrooms*. Paper presented at the BERA 1999 Conference, Brighton.

Cox, M, Webb, M, Abbott, C, Blakeley, B, Beauchamp, T and Rhodes, V (2003) *ICT and Pedagogy: A Review of Research Literature*. London: DfES

Creating Spaces (2003) *Keys to Imagination Report to Arts Council of England*. Online at: **www.artscouncil.org.uk** (retrieved 12 December 2004).

Cronbach, L J (1975) Beyond the two disciplines of scientific psychology, *American Psychologist*, 30: 116–27.

Cubeisy, E and Cox, A (2004) Delivering the vision, in Selinger M (ed), *Connected Schools*. London: Premium Publishing.

Cutler, M (2004) Exploring science locally and sharing insights globally, *School Science Review*, 86(314): 33–41.

Davison, J (2000) Literacy and social class, in Davison J and Moss J (eds), *Issues in English Teaching*. London: Routledge.

Dede, C (1998) *Learning about Teaching and Vice Versa*. Paper presented at the Conference of the Society for Information Technology in Education, Washington, DC, USA

Denning, T (1997) *IT and Pupil Motivation: A Collaborative Study of Staff and Pupil Attitudes and Experiences*. Coventry: NCET

DfEE (1998) *The National Literacy Strategy: Framework for Teaching*. London: DfEE

DfEE (1999a) *The National Numeracy Strategy – Framework for Teaching Mathematics*. London: DfEE

DfEE (1999b) *The National Curriculum for England: Information and Communication Technology*. London: DfEE

DfEE (n.d.) *Teaching in England*. Online at: **www.teachernet.gov.uk/teachinginengland/detail.cfm?id=523** (retrieved 26 January 2005).

DfEE/QCA (1999a) *Music National Curriculum*. London: QCA

DfEE/QCA (1999b) *ICT National Curriculum*. London: QCA

DfEE/QCA (n.d.) *Music in the National Curriculum*. Online at: **www.ncaction.org.uk/subjects/music/ict-lrn.htm** (retrieved 26 January 2005).

DfEE/QCA (n.d.) *Spotting Creativity*. Online at: **www.ncaction.org.uk/creativity/spot.htm** (retrieved 26 January 2005).

DfES (1999) *National Numeracy Strategy Framework for Teaching Mathematics*. Norwich: Stationery Office.

DfES (2000) *National Curriculum Handbook for Primary Teachers in England*. Online at: **www.nc.uk.net** (retrieved 10 January 2005).

DfES (2001a) *SEN Code of Practice* (2001). Online at: **www.teachernet.gov.uk/_doc/3724/SENCodeOfPractice.pdf** (retrieved 31 January 2005).

DfES (2001b) *ImpaCT2: Emerging Findings from the Evaluation of the Impact of Information and Communications Technologies on Pupil Attainment*, NGfL Research and Evaluation Series. London: DfES

DfES (2003a) *GCDI Models and Images: Using models and images to support mathematics teaching and learning in Years 1 to 3*, 0508-2003. Norwich: Stationery Office.

DfES (2003b) *Teaching Literacy and Mathematics in Year 3*, 0495-2003. Norwich: Stationery Office.

DfES (2003c) *Excellence and Enjoyment*. Online at: **www.standards.dfes.gov.uk/ primary/publications/literacy/63553/** (retrieved 24 January 2005). [10]

DfES (2004a) *Learning and Teaching Using ICT: Leadership Team Toolkit*, 0369-2004. Norwich: Stationery Office.

DfES (2004b) *Primary National Strategy ICT CD-ROM*, 0473-2004 (available from prolog: tel. 0845 602 2260).

DfES (2004c) *Problem Solving*, 0247-2004. Norwich: Stationery Office.

DfES (2004d) *Excellence and Enjoyment: A Strategy for Primary Schools*. London: DfES

DfES (2004e) *Excellence and Enjoyment: Learning and Teaching in the Primary Years*. London: DfES

DfES (2004f) Citizenship at Key Stages 1 and 2 (Year 1-6) Unit 05: Living in a diverse world, *The Standards Site*. Online at: /**www.standards.dfes.gov.uk/schemes2 /ksl-2citizenship/cit05/?view=get** (retrieved 20 December 2004).

DfES (2004g) *Putting the World into World-Class Education. An International Strategy for Education, Skills and Children's Services*. London: DfES Online at: **www.global gateway.org.uk/PDF/World%20Class%20Education.pdf** (retrieved 29 December 2004).

DfES (n.d.) *Consultation on Classification of Special Educational Needs (2002–2003)*. Online at: **www.dfes.gov.uk/consultations/conResults.cfm?consultation Id=1200** (retrieved 23 November 2004).

Doll, J and Ajzen, I (1992) Accessibility and stability of predictors in the theory of planned behavior, *Journal of Personality and Social Psychology*, 63(5): 754–65.

Dunn, R, Dunn, K and Price, G E (1989) *Learning Style Inventory*. Lawrence, KS: Price Systems.

Dyslexia Institute (n.d.) *What Is Dyslexia?* Online at: **www.dyslexia-inst.org.uk/ faqs.htm#What_is** (retrieved 18 January 2005).

Eagleton, T (1983) *Literary Theory: An Introduction*. Oxford: Blackwell.

Elliman, N A, Green, M W, Rogers, P J and Finch, G M (1997) Processing efficiency theory and the working memory system: impairments associated with sub-clinical anxiety, *Personality and Individual Differences*, 23: 31–5.

Ellis, V (2001) Analogue clock/digital display: continuity and change in debates about literacy, technology and English, in Loveless A and Ellis V (eds), *ICT, Pedagogy and the Curriculum: Subject to Change*. London: Routledge.

Ellis, V with Long, S (2004) Negotiating contrad(ICT)ions: teachers and students making multimedia in the secondary school, *Technology, Pedagogy and Education*, 13(1): 11–28.

Eurydice (2004) *Key Data on Information and Communication Technology in Schools in Europe 2004 Edition*. Brussels: Eurydice. Online at: **www.eurydice.org/ Documents/KDICT/en/FrameSet.htm** (retrieved 29 December 2004).

Evans, M (2002) *Open Windows: Becoming an e-Learning School*. National College for School Leadership. Online at: **www.ncsl.org.uk/mediastore/image2/evans -open-windows.doc** (retrieved 12 January 2005).

Fabry, D and Higgs, J (1997) Barriers to the effective use of technology in education, *Journal of Educational Computing*, 17(4): 385–95.

Facer, K (2002) *What Do We Mean by the Digital Divide? Exploring the Role of Access, Relevance and Resource Networks*, Paper presented at Toshiba/BECTa Digital

Divide seminar, 19 February. Online at: **www.becta.org.uk/page_ documents /research/digidivseminar.pdf** (retrieved 7 July 2004).

Flavell, J (1976) Metacognitive aspects of problem-solving, in Resnick L (ed), *The Nature of Intelligence*. Hillsdale, NJ: Erlbaum Associates.

Forcheri, P and Molfino, M T (2000) ICT as a tool for learning to learn, in Watson D M and Downes T (eds), *Communications and Networking in Education*. Boston, MA: Kluwer Academic Press.

Forsyth, I (2001) *Teaching and Learning Materials and the Internet*, 3rd edn. London: Kogan Page.

Frank, M, Reich, N and Humphreys, K (2003) Respecting the human needs of students in the development of e-learning, *Computers in Education*, 40(1): 57–70.

Fraser, A (1999) Colleges should tap the pedagogical potential of the World Wide Web, *Chronicle of Higher Education*, 6 August, section B, p. 8.

Friere, P and Macedo, D (1987) *Literacy: Reading the Word and Reading the World*. Hadley, MA: Bergin & Hadley.

Furnell, S (2003) *Cybercrime: Vandalising the Information Society*. London: Addison Wesley.

Gamble, N and Easingwood, N (eds) (2001) *ICT and Literacy*. London: Continuum.

Gardner, H (1983) *Frames of Mind: A Theory of Multiple Intelligences*. New York: Basic Books.

Gardner, H (1993) *Frames of Mind: The Theory of Multiple Intelligences*, 2nd edn. London: Fontana.

Gardner, H and Hatch, T (1989) Multiple intelligences go to school: educational implications of the theory of multiple intelligences, *Educational Researcher*, 18(8): 4–9.

Gibson, J J (1979) *The Ecological Approach to Visual Perception*. Boston: Houghton.

Gibson, W (1995) *Neuromancer*. London: Harper Collins.

Gilster, P (1997) *Digital Literacy*. New York: John Wiley & Sons.

Graves, D (1983) *Writing: Teacher and Children at Work*. London: Heinemann Educational.

Greenfield, S (2003) *Tomorrow's People: How 21st Century Technology Is Changing the Way We Think and Feel*. London: Penguin.

Halliday, M A K (1975) *Learning How to Mean: Explorations in the Development of Language*. London: Arnold.

Harrison, C, Comber, C, Fisher, T, Haw, K, Lewin, C, Lunzer, E, McFarlane, A, Mavers, D, Scrimshaw, P, Somekh, B and Watling, R (2002) *ImpaCT2: The Impact of Information and Communication Technologies on Pupil Learning and Attainment* [report to the DfES]. Coventry: BECTa.

Hayward, B, Alty, C, Pearson, S and Martin, C (2003) *Young People and ICT 2002*. London: DfES Online at: **www.becta.org.uk/page_documents/research/ full_report.pdf** (retrieved 7 July 2004).

HMI 555, *The National Literacy Strategy: The First Four Years 1998–2002*. London: Ofsted.

Holmes, E (2003) *School Twinning*. Online at: **www.elizabethholmes.co.uk/a43. html** (retrieved 20 December 2004).

Hooper, S and Reiber, L P (1995) Teaching with technology, in Ornstein A (ed), *Teaching: Theory into Practice*. Neeham Heights, MA: Allyn & Bacon.

Institute for the Advancement of Research in Education (2003) *Graphic Organizers: A Review of Scientifically Based Research*. Online at: **www.inspiration.com/ vlearning/research/index.cfm** (retrieved 12 December 2004).

Jackson, C and Lawty-Jones, M (1996) Explaining the overlap between personality and learning style, *Personality and Individual Differences*, 20(3): 293–300.

John, P D (2004) Teaching and learning with ICT: new technology, new pedagogy? *Education, Communications and Information*, 4(1): 101–9.

John, P D (2005, in press) The sacred and the profane: subject sub-cultures, pedagogical practice and teachers' perceptions of the classroom uses of ICT, *Educational Review*.

John, P D, Baggot La Velle, L M, Sutherland, R and Dale, R (2004) Devices and desires: subject sub-cultures, pedagogical identity and the challenge of information and communications technology, *Technology, Pedagogy and Education*, 13(3): 307–27.

John, P D and Sutherland, R (2004) Teaching and learning with ICT: new technology, new pedagogy? *Education, Communication and Information*, 4(1): 101–8.

Joiner, R W (1998) The effect of gender on children's software preferences, *Journal of Computer Assisted Learning*, 14: 195–8.

Joiner, R, Messer, D, Littleton, K and Light, P (1996) Gender, computer experience and computer-based problem solving, *Computers and Education*, 26(1–3): 179–87.

Kelly, K (2003) New independence for Special Needs students, in Gordon D (ed), *The Digital Classroom: How Technology Is Changing the Way We Teach and Learn*. Cambridge, MA: Harvard Education Letter.

Kemmis, S, Atkin, R and Wright, E (1977) *How Do Students Learn?*, Working Papers on Computer Assisted Learning, Occasional Publication 5. UNCAL: UEA

Kirkman, C (2000) A model for the effective management of information and communications technology development in schools derived from six contrasting case studies, *Journal of Information Technology for Teacher Education*, 9(1): 37–52.

Kress, G (1982) *Learning to Write*. London: Routledge.

Kress, G (2000) *Literacy in the New Media Age*. London: Routledge.

Kress, G and van Leeuwen, T (1996) *Reading Images: The Grammar of Visual Design*. London: Routledge.

Lachs, V (2000) *Making Multimedia in the Classroom*. London: Routledge.

Lanham, R (1993) *The Electronic Word: Democracy, Technology and the Arts*. Chicago: University of Chicago Press.

Lankshear, C (1997) *Changing Literacies*. Buckingham: Open University Press.

Lankshear, C and Knobel, M (2003) *New Literacies: Changing Knowledge and Classroom Learning*. Buckingham: Open University Press.

Laval, E (2002) 'Shared construction of knowledge through electronic mail communication'. Unpublished PhD dissertation, University of Bristol.

Leask, M and Meadows, J (eds) (2000) *Teaching and Learning with ICT in the Primary School*. London: RoutledgeFalmer.

Leutner, D and Plass, J L (1998) Measuring learning styles with questionnaires versus direct observation of preferential choice behavior in authentic learning situations: the visualizer/verbalizer behavior observation scale (VV-BOS), *Computers in Human Behavior*, 14(4): 543–57.

Levinson, P (2003) *Real Space*. London: Routledge.

Lim, C P (2001) Object of the activity systems as a major barrier to the creative use of ICT in schools, *Australian Journal of Educational Technology*, 17(3): 295–312.

Locke, T and Andrews, R (2004) A systematic review of the impact of ICT on literature-related literacies in English 5–16, in *Research Evidence in Education Library*. London: EPPI-Centre, Social Science Research Unit, Institute of Education.

Long, S (2001) What effect will digital technologies have on visual education in schools? in Loveless, A and Ellis, V (eds), *ICT, Pedagogy and the Curriculum: Subject to Change*. London: Routledge.

Loveless, A (1997) Visual literacy and new technology in primary schools: the Glebe School Project, *Journal of Computing and Childhood Education*, 8(2/3): 98–110.

Loveless, A (2003) *The Role of ICT*, 2nd edn. London: Continuum.

Loveless, A with Taylor T (2000) Creativity, visual literacy and ICT, in Leask M and Meadows J (eds), *Teaching and Learning with ICT in the Primary School*. London: Routledge, pp. 65–80.

Lundin, U (2004) Learning communities for students and teachers, in Selinger M (ed.), *Connected Schools*. London: Premium Publishing.

Makaton Vocabulary Development Project (n.d.) Online at: **www.makaton.org/ about/mvdp_anniv.htm** (retrieved 12 January 2005).

Marton, F, Hounsell, D and Entwistle, N (eds) (1997) *The Experience of Learning*. Edinburgh: Scottish Academic Press.

Matthewman, S, Blight, A and Davies, C (2004) What does multimodality mean for English? Creative tensions in teaching new texts and new literacies, *Education, Communications and Information*, 4(1): 153–77.

Mavers, D, Somekh, B and Restorick, J (2002) Interpreting the externalised images of pupils' conceptions of ICT: methods for the analysis of concept maps, *Computers and Education*, 38: 187–207.

McDonald, H and Ingvarson, L (1997) Technology: a catalyst for educational change, *Journal of Curriculum Studies*, 29(5): 513–27.

MCEETYA (2002) *National Report on Schooling in Australia 2002*. Online at: **http:// cms.curriculum.edu.au/anr2002/index.htm** (retrieved 29 December 2004).

McFarlane, A (1997) *Information Technology and Authentic Learning*. London: Routledge.

McKeown, S (2000) *Unlocking Potential. How ICT Can Support Children with Special Needs*. Birmingham: Questions Publishing.

McKeown, S (2005) *Using ICT to Support Dyslexia*. London: BETT Special Educational Needs Fringe guest lecture.

McLean, G and Russell, B (1995) *Teacher Support Materials for the Application of Laptop Computers to the Primary Key Learning Areas*. New South Wales: Batlow Technology College.

Mosely, D and Higgins, S (1999) Ways forward with ICT: effective pedagogy using information and communications technology for literacy and numeracy in primary schools. Online at: **www.ncl.ac.uk/ecls/research/project_ttaict/ TTA_ICTpdf** (retrieved 11 December 2002).

Muffoletto, R (2001) An inquiry into the nature of Uncle Joe's representation and meaning, *Reading Online*, 4(8). Online at: **www.readingonline.org/ newliteracies/lit_index.asp?HREF=/newliteracies/muffoletto/ index.html** (retrieved 12 December 2004).

Mujis, D and Reynolds, D (2001) *Effective Teaching: Evidence and Practice*. London: Paul Chapman.

Mumtaz, S (2000) Factors affecting teachers' use of information and communications technology: a review of the literature, *Journal of Information Technology for Teacher Education*, 9(3): 319–41.

National Advisory Committee on Creative and Cultural Education (1999) *All Our Futures: Creativity, Culture and Education*. London: QCA

National Autistic Society (n.d.) *What Is Autism?* Online at: **www.nas.org.uk/nas/ jsp/polopoly.jsp?d=299** (retrieved 18 January 2005).

Norman, D (1988) *The Psychology of Everyday Things*. New York: Basic Books.

Novak, J D and Gowin, D B (1984) *Learning How to Learn*. New York: Cambridge University Press.

Ofsted (2002) *The National Literacy Strategy: The First Four Years 1998–2002*, HMI 555. London: Ofsted.

Ofsted (2004) *ICT in Schools: The Impact of Government Initiatives* (Primary). London: Ofsted.

Olivero, F, John, P D and Sutherland, R (2004) Seeing is believing: using videopapers to transform teachers' professional knowledge and practice, *Cambridge Journal of Education*, 34(2): 179–93.

Olson, J (2000) Trojan horse or teacher's pet. Computers and the culture of the school, *Journal of Curriculum Studies*, 32(1): 1–9.

Orton Dyslexia Society (1995) *What Is Dyslexia?* Online at: **www.interdys.org/ servlet/compose?section_id=5&page_id=95#What%20is%20dyslexia** (retrieved 18 January 2005).

Papert, S (1993) *Mindstorms: Children, Computers and Powerful Ideas*. New York: Perseus Publishing.

Passey, D, Rogers, C, Machell, J and McHugh, G (2004) *The Motivational Effect of ICT on Pupils*, DfES Research Report RR523. University of Lancaster.

Passey, D, Rogers, C, Machell, J, McHugh, G and Allaway, D (2003) *The Motivational Effect of ICT on Pupils: Emerging Findings*. London: DfES

Pearson, M and Somekh, B (2000) *Concept-mapping as a Research Tool: A Study of Primary Children's Representations of Information and Communication Technologies (ICT)*, Paper presented at the British Educational Research Association Conference, Cardiff University, 7–10 September 2000. Online at: **www.leeds. ac.uk/educol** (retrieved 12 December 2004).

Penley, C and Ross, A (1991) *Technoculture: Cultural Politics*, Vol. 3. Minneapolis, MN: University of Minnesota Press.

Perkins, D N (1993) Person-plus: a distributed view of thinking and learning, in Saloman G (ed), *Distributed Cognitions: Psychological and Educational Consider-ations*. Cambridge: Cambridge University Press.

Pittard, V, Bannister, P and Dunn, J (2003) *The Big pICTure: The Impact of ICT on Attainment, Motivation and Learning*. Nottingham: DfES

Plymouth Grid for Learning (n.d.) *Below Age-Related Expectations* (BARE) project. Online at: **www.pgfl.plymouth.gov.uk/wbcm/newsevents/nelinkext. asp?url=http://www.recordingandassessment.co.uk** (retrieved 18 January 2005).

Preston, C, Cox, M J and Cox, K M (2000) *Teachers as Innovators: An evaluation of teachers' motivation in the use of ICT*. A report funded by the Teacher Training Agency, Oracle and Compaq, published by MirandaNet in collaboration with the

Institute of Education, University of London. Online at: **www.mirandanet.ac.uk/pubs/tes_art.htm.**

PricewaterhouseCoopers (PwC) (2001) *Teacher Workload Study: Final Report.* DfES Online at: **www.teachernet.gov.uk/_doc/3165/Final%20%Report%205%20December%20CK3Dec2.doc** (retrieved 12 May 2003).

Radabaugh, M (1988) Cited in *National Council on Disability: Study on the Financing of Assistive Technology Devices and Services for Individuals with Disabilities* (1993). Online at: **www.ncd.gov/newsroom/publications/1993/assistive.htm#6** (retrieved 31 January 2005).

Reid, M, Burn, A and Parker, D (2002) *Evaluation Report of the Becta Digital Video Pilot Project.* Coventry: BECTA Online at: **www.becta.org.uk/research/research.cfm?section=1&id=532** (retrieved 12 December 2004).

Riding, R J (1991) *Cognitive Styles Analysis.* Birmingham: Learning and Training Technology.

Riding, R J (2002) *School Learning and Cognitive Style.* London: David Fulton.

Riding, R J and Grimley, M (1999) Cognitive style, gender and learning from multimedia materials in 11 year old children, *British Journal of Educational Technology,* 30(1): 43–56.

Riding, R J and Rayner, S (1998) *Cognitive Styles and Learning Strategies: Understanding Style Differences in Learning and Behaviour.* London: David Fulton.

Riding, R J and Read, G (1996) Cognitive style and pupil learning preferences, *Educational Psychology,* 16: 81–106.

Riding, R J and Wigley, S (1997) The relationship between cognitive style and personality in further education students, *Personality and Individual Differences,* 23: 379–89.

Robert Gordon University, The (n.d.) Online at: **www.scotland.gov.uk/library/ict** (retrieved May 2004).

Rockman, S (1997–2000) *Results of Research into Student Use of Laptop Computers to Learn Anytime, Anywhere.* San Francisco, CA: Microsoft Corporation.

Rockman, S (1998) Powerful tools for schooling: second year study of the laptop program, *San Francisco Results of Research into Student Use of Laptop Computers to Learn Anytime, Anywhere.* San Francisco, CA: Microsoft Corporation.

Rogers, E M (1983) *Diffusion of Innovations,* 3rd edn. New York: Macmillan.

Rosenfeld, M and Rosenfeld, S (2004) Developing teacher sensitivity to individual learning differences, *Educational Psychology,* 24(4): 465–86.

Ryman, J (2004) Children's perception on having an IWB in their classroom. Online at: **www.ict.oxon-lea.gov.uk** (retrieved 10 June 2004).

Selinger, M (2005) *What Is Content?* Paper to be presented at WCCE2005 (The World Congress on Computers in Education), Cape Town, South Africa, July 2005.

Selinger, M and Gibson, I (2004) Cultural relevance and technology use: ensuring the transformational power of learning technologies in culturally defined learning environments, in Cantoni L and McLoughlin C (eds), *Proceedings of EdMedia 2004,* 21–26 June, Lugano, Switzerland.

Selinger, M, Littleton, K, Kirkwood, A, Wearmouth, J, Meadows, J, Davis, P, Taylor, J, Lincoln, C and Lochun, S (1998) *Educational Internet Service Providers Project, Final Evaluation Report.* London: DfEE

Shannon, C E (1949) *The Mathematical Theory of Communication.* Chicago: University of Illinois Press.

Sheppard, B (2000) *Organisational Learning and the Integration of Information and Communication Technology in Teaching and Learning*, Paper presented at the annual meeting of the American Educational Research Association (AERA), New Orleans, LA, 24–28 April.

Simpson, M *et al.* (1999) Using information and communications technology as a pedagogical tool: who educates the educators? *Journal of Education for Teaching*, 25(3): 247–62.

Smith, H (2001) *Smart Board Evaluation: Final Report*. Kent NGfL Online at: **www.kented.org.uk/ngfl/whiteboards/report.html** (retrieved 22 January 2003).

Smith, J (2002) Learning styles: fashion fad or lever for change? The application of learning style theory to inclusive curriculum delivery, *Innovations in Education and Teaching International*, 39(I): 63–70.

Smith, M K (2002) Howard Gardner and multiple intelligences, *Encyclopaedia of Informal Education*. Online at: **www.infed.org/thinkers/gardner.htm** (retrieved 10 February 2004).

Smith, P and Hagues, N (1993) *NFER-NELSON Non Verbal reasoning 10 & 11 Manual*. Windsor: NFER-NELSON.

Snyder, I (ed) (2002) *Silicon Literacies: Communication, Innovation and Education in the Electronic Age*. London and New York: Routledge.

Solomon, C and Papert, S (1972) Twenty things to do with a computer, *Educational Technology Journal*, April.

Somekh, B, Lewin, C, Mavers, D, Fisher, T, Harrison, C, Haw, K, Lunzer, E, McFarlane, A and Scrimshaw, P (2002) *ImpaCT2: Pupils' and Teachers' Perceptions of ICT in the Home, School and Community*. Coventry: BECTA Online at: **www.becta.org.uk/research/research.cfm?section=1&id=539** (retrieved 12 December 2004).

South Texas Community College (STCC) (2002) *Student Perceptions of the Use and Educational Value of Technology at the STCC Starr County Campus*. Online at: **www.stcc.cc.tx.us/~research/reports/pdfs/Student_Perceptions_Technology.pdf** (retrieved 22 January 2005).

Special Educational Needs and Disability Act 2001. Online at: **www.legislation.hmso.gov.uk/acts/acts2001/20010010.htm** (retrieved 31 January 2005).

Sternberg, R J (1997) *Thinking Styles*. Cambridge: Cambridge University Press.

Sutherland, R, Breeze, N, Gall, M, Godwin, S, Mattewman, S, Shortis, T and Triggs, P (2002) *Pedagogy and Purpose for ICT in Primary Education*. Online at: **www.interactiveeducation.ac.uk/out_sut.pdf** (retrieved 26 January 2005).

Swanwick, K (1999) *Teaching Music Musically*. London: RoutledgeFalmer.

Swanwick, K and Tillman, J (1986) The sequence of musical development, *British Journal of Music Education*, 3(3): 305–39.

Times Education Supplement (2004a) *Express Yourself*. September.

Times Education Supplement (2004b) *TES Online: The Joys of Text*, 14 May.

Times Education Supplement (2004c) *TES Online: The Creation Story*, 14 May.

Tobin, P and Shrubshall, C (2002) *How to Access and Manage Creativity in Organisations: A Collection of Perspectives*. London: Royal Society of Arts, p. 18.

Toffler, A (1970) *Future Shock*. New York: Pan Books.

Torjussen, M and Coppard, E (2002) Potential into practice: developing ICT in the primary classroom, in Loveless, A and Dore B (eds), *ICT in the Primary School*. Buckingham: Open University Press.

Triggs, P and John, P D (2004) From transaction to transformation: ICT, professional development and the formation of communities of practice, *Journal of Computer Assisted Learning*. 20(6): 426–39.

Triggs, P and Scott Cook, E (2002) *E-Mail a Viking: An Exploration of How Using E-Mail Shapes Children's Writing*, BERA Working Paper. University of Bristol.

TTA (2002) *Qualifying to Teach*. London: Teacher Training Agency.

Twining, P (2001) ICT and the nature of learning, in Praechter C, Edwards R, Harrison R and Twining P (eds), *Learning, Space and Identity*. London: Paul Chapman.

Tyldesley, A (n.d.) *What Is the Place of ICT in the Literacy Hour?* Online at: **www.mape.org.uk/curriculum/english/ict.htm** (retrieved 4 January 2005).

Tyrer, R, Parker, M, Lee, C, Gunn, S, Pitman, M and Townsend, M (2004) *A Toolkit for the Effective Teaching Assistant*. London: Paul Chapman.

Valdez, G, McNabb, M, Anderson, M, Hawkes, M and Raack, L (1999) Computer-based technology and learning: evolving uses and expectations. Online at: **www.ncrel.org/tplan/cbtl/toc.htm** (retrieved 10 June 2004).

Valle, A, Cabanach, R G, Nuñez. J C, González-Pienda, J, Rodríguez, S and Piñeiro, I (2003) Multiple goals, motivation and academic learning, *British Journal of Educational Psychology*, 73: 71–87.

Venezky, R L (2004) Introductory paper: technology in the classroom: steps toward a new vision, *Education, Communication and Information*, 4(1): 2–22.

Vygotsky, L S (1978) *Mind in Society: The Development of Higher Psychological Processes*, eds Cole M, John-Steiner V, Scribner S and Souberman E. London: Harvard University Press.

Waite, S J (2004) Tools for the job: a report of two surveys of ICT use for literacy in primary schools in the West of England, *Journal of Computer Assisted Learning*, 20: 11–20.

Wallace, P (1999) *The Psychology of the Internet*. New York: Cambridge University Press.

Wann, J and Mon-Williams, M (1996) What does virtual reality need? Human factors issues in the design of three-dimensional computer environments, *International Journal of Human-Computer Studies*, 44: 829–47.

Wheeler, S (2001) Information and communication technologies and the changing role of the teacher, *Journal of Educational Media*, 26(1): 7–18.

Wheeler, S, Waite, S and Bromfield, C (2001) *Promoting Creative Thinking Through the Use of Web Resources*, Paper presented at the Romanian Internet Learning Workshop, Sumuleu Cuic, Romania, August.

Wheeler, S, Waite, S J and Bromfield, C (2002) Promoting creative thinking through the use of ICT, *Journal of Computer Assisted Learning*, 18(3): 367–78.

Whelan, R, (2000) *How schools can get the most from their information resources*. Online at: **www.en.eun.org** (retrieved 10 June 2004).

Wild, M (1995) Using CD-Rom storybooks to encourage reading development. Item 5 of set: *Research Information for Teachers, 2*. Canberra, Australia: ACER

Williams D et al. (1998) *Teachers' ICT Skills and Knowledge Needs. Final Report to SOEID*.

Woodrow, D (2001) Cultural determination of curricula, theories and practices, *Pedagogy, Culture and Society*, 9(1): 5–27.

Wragg, E (2001) Your number's up, *TES Primary*, January, p. 21.

Wragg, E C and Brown, G (2001) *Questioning in the Primary School*. London: Routledge.

Yee, D L (2000) Images of school principals' information and communication technology leadership, *Journal of Information Technology for Teacher Education*, 9(3): 287–302.

Zar, Jerrold H (n.d.) Spellchecker poem 'Candidate for a Pullet Surprise'. Northern Illinois University. Online at: **http://garnet.acns.fsu.edu/~phensel/Teaching/spelling.html** (retrieved 4 January 2005).

24 Hour Museum 120

acquisition of skills and knowledge 100
active participation 96
adaptation of knowledge 101
adapted keyboards 103, 104-5
adoption of new technologies, promotion 24
adult support 75-6
adventure quest 43
analytics 149, 156
anti-virus software 93, 94
anxiety
  and the use of ICT 146, 157
  see also technophobia
Anytime, Anywhere initiative 164
application of knowledge 101
art education and digital technologies 118
art galleries, use of the World Wide Web 120
ASD
  case study of pupil with 105-7
  triad of impairments 105
assessment
  as a framework for creativity 135
  in a 'school without walls' 178-82
  see also online assessments; risk assessment
attainment, relationship between ICT and 143, 151, 155, 159, 169
auditory learning 68, 145
Australia, ICT policies and practice 190
authentic writing 195
Autistic Disorder Spectrum see ASD
automaticity 97

BARE project (below age related expectation) 99
BECTa 141, 189
BECTa Digital Video Pilot Project 121
BECTa 'Young People and ICT' survey 153
behaviour management and the use of laptops 173
benefits of ICT 12
'The Big Breakfast' project 117-8
Blackcat's Compose 74, 78
'Bobby' web-testing site 91
bodily-kinaesthetic intelligence 72
British Educational and Communications Technology Agency see BECTa
British Film Institute (BFI) 121

change
  categories of response 10-11
  management of 163, 170
  by pupils with ASD 105-6
change agency 11-12
chat rooms 87
Chrisi Bailey Award 125
citizenship agenda, contribution of e-twinning 196
classrooms
  ICT to support languages, cultures and learning styles in 199
  see also global classroom; multicultural classrooms
ClozePro software 108f, 109
Code of Practice 95, 100
cognitive skills, levels 56-8
cognitive style 144-5
collaboration 75
  between schools see e-twinning
  and scaffolding learning 156

collaborative learning 54, 97
collaborative planning with peers 24
COMENIUS 195
Comenius Space 193
communication 49-50
  importance to those with learning difficulties 151
  levels 151-2
  managing the development of 96
  see also e-pal communication; social communication; symbol communication systems
communication difficulties, use of ICT for 96-8
communication skills, development 94, 95-6
community learning 54
completion of tasks 156-7
composing music
  as a problem-solving activity 68, 69, 75, 77f
  see also Blackcat's Compose
computer hackers 93
computer programs see programs
computer screens 119
  see also touch-screens
computer suites 163, 164, 165, 167, 173
computer-based worksheets 29
computers
  differentiated use 153-4, 156
  as a medium for creativity 133
  ratio of pupils to 190
  social uses by females 151
  see also home computers; laptop computers; networked computers; 'zombie' computers
concept maps, software applications 125-6
confirming, testing and 50
conformity 167
Conjectural paradigm 154, 155
consultation on internet use 83, 89
'Contact a Family' 98
content-free software 52, 54
contexts for learning see learning contexts
continuity of product 34
Core subjects of the National Curriculum
  emphasis on 59-60
  see also literacy; numeracy
Counter program 53
countries
  sharing of practice between 190-2
  see also Australia; Europe; UK
creating with ICT 122-3
creative action 186
creative cognition model 186f
Creative Partnerships 167
creative teaching 8, 134, 136
creative thinking 133-4
  using ICT to develop 184
creativity 132-42, 159, 167
  barriers 135
  definition 69, 132-3
  ICT as an aid 89-70
  and ICT in literacy teaching 138-40
  and ICT in numeracy teaching 136
  ICT as a tool 134
  music and 68
  and musical expression 140
  and problem-solving 136-7
  in science teaching 141-3

and teaching roles 142
   use of imagination and curiosity 133
critical literacy approach 26-7
critical thinking skills and the use of laptop
   computers 165
culture
   creating connections through e-pal
      communication 88
   effect on teaching style 198
curriculum
   embedding ICT see embedding ICT
   as a framework for creativity 135
   of the future 183
   ICT in 189
   learning across 54-6
   see also National Curriculum
cyberspace 81

DARE site 120
data projectors 27
'datalogging' 141-2
deep approaches to learning 146
demonstrating 48
denial of service 92
developmental checklists 99
differential use of ICT 143
diffusion of innovation 9-11
digital divides 16-17, 18, 197
   and pupils with SEN 112
digital literacy 16–17
   definition 26
digital pathogens 92
digital photography 17, 123, 127, 129, 130
digital projectors 54
digital video 127, 130, 133
   see also BECTa Digital Video Pilot Project
direct teaching 73
do2learn website 106
domains 72
drill and practice tests 145
'drill and skill' 51
dyslexia 107-8
   using ICT to support learners with 108-10

e-contact activities, supervision of 85
e-learning environment in a 'school without walls'
   182-4
e-mail
   advantages 7
   communication opportunities 152
   symbol-based 111
   see also spam
e-pal communication 87
e-twinning 193-6
   links to UK education policy 196-7
Early Adopters 10
Early Majority 10-11
editing work in progress 69-70, 97
Educational Reform for a Knowledge Economy
   (ErfKE) 191
educational systems 198
   see also schools
Electric December 125
electronic storybooks 31-2
Emancipatory paradigm 154
embedding ICT 1, 17-25, 46-7, 63
   in music teaching 63
   stages 23-4
   use of portable laptops 174
'emoticons' 87
ENIS (European Network of Innovative Schools)
   193
eSchola 193

Europe, ICT policies and practice 188-90
European Schoolnet Community Environment 193
European Schoolnet (EUN) 192-3
evolution 47
Excel spreadsheets 50, 52
'Excellence and Enjoyment' 167
experiential learning 100
extravert personalities 145, 156
Eye to Eye project 121

familiarisation 24, 46-7
'fat pictures' 124-5
feedback 50
   speed of 33-4
'file manipulation' 153
filtering information on the Internet 87
filtering software 85-7
firewall software 93
firewalls 92
fixity 137
'flow', facilitation by technology 34
fluency 100
Foundation subjects in the National Curriculum 61
free play 154, 159
Future Shock 11-12

galleries, use of the World Wide Web 120
Gardner's theory of multiple intelligences 71-2, 73,
   132, 144
gender and the use of ICT 147, 151
generalisation 101
geography 141
global classroom 187-200
   e-twinning see e-twinning
   ICT policies and practice across Europe and
      Australia 188-90
   ICT to support languages, cultures and
      learning styles 199
   sharing of practice between countries 190-92
      European Schoolnet 192-3
   technology dissonance 197-8
Global eSchools and Communities Initiative
   (GeSCI) 191, 192
global learning resources 199
global phenomenon, internet as a 75, 80-1
global society, key concepts 197
globalisation 114, 175
government policies 163, 167-9
graphic organisers 126
graphical user interface 119
group work in literacy, digital tools 29-30
group work in music teaching 67

hackers 82
hardware
   purchase and maintenance 189-90
   see also computers
highlighting teaching points 32
home computers 16
   use 164
      effect on classroom use 152-4
home school learning 185
How to Support Children Using ICT in Music 63
html 33
human capital 176-7
hyperlinks 32, 33
   use in adventure quest 43
hypertext 124

icons 117, 119, 122
   use in SEN 120
ICT National Curriculum 69, 163
ICT suites 163, 164, 165, 167, 173

iEARN 195
IEPs (individual education plans) 98
Illuminations 49
ILPs (individual learning plans) 178, 180, 181
image manipulation software 123
imagers 149
imagination 133
    and pupils with ASD 105
Imfundo: Partnership for IT in Education 190-1
Impact2evaluation 125-6
implementation of ICT 163-5
    factors for 20t
inclusion
    of children with SEN 95
    in a 'school without walls' 179, 184
    and the use of laptops 173
independent learning 54, 97
    in literacy 29-30
    in music 69
individual differences
    ICT and 143
    language to conceptualise 157
    sources 144-6
        cognitive style 144-5
        deep and surface approaches to learning
            146
        personality 145
        tasks 155-7
        visual, auditory and kinaesthetic learning
            145
individual education plans (IEPs) 98
individual learning cycle 181-2
individual learning plans (ILPs) 178, 180, 181
individualised learning 177
    in music 74
information
    accessing and analysing 48
    importance to gifted and talented pupils 151
    processing 96
    transmitting and receiving 96
innovation
    case study on adoption 19-24
    see also diffusion of innovation
Innovators 9
Inspiration and Kidspiration 126
instant messaging 152
Instructional paradigm 154
integration
    as a stage in embedding ICT 24, 47
    and teachers' beliefs 12-16
intelligence, types of 70-1, 132
IntelliKeys overlay keyboards 103
interaction 97, 157
    in music teaching 67
    and the use of IWBs 22
interactive storybooks 31-2
Interactive Teaching Programs (ITPs) 56, 58
    for data handling 49-50
    use for division 47-8
interactive whiteboards see IWBs
Internet 7, 80-93
    access for pupils with SEN 111
    evaluation of web resources 89-91
    as a global phenomenon 75, 80-81
    and learning independently 54
    learning opportunities 86-7
    and provision of a real audience 29-30, 81
    removal of capability from laptops 171
    safety and security issues
        balancing advantages and benefits with 87
        reflective exercise 82-5, 86, 88-9
        solutions 85-7
    spam 92-3

websites for 93
zombies, digital pathogens and hackers 92
    see also World Wide Web
Internet browser, symbol-based 111
interpersonal intelligence 72
intranets 85
intrapersonal intelligence 72
introvert personalities 145
IWBs 7, 17, 73
    case study on adoption of 19-24
    combination of laptop computers and 22
    effect on interaction in teaching 22
    and a kinaesthetic approach to language 28,
        29, 32, 33
    and learning in a community 54
    and the management of learning in music 74
    and pupil motivation 21

Jackson's Learning Styles Profiler 157
Jordan Education Initiative 191-2

Key Stages 1 and 2 18
    National Curriculum Music programmes of
        study 64
keyboards
    adapting 102, 103
    see also QWERTY keyboards
kinaesthetic learning 33, 68, 145
    and the use of IWBs 28, 32, 33
knowledge, storing 96
'knowledge society' 114

labels 157
Laggards 11
laptop computers 165
    children's perceptions 165-7
    combination of IWBs and 22
    see also wireless laptops
'Laptops for Teachers' 22
Late Majority 11
learning
    deep and surface approaches 146
    levels 101-2
    personalisation of 143
    see also collaborative learning; home school
        learning; independent learning; individual
        learning cycle; individual learning plans
        (ILPs); individualised learning; scaffolding
        learning
learning in a community 54
learning contexts 53-6
    provision of different 154-6
Learning Gateways 183, 184
learning styles 144
    supporting individual 28, 49, 72-3, 97
    VAK model 68, 73
    see also auditory learning; kinaesthetic
        learning; visual learning
Learning Styles Inventory 144, 149
'lexicon of learning' 157
linguistic intelligence 71
literacy 26-45
    case studies of learners' experiences 34-44
        investigating 'shun' 34-7
        predicting phonic letter strands 37-41
        Quorum Tools 42-4
        Wordwalls 41-2
    case study on using visual literacy to
        develop awareness of 126-30
    creative use of ICT in teaching 139-40
    definition 26
    and ICT strategies 29-32
    merging of media literacy and 30

models 26-7
see also digital literacy; National Literacy
    Strategy (NLS); visual literacy
'literacy learners', benefits of ICT 32-4
logical-mathematical intelligence 71
looking with ICT 119-22

maintenance of knowledge 101
Makaton 95
'malware' 92
mathematics, ICT as a learning tool 51-3
media literacy 30-2
media stage 30
metacognition 66
Microsoft Class Server 184
Miller, Edward 91
mimicry 122-3
mind maps, software applications 30, 125
modelling 47-8, 63, 159
monitoring pupil responses 98-9
motivational outcomes of ICT 21, 34, 62, 97, 159
mouse control skills, development 104-5
multi-sensory interface 33
multicultural classrooms 198
multimedia 145
multimedia interface 33
multimodality 124-5
'multiple digital divides' 16
multiple intelligences, theory of 71-2, 73, 132, 144
museums, use of the World Wide Web 120
music 60-78
    application of national initiatives 62-5
    benefits of ICT 63
    elements and associated vocabulary 76t
    employing adult support 75-6
    examples of equipment 77
    individual, paired or small group learning
        74-5
    promoting creativity and teaching 66-70
    scaffolding learning in 70-3
    teaching musically 67
    websites for 78
    whole-class teaching 67, 73-4, 77f
'music as discourse' 67
Music National Curriculum 63, 64, 66-8
musical development 66-7
musical expression through ICT 140
musical intelligence 71-2
musicphobia 60-2
myEUROPE 193
myEUROPE Web site 193

National Curriculum
    emphasis on Core subjects 60-1
    time constraints 135
    see also ICT National Curriculum; Key Stages 1
        and 2; Music National Curriculum
National Grid for Learning (NGfL) 1, 163
National Literacy Strategy (NLS) 26, 42, 63
    and plenary sessions 73-4
National Numeracy Strategy 63
    and direct teaching 73
NC (National Curriculum) in Action website 178
networked computers 17
    and learning collaboratively 54
'New Literacy' movement 27
New Opportunites Funding (NOF) 8, 163
NFER-Nelson non-verbal reasoning tests 10 and 11
    148
NGfL (National Grid for Learning) 1, 163
numeracy 48-59
    creative use of ICT in teaching 136
    learning contexts 53-6

lesson example 56-8
use of ICT 46-7
    as a learning tool 51-3
    to support teaching 47-51
    websites for 58-9
    see also National Numeracy Strategy

observation
    and assessment of learning style 149
    importance of 98-9
observation schedule 158f
OECD 190
online assessments 178, 180, 184
online communities, participation by pupils with
    SEN 111
opaque technologies 18
open-ended tasks 145, 159
    creation of more structure in 156
outcomes of ICT use 7

painting software 122-3
paired work in music 75, 77f
parent helpers, role in scaffolding learning in music
    75-6
parents
    consultation with 83, 89
    objections to internet use 82, 88
PECS (Picture Exchange Communication System)
    106
pedagogy
    importance of effective explanations 159
    see also teaching
personalisation of learning 143
personalising ICT 143-60
    classroom study 147-54
        findings 151-5
    individual differences see individual
        differences
    labels 157
    provision of different contexts for learning
        154-6
personality and the differential use of ICT 145
photographs on the internet 85
physically disabled children, accessing technology
    102-4
Pickford's site 121
Picture Communication System (PCS) symbol
    system 106
Picture Exchange Communication System (PECS)
    105
planning
    link with assessment in a 'school without
        walls' 181-2
    for writing 30-1
    see also collaborative planning with peers
plenary sessions 73-4
    and the use of visual display technologies 32
PMLD, case study of pupil with 101-5
positive practice 24
'post-critical literacy' studies 27
PowerPoint 31, 32
practical utility, ICT as 17
predictive word processors 109
presentation 33, 49-50, 155
    and a surface approach to learning 146
presentation software 31
Primary National Strategy 73
    key aspects of ICT 51
    key aspects of learning 54-6
    and peer talking 152
Primary National Strategy website 154
printed text 33

problem-solving 73
  composing music as 68, 69, 75, 77f
  as a creative strategy 136-7
  and the use of laptop computers 165
product, continuity of 34
professional practice 12-13
professional understanding 182
programs
  individual use 152-3
  moving between 153
'provisionality' 53
'psychological arrival' 11-12
pupil-to-computer ratios 190
pupils
  disconnect between lives in and out of school
    187-8
  response to ICT 156

QCA's NC (National Curriculum) in Action website
  178
Quorum Tools 43
QWERTY keyboards 34

re-presentation of information 49-50, 155
real audiences 29-30, 81
Record of Achievement format 100
redrafting 155
reflection 24
reflective sessions 32
reorientation 49
resources
  for ICT 9
  schools as 177
  see also global learning resources; virtual
    reality (VR) resources; web resources
responses of teachers 7-8
Revelatory paradigm 154, 155
Riding's Cognitive Styles Analysis approach 144-5,
  149
risk assessment 169-70
Roger's diffusion of innovation model 9-11

'safe environment', provision of 70
SAW (Science Across the World) 196
scaffolding learning 155
  of ICT 154
  in music 70-3, 74
  role of teaching assistants and parent helpers
    75-6
  use of collaboration 156
scanners 123
School Managers Centre 193
schools
  availability of space 173
  collaboration between see e-twinning
  purposes 177
  see also classrooms
schools of the future 161-86
  'school without walls' 175-86
    and assessment 178-82
    creative action 186
    e-learning environment 182-4
    home school learning 185
    and the importance of human capital 176-7
    provision in 179-80
    technology needs 183
  use of wireless technologies and laptop
    computers 162-75
    case study into children's perceptions of the
      stack system and laptops 165-7
Science Across the World (SAW) 196
science and the use of ICT 18, 141-2
screen interface 33

'screen reading' software 110
self-esteem 155, 156
SEN 94-113
  case studies 101-10
    communication development for a pupil
      with PMLD 101-4
    meeting the needs of a pupil on the ASD
      105-7
    supporting writing difficulties 107-10
  categories 95
  developing ICT-based interventions 97-9
  emerging trends 110-11
  learning objectives 100-101
  obtaining information 98-100
    identifying pupils' strengths in their use of
      ICT 99-100
    importance of observation 98-9
  pupils with communication difficulties 96-7
  resources for 112-13
  use of icons 120
SENDA (Special Educational Needs Disability Act)
  (2001) 95, 100
'sense of ownership' issue 164
sentence level work 28-9
shared reading 27
shared writing 27
  supporting 43-4
'Show me' 120
'Silicon Literacies' 45
'SILVER' standard 89-91
small-group work in music 74, 76f
social communication 97
  and pupils with ASD 105
social interaction and pupils with ASD 105
sound 97
  as an aid to independent working 32
space, availability of 173
spam 92-3
spam detection software 92
spatial intelligence 71
special educational needs see SEN
Special Educational Needs Disability Act (SENDA)
  (2001) 95, 100
speech recognition software 110
spellcheckers 31, 139-40
Spotting Creativity 68
spreadsheets 49, 51, 53
stack system
  children's perceptions 165-7
  problems 174
'standardisation' of teachers' professional
  judgements 182
states 144
story writing, editing 70
storyboarding software 31
storyboards 30, 128
subject, ICT as a 18
surface approaches to learning 146
switching devices 102, 103
symbol communication systems 105-7, 111, 120
  and developing understanding 106-7
  see also 'emoticons'; Makaton
Symbol World 111

talk to aid learning 151-2
tasks
  completion 155-6
  see also open-ended tasks
teacher attitudes
  case study on adoption of innovation and
    19-24
  on usefulness of ICT 21-3
teacher beliefs 12-16

teacher demonstration, ICT as an aid 32
teachers
    professional understanding 182
    responses to ICT 7-8
        psychological aspects 8-9
    role 177
        creative engineering 142
    in a 'school without walls' 178
    training 8, 23
teaching
    effect of multicultural classrooms on 198
    see also creative teaching; direct teaching;
        pedagogy
teaching assistants, role in scaffolding learning in
    music 75-6
technologies
    adoption of new 24
    barriers to full exploitation 13
    transparent or opaque 18
    see also visual display technologies
technology dissonance 197-8
technophobia 8-9
Teddy Bear project 195
testing and confirming 50
tests of cognitive and learning style 144-5
    using theoretical models without 149-51
text
    relationship between the visual and 116
    see also printed text
thinking with ICT 125-6
thinking skills, levels 56-8
touch-screens 102
training 8, 23
traits 144
Transforming the Way We Learn 1
transparent technologies 18

UK
    education policy 163, 167-9
        contribution of e-twinning 196-7
    use of ICT 192
underutilisation of ICT, factors for 9
UNESCO 190
usefulness of ICT 21-3
utilisation 47

VAK model of preferred learning styles 67, 72
verbalisers 149, 152, 156
video 127, 131, 133
    see also BECTa Digital Video Pilot Project
Virtual Library Museums page 120
virtual reality (VR) resources 121
Virtual School 193
virus protection software 92, 93
viruses 92
visual display technologies 97
    and reflective and plenary sessions 32
    and sharing texts 27
visual learning 67, 145

visual literacy 16-17, 114-30
    case study 126-30
    challenges of 116-17
    definitions 116-17
    'fat pictures' 124-5
    from manipulation to making meaning 123
    looking, creating and thinking with images 119-23
    role of ICT 117-19
    and thinking with ICT 125-6
visualisers 27
Vygotsky, L. S. 27, 29, 70-1, 73, 75

Ways of Seeing 115
web browsers, symbol-based 111
web pages 81
    checks and balances for 87-8
web resources
    evaluation 89-91
    on lesson activities 121
whole-class teaching in music 67, 73-4, 77f
whole-class word level work 28-9
wholists 149, 152, 156
Widgit software 106, 111
wireless laptops 170-5
    advantages
        flexibility, deployment and cross-curricular
            use 174
        inclusion and behaviour management 173
        matching pupils' expectations and needs 173
        space saving 172
    disadvantages 170-2
        battery life and charging routines/needs 170
        health and safety 172
        losing parts 170
        portability, damage and accountability 171
        wireless capability 171
word processing 146
    see also predictive word processors
WordWalls 41-2
worksheets 29
World Links 195
World Wide Web
    access to visual images through 120-1
    use of the visual 116
    see also Internet; web pages
writing
    planning in 30-1
    for real audiences 29-30
    see also authentic writing; shared writing
writing difficulties, case study of using ICT to
    support 107-10
writing stories, editing work in progress 70

'Young People and ICT' survey 153

'zombie' computers 92
zone of proximal development (ZPD), theory of 27,
    70-1, 73